ANCIENT
aLien
ANCESTORS

D1414431

ANCIENT ALIEN ANCESTORS

Advanced Technologies That Terraformed Our World

Will Hart

Bear & Company
Rochester, Vermont • Toronto, Canada

Bear & Company
One Park Street
Rochester, Vermont 05767
www.BearandCompanyBooks.com

Bear & Company is a division of Inner Traditions International

Library of Congress Cataloging-in-Publication Data

Names: Hart, Will, 1946– author.
Title: Ancient alien ancestors : advanced technologies that terraformed our
    world / Will Hart.
Description: Rochester, Vermont : Bear & Company, [2017] | Includes
    bibliographical references and index.
Identifiers: LCCN 2016051939 (print) | LCCN 2016054721 (e-book) |
    ISBN 9781591432531 (pbk.) | ISBN 9781591432548 (e-book)
Subjects: LCSH: Civilization, Ancient—Extraterrestrial influences.
Classification: LCC CB156 .H359 2017 (print) | LCC CB156 (e-book) |
    DDC 001.942—dc23
LC record available at https://lccn.loc.gov/2016051939

Printed and bound in the United States by P. A. Hutchison Company

10 9 8 7 6 5 4 3 2 1

Text design and layout by Debbie Glogover
This book was typeset in Garamond Premier Pro with Aguda and Gill Sans MT
Pro used as display fonts

To send correspondence to the author of this book, mail a first-class letter to the
author c/o Inner Traditions • Bear & Company, One Park Street, Rochester, VT
05767, and we will forward the communication, or contact the author directly at
www.ancientalienancestors.com.

Contents

. . . .
The Contact and Colonization of the Earth

I see some kind of intelligent being, like us, skipping around the universe from planet to planet as, let's say, the South Pacific Indians do on the islands, where they skip from island to island. . . . I think that's what the [alien] space program is all about.

ASTRONAUT AL WORDEN

This is the second book in this series. The first volume, *The Genesis Race,* primarily examined artifacts, sacred texts, and oral traditions from human history that tell of "gods" descending from outer space to Earth. These aliens "gods," the Genesis Race, had as their mission to seed life on the planet and to extend their civilization through the creation of humankind.

In this volume I present the scientific basis for the theory of *directed panspermia,* which posits that life, via microorganisms, was shipped to Earth by an extraterrestrial civilization.

The theory was first proposed by the late Nobel Prize–winning microbiologist Sir Francis Crick, cofounder of the shape and design of the DNA molecule in the 1950s.

This book makes it clear that the concept of *The Genesis Race* is a theoretical framework that goes beyond the general theory and shows that there is extensive ancient and modern-day evidence of extraterrestrial involvement, contact, and colonization of the earth.

This series is not just a simple cataloging of historical and present-day enigmas and anomalies.

I examine the current state of astronomy, space exploration, astrophysics, biology, genetics, and modern-day unidentified flying object (UFO) sightings and contacts. Ancient oral traditions and texts are replete with accounts of contact with this advanced civilization. It is important to establish the fact that our human ancestors clearly made every attempt to convey for posterity the gist of their experiences with this race.

However, since they lacked any knowledge of sophisticated technology the best they could do was to describe the spacecraft as bright, shiny, luminous clouds or fiery chariots.

In the Bible, Ezekiel's portrayal of the craft that landed in front of him is perhaps the clearest account ever given of an ancient UFO. He tells of a "humanlike" *man* he calls the Lord sitting inside the craft in a high-backed chair, which he describes as a throne.

For some curious reason this fact has been lost to both Judaism and Christianity. In fact, the Bible is full of references to UFO sightings and encounters, as are the oral traditions of ancient cultures such as the Dogon of northern Africa.

The recent, post–World War II rise in UFO sightings by highly credible witnesses is consistent with our earliest oral traditions and written accounts.

Directed panspermia (which I shall refer to as Cosmic Ancestry II because I have included the evidence of ET visits in the form of enigmatic, archaeological evidence to the original theory) is simply the idea that the seeds of life originated elsewhere and were deliberately shipped to earth from an extraterrestrial planet long ago. To that basic concept, I have added the evidence in support of the notion that these same extraterrestrials actually set foot on earth and intervened in human history. Cosmic ancestry and extraterrestrial visitation are not new phenomena that exist outside the bounds of science. Today, most scientists agree that the earth is not an exceptional planet, that it probably is not the only one in the universe that houses life and intelligent beings.

Hundreds of millions, if not tens of billions of planets in our galaxy alone are now projected to contain some form of life, and some of them have likely produced civilizations that evolved long before things got started on Earth.

In fact, directed panspermia (Cosmic Ancestry II), via the Genesis Race, only requires that one civilization in the entire universe triumphed over every obstacle and has been able to travel the vast expanses of space-time to transmit life to other worlds.

SECTION I

· · · · · · · ·

DIRECTED PANSPERMIA
The Seeding of Our World

1
....
Cosmic Seeds of Life

The notion that life originated elsewhere in the universe and later arrived on Earth is not the stuff of any science fiction writer's imagination. Today it is a solid scientific theory that explains how life came to Earth from the cosmos.

The first documented mention of the idea appears in the writings of the fifth-century-BCE Greek philosopher Anaxagoras. He called his thesis *panspermia,* a Greek term that means "seeds everywhere."

More than two millennia later, on April 9, 1864, the French chemist Louis Pasteur reported his experiment disproving spontaneous generation. This was a devastating blow to Charles Darwin's theory regarding the origin of life on Earth, which held that life began as a direct result of *spontaneous generation.* In other words, nonliving things spontaneously produced living things.

Then, in the 1870s, the British physicist Lord Kelvin (William Thomson) and the German physicist Hermann von Helmholtz reinforced Pasteur's findings and argued that life might have originated in space and been transported to Earth.

Next, in the first decade of the 1900s, the Swedish chemist and Nobel laureate Svante Arrhenius theorized that bacterial spores—propelled through space by light pressure—were the mechanism that seeded life on Earth.

In his day, the concept was pure scientific speculation because it had not been proven that life-forms could survive the extreme conditions of interstellar space. In fact, most scientists at the time were not convinced that any could. However, science has since shown that such life-forms, called *extremophiles,* do indeed exist.

Fig. 1.1. Life from the Cosmos. Photo courtesy of NASA.

In the 1960s, Sir Fred Hoyle and Chandra Wickramasinghe were trying to identify the contents of interstellar dust by finding something that would match its infrared signature. Hoyle was an astronomer and Wickramasinghe an astrobiologist, and neither was out to prove the tenets of panspermia.

More than three decades ago Hoyle and Wickramasinghe began arguing the case for the widespread occurrence of microbial life in the universe. They drew their conclusions from studies of interstellar dust grains and found a vast array of molecules to be present in space, which they believed to represent components that may have derived from biology.

When they began working on this problem in the early 1960s, the standard theory posited that the spectrum of cosmic dust could be adequately explained as obtained from nonliving graphite grains. A new look at the interstellar dust permeating the universe has revealed hints of organic matter that could be created naturally by stars, scientists say.

Researchers at the University of Hong Kong observed stars at different evolutionary phases and found that they are able to produce complex organic compounds and eject them into space, filling the regions between stars.

But an imperfect match between the theoretical and actual spectrums—and an implausible account of the formation of the grains—pushed Hoyle and Wickramasinghe to explore other possibilities. In their work—and that of other astronomers and astrobiologists—molecules that were more closely related to biological entities began to enter the picture.

As their research proceeded, other noted researchers reported finding polycyclic aromatic molecules in interstellar dust signatures. Then, in 1972, persuasive evidence showing that the dust contained porphyrins was also obtained. Porphyrins are carbon-based molecules—not rocks; that is, they came from something that probably once was what we would call "alive."

Next, in 1974, Wickramasinghe demonstrated that complex organic polymers, specifically molecules of polyformaldehyde, existed in space. These molecules are closely related to cellulose, which is very abundant in living, biological forms.

By 1975, Hoyle and Wickramasinghe were convinced that organic polymers were a substantial fraction of interstellar dust. Of course, this line of reasoning was considered wildly speculative at that time.

After the middle 1970s, they turned their attention to an apparent anomaly in the spectrum. This spectral feature could be explained if the grains of dust were of a specific size and translucent as well. After trying to fit every known factor to conform to the spectral data and failing, they decided to look at the spectrum for bacteria.

Dried bacteria refract light as irregularly shaped, hollow spheres, which did fit the data, and the pair discovered that their size range was also appropriate. The match between the spectrums for dried bacteria and the ones from the interstellar grains were nearly perfect. Hoyle and Wickramasinghe concluded that the grains were probably dried, frozen bacteria.

Today the panspermia theory posits that the seeds of life proceed when microbes become trapped in debris that is ejected into space after collisions between planets that harbor life and small solar system bodies. These living organisms (bacteria) travel in a dormant state for prolonged periods of time before colliding randomly with other planets or intermingling with protoplanetary disks.

According to the theory, if a given planet presents the right conditions, the bacteria become active and the process of evolution begins. Panspermia is not meant to address the ultimate question of how life began. It only addresses the issue of the mechanisms and methods that cause life to spread and be sustained, and how life arrived on Earth.

The theory does not claim that life only originated at a specific point and was subsequently spread throughout the entire universe. Instead it argues that, once started, it may have been able to spread to other environments suitable for replication via microbes traveling through space.

Today the notion of interplanetary transfer of material is well documented, as shown by meteorites of Martian origin found on Earth. Of course, this was unknown to Anaxagoras or the later nineteenth-century panspermia proponents. This evidence was forthcoming as a direct result of late-twentieth-century space exploration.

The proof that extremophiles do exist and that they do travel through space is a strong piece of evidence in support of some form of panspermia. Some bacteria grow at temperatures as high as 113°C.

At the other end, microbes can thrive at temperatures as low as −18°C; many can be preserved in liquid nitrogen at −196°C. Researchers have found that they can also tolerate high doses of ionizing and ultraviolet radiation, extreme pressure, and so forth.

These observations suggest that it is difficult to define the conditions that favor life, which makes it harder for science to claim that life is unique to Earth.

Mounting data derived from space probes support the panspermia theory, which predicts the existence of extremophiles. If the interstellar dust was devoid of any signs of life and our space probes had not discovered extremophiles, then panspermia would not fit the data.

There is yet another piece of evidence that supports panspermia—the discovery that water also is not unique to Earth.

Mars is believed to have contained water in the past. Space scientists are also excited about the idea of the possible presence of life on Europa, one of Jupiter's moons, which has been fueled by speculations that this moon may have underground oceans. In fact, in recent years the National Aeronautics and Space Administration (NASA) has found evidence of ice on the moon and Mercury.

The fact that water is relatively common on other planetary bodies would also strongly support the idea of extraterrestrial life. Organic matter is composed of compounds that contain carbon. All living things on Earth are carbon-based, something well known by *Star Trek* fans.

A variety of organic compounds have been detected in meteorites that have landed on Earth, including amino acids, which are the building blocks of proteins—the latter being one of the primary components of living cells.

The presence of carbon-based matter in meteorites supports the possibility that life on our planet could have come from outer space. But even though life on Earth is composed of organic matter, that, in itself, is not considered life. We cannot yet conclusively prove that life exists in outer space and was transported to Earth via bacteria. Nonetheless, we are getting closer to that conclusion.

For the sake of argument, we shall put ourselves at the point in time when the compiled evidence is so strong that it leads science to conclude that life originated elsewhere in space. Now we must still determine how life arrived on Earth.

There is another theory that goes beyond the simple and random spread of life via microbes embedded in rocks or pushed by light waves. *Directed panspermia* takes the theory a quantum leap further by proposing that the microbes that arrived on Earth were intentionally sent here by a highly advanced civilization.

Once again this may sound like the stuff of science fiction novels, but it is not. As previously noted, Francis Crick proposed the theory in the 1950s. Given Crick's unimpeachable scientific credentials, being the codiscoverer of the DNA molecule, no one can dismiss this theory out of hand without having himself or herself come under close scientific scrutiny.

Crick presented his view of directed panspermia and the arguments in support of this theory in a small and little-known book titled *Life Itself: Its Origin and Nature,* published in 1981.

At the time, Crick was a member of the Medical Research Council Laboratory of Molecular Biology in Cambridge, England. L. E. Orgel, a British chemist, worked for the Salk Institute for Biological Studies, based in San Diego, California. In a paper they coauthored in 1973, they wrote the following:

> It was not until the middle of the nineteenth century that Pasteur and Tyndall completed the demonstration that spontaneous generation is not occurring on the Earth nowadays. Darwin, and a number of other biologists, concluded that life must have evolved long ago when conditions were more favourable. Some other scientists, however, drew a quite different conclusion. They supposed that if life does not evolve from terrestrial nonliving matter nowadays, it may never have done so. Hence, they argued, life reached the earth as an 'infection' from another planet.[1]

They also addressed the issue of undirected panspermia:

> It now seems unlikely that extraterrestrial living organisms could have reached the earth either as spores driven by the radiation pressure from another star or as living organisms imbedded in a meteorite. As an alternative to these nineteenth-century mechanisms, we have considered Directed Panspermia, the theory that organisms were deliberately transmitted to the earth by intelligent beings on another planet. We conclude that it is possible that life reached the earth in this way.[2]

As a prerequisite to proposing their alternative to Darwinian evolution, Crick and Orgel raised numerous scientific objections to that theory. The scientists were not at all convinced that enough time had elapsed on Earth to account for the sudden appearance of complex organisms about three billion years ago.

Crick's work with DNA afforded him knowledge and observations unavailable to previous evolutionists. He had intimate knowledge of the astonishing complexity of DNA, had researched and confirmed the absence of evidence for a primordial soup, had observed that life appeared suddenly and with complexity in the fossil record, and had confirmed the absence of any fossil evidence for transitional (missing links) forms of life.

In fact, it was Crick and his DNA codiscover, the American molecular biologist, geneticist, and zoologist James Dewey Watson, who proved that any single paired strand of human DNA contains the information to direct the one hundred trillion cells in the human body. DNA also has the capability of both reproducing and repairing itself. It is a molecular chain of approximately one billion nucleotides that form combination strings of four specific chemicals that function like a coded computer program. The pair has to be ultimately credited with discovering the basis for all subsequent DNA research, as well as the principles of bioengineering.

For their part, Crick and Orgel, not convinced that undirected panspermia was a strong enough mechanism to support the arrival of the seeds of life on Earth, proposed that an advanced civilization had packed a space probe with microbes and sent it to "infect" Earth with the seeds of life. In his book *Life Itself* Crick summed up his views in the following statement:

> Directed Panspermia—postulates that the roots of our form of life go back to another place in the universe, almost certainly another planet; that it had reached a very advanced form there before anything much had started here; and that life here was seeded by microorganisms sent on some form of spaceship by an advanced civilization.[3]

In fact, both panspermia and directed panspermia predict the absence of transitional life-forms, the missing links that evolutionists have tried to uncover, in vain, ever since Darwin proposed his theory a hundred and fifty years ago.

The public is given the false impression that the only missing link not accounted for is the one that separates apes and humans. The fact is that there are thousands of missing links in the plant and animal kingdoms. For example, the question arises, Where are the missing links that should exist between the nonflowering plants and flowering plants?

In addition, where are the missing links that should connect nonpollinating insects and bees that are necessary to pollinate the flowering plants?

In other words, why do flowering plants and bees, which depend on each other, suddenly appear in the record without any intermediate forms? These issues vex hardcore Darwinians, and they were one fact that compelled Crick and Orgel to formulate the theory of directed panspermia.

Hoyle was also concerned about the problem, and he summed up his view of the missing links by comparing them to how computer hardware is upgraded. He wrote:

> We saw there that intermediate forms are missing from the fossil record. Now we see why, essentially because there were no intermediate forms. When a computer is upgraded, there are no intermediate forms. The new units are wheeled in beside the old computer, the electrical connections are made, the electric power is switched on, and the thing is done.[4]

Clearly the work and conclusions of Hoyle and Wickramasinghe both agree with and differ from those of Crick and Orgel. Nonetheless, we do not necessarily have to make it an either-or proposition. The universe—as exhibited by the multitude of survival strategies employed by species on Earth—does not appear to be the kind of gambler who bets the farm on everything.

It is more likely that both strategies are used to ensure the spread and continued existence of life, which must be maintained as much as possible in an often very hostile universe.

Now let us review a list of some of the hard scientific evidence in support of the idea that the seeds of life originated in outer space and arrived on Earth very late in the cosmic scheme of things.

September 24, 1970: For the first time, an unmanned spacecraft delivered a lunar "soil" sample to Earth. The Soviet Union's Luna 16 spacecraft returned from the moon's Sea of Fertility with 101 grams of lunar regolith in a hermetically sealed container.

February 1972: Only 120 kilometers from the Luna 16 site on the moon, Luna 20 used a drill with a ten-inch, hollow-core bit to collect another regolith sample, which was also hermetically sealed.

1979: The sealed containers from the Luna missions were promptly delivered to a laboratory in 1972 to be examined and photographed. But even after hundreds of the pictures were published in an atlas in 1979, the biological nature of some of the particles was not noticed at first glance.

1984: A meteorite that had been blasted off from the surface of Mars about fifteen million years ago was found in Antarctica by a team of scientists searching for meteors. The space rock was named Allan Hills 84001 (ALH 84001).

May 19, 1995: Two scientists at California Polytechnic State University showed that bacteria can survive without any metabolism for at least twenty-five million years; they opined that they might be immortal.

November 24, 1995: The *New York Times* described bacteria that can survive radiation much stronger than any that Earth has ever experienced.

August 7, 1996: After a decade of research, NASA announced that researchers had found evidence of ancient life in meteorite ALH 84001 from Mars.

July 29, 1997: A NASA scientist announced evidence of fossilized microscopic life-forms in a meteorite not from any known planet.

Spring 1998: A microfossil that was found in a meteorite and photographed in 1966 was recognized by a Russian microbiologist as a magnetotactic bacterium.

Fall 1998: NASA's public position on life from space shifted dramatically.

January 4, 1999: NASA officially recognized the possibility that life on Earth comes from space.

March 19, 1999: NASA scientists announced that two more meteorites held even stronger fossilized evidence for past life on Mars.

April 26, 2000: The German team operating the mass spectrometer on NASA's Stardust mission announced the detection of very large organic molecules in space. (Nonbiological sources for organic molecules so large were not then known.)

October 19, 2000: A team of biologists and a geologist announced the revival of bacteria that are 250 million years old, strengthening the case that bacterial spores can be immortal.

December 13, 2000: A NASA team demonstrated that the magnetosomes in Mars meteorite ALH 84001 are biological.

May 11, 2001: Geologist Bruno D'Argenio and molecular biologist Giuseppe Geraci from the University of Naples announced that they had found extraterrestrial bacteria inside a meteorite estimated to be more than 4.5 billion years old.

June 2002: Geneticists reported evidence that the evolutionary step from chimps to humans was assisted by viruses.

August 2, 2004: Very convincing electron microscope photos of fossilized cyanobacteria in a meteorite were reported by NASA astrobiologist Richard B. Hoover.

January 25, 2005: J. Craig Venter, a biologist involved in sequencing the human genome, endorsed panspermia.

May 10, 2007: Eminent biologist E. O. Wilson endorsed panspermia.

April 18, 2008: Richard Dawkins, an evolutionary biologist, endorsed panspermia.

April 7, 2009: Stephen Hawking, a world-renowned physicist, endorsed panspermia.

May 2, 2009: Freeman Dyson, a physicist and mathematician, spoke favorably about panspermia.

February 26, 2010: Neil deGrasse Tyson, an astrophysicist, endorsed panspermia in a ten-minute video, *Cosmos: A Spacetime Odyssey,* episode 11.

May 10, 2010: *We Are Not Alone: Why We Have Already Found Extraterrestrial Life,* a book about astrobiology by Dirk Schulze-Makuch and David J. Darling that includes the topic of panspermia, was published.

January 25, 2011: Chandra Wickramasinghe had a new article, "Viva Panspermia," available online.

February 28, 2011: A two-hour video program about panspermia and related topics became available on the Internet, "Finding Life beyond Earth," NOVA, 2011, available on YouTube.

August 24, 2011: Panspermia is more likely than we thought, a new analysis revealed. Website: panspermia.org, Brig Klyce, article, "Introduction: More than Panspermia."

September 1, 2011: An article titled, "Earth Could Spread Life across The Milky Way," by Tammy Plotner, appeared on Universe Today, the space and astronomy news blog, www.universetoday .com (accessed March 20, 2017).

October 10, 2011: The new terms *neopanspermia* and *pathospermia* were introduced in a paper available online. In addition to explaining the origin of life, a form of panspermia suggests that life is continually arriving on Earth from space. This possibility Milton Wainwright termed *neopanspermia* (neo = "new"). Hoyle and Wickramasinghe also suggest that pandemic diseases may originate from space, an idea covered by the terms *pathopanspermia* or *pathospermia*.

February 13, 2015: Scientists (U. of Buckingham) in the UK have examined a tiny metal circular object and are suggesting it might be a microorganism deliberately sent by aliens to create life on earth. "UK Scientists. Aliens May Have Seeded Life on Earth." The minuscule object was discovered by astrophysicist Milton Wainwright.

Mounting evidence supporting some form of panspermia seeding Earth with life in the remote past is gaining momentum every year as new data from space probes is made available. The publicly disclosed acceptance of the theory by eminent scientists in recent years is indicative of the paradigm shift in the scientific community.

We should be clear that the acceptance of the theory of panspermia does not mean that the theory of directed panspermia has also been accepted. However, it may represent an important first step in that direction.

The Genesis Race theory goes beyond all forms of panspermia and directed panspermia by positing not only that life was seeded on Earth by an advanced extraterrestrial civilization, but that the same civilization also intervened in the evolutionary process to create humans and to generate civilization.

The first book in this series largely dealt with the cultural and archaeological evidence in support of this theory. The current volume focuses more on the modern scientific evidence while including additional cultural and archaeological evidence.

CONCLUSION

The theory of panspermia, the idea that the seeds of life exist throughout the universe, originated in ancient times. While Darwin proposed that life began on Earth via spontaneous generation, that theory was disposed of by Louis Pasteur in the nineteenth century. Thereafter, panspermia was resurrected in the late nineteenth and early twentieth centuries and refined by Hoyle and Wickramasinghe.

Then Crick and Orgel proposed that seeds of life, microorganisms, were intentionally dispatched to Earth by an advanced civilization. The tenets of undirected panspermia have become increasingly accepted by mainstream scientists. The Genesis Race theory (Cosmic Ancestry) takes directed panspermia to its conclusion.

2

Where Is Everybody?

A literal interpretation of Fermi's Paradox embraces a number of invalid assumptions. It therefore has irreconcilable problems, putting it in conflict with reality. Some misguided individuals attempt to use Fermi's Paradox as if it were proof that Earth is the only home of intelligent life in the Universe. They are erroneous and likely misunderstand the original point of Professor Fermi's question.

BILL M. TRACER

FERMI'S PARADOX

Enrico Fermi was a highly distinguished, world-renowned physicist. In 1950, he addressed the issue of whether there was intelligent life in the universe, and if there was, why had it not contacted Earth?

He came to the conclusion that there was an apparent contradiction between the high estimates of the *probability* of the existence of extraterrestrial civilizations and humanity's apparent lack of contact with, or observational evidence for, such civilizations. The basic points of Fermi's argument follow:

- The sun is a young star. There are billions of stars in the galaxy that are billions of years older.
- If Earth is typical, some of these stars likely have planets with intelligent life.

Fig. 2.1. Is there intelligent life elsewhere? Photo courtesy of NASA.

- Presumably, some of these civilizations will develop interstellar travel, as Earth seems likely to do.
- At any practical pace of interstellar travel, the galaxy can be completely colonized in just a few tens of millions of years.
- The observable universe is currently believed to have at least eighty billion galaxies.

According to this line of thinking, Earth should have already been colonized or at least visited long ago. However, according to Fermi, no convincing evidence of this exists. Hence, his famous question, which is said to have been raised during a lunchtime conversation with other physicists about the possibility of extraterrestrial life:

Where is everybody?

The Fermi paradox can be summed up in the following way: The apparent size and age of the universe suggest that many technologically advanced extraterrestrial civilizations ought to exist. However, this hypothesis seems contradicted by the lack of observational evidence to support it.

But there is a large fly in Fermi's ointment; his assertion that there was no evidence in the historical and archaeological records was based on the assumption that conventional scholars could explain and dismiss all of history's mysteries.

While he declared there was no evidence, he also failed to even acknowledge that there were anomalies in the historical and archaeological records, which he had not analyzed and therefore not dismissed on any clear scientific basis.

Though his argument is internally consistent with the known astronomical facts, I would beg to differ about the assertions concerning colonization and contact. Fermi, and the majority of his colleagues, failed to examine the archaeological, historical, and cultural evidence the way he examined the physics of space-time, energy, and matter.

Lacking that rigor, he made a false assumption by asserting there was no evidence to support contact and colonization in Earth's or humanity's records.

We need to know what archaeological evidence, if any, Fermi investigated to arrive at that conclusion. Did he systematically collect and analyze the data contained in the Great Pyramid? Or did he simply accept the conventional interpretations offered by archaeologists? The latter was obviously the case.

Did he know that the base of the Great Pyramid was leveled with such precision that we could only duplicate it today using laser leveling technology? (This analysis was conducted by the engineering firm Daniel Mann Johnson & Mendenhall.)

Have any of our physicists and astronomers carefully considered the fact that no mummies were ever found in any of the major pyramids?

In addition, have these physicists ever thought through the reasons the Great Pyramid lacks predecessors, the hundreds or even thousands of smaller, less sophisticated pyramids it would have taken to gain the knowledge, skills, and organizational infrastructure needed to build it or them?

We must wonder why a scientist of Fermi's stature would make such a blanket statement without supporting it in any way. Unfortunately, here we are faced with one of the severe weaknesses of our own civilization: *overspecialization*.

Fermi was a stellar physicist, but he appears to have been just another bozo on the bus the moment he stepped out of his specialty to weigh in where many disciplines need to be involved.

I have repeatedly invited hard scientists to apply their knowledge, technologies, and skills to make a thorough investigation of the Great Pyramid. Now they must also include the geological and geographical facts raised in the next chapter. I hope they will be happy to load all of the data they have accumulated over decades of research into a Cray supercomputer to see what results it comes up with.

Now I have my own paradox to present to the scientific community:

Since you dismiss the histories handed down by our ancestors as being nothing more than mere myths (apparently spun by ignorant, childish minds) that have no intrinsic value or relevancy to scientific investigations, then why do you, contrarily, insist that they were intelligent enough to engineer plant genetics, build the Great Pyramid, and invent the sexagesimal numeric system that is still the basis of timekeeping?

You see, you cannot have it both ways; either our ancestors knew what they were talking about and doing, or they did not, so which way is it? The Sumerians were quite clear in their historical documents: *another race of beings, the Anunnaki, built that civilization.* The Sumerians were merely workers taking orders or scribes keeping track of inventories and events.

The late astronomer Carl Sagan had enough insight into human nature, politics, and history to realize that there were historical and archaeological mysteries that raised questions that needed serious investigation.[1] But even his ideas fell on deaf ears, and Sagan was the main public spokesman for the scientific community back in the 1970s.

Physicists, astronomers, and other scientists are so focused on their own narrow fields that they do not take the time to do serious research into other fields. Instead, they seem to simply accept the "findings" and "interpretations" of the archaeological and historical communities as having been scientifically verified.

As we shall soon see, that is a big mistake, since such is not the case.

Despite the apparent paradox raised by Fermi, he actually confirmed two key supports for the Genesis Race theory: (1) there are billions of stars older than our sun, and (2) some of these stars evolved intelligent life and interstellar travel.

The physicist seems not to have considered the possibility that a superior civilization might prefer to remain concealed from its colonized planets. There is no reason to assume that any advanced race would or should act in ways we consider logical to prove their existence.

This is why the Search for Extraterrestrial Intelligence (SETI) project is based on a series of false presumptions.

Just because we have gone the radio, electromagnetic, technological route does not mean an extraterrestrial civilization would have done the same. Or if they had, that they would openly broadcast that fact.

Turned around, there actually seems to be a very good and simple explanation for the absence of evidence showing discernable contact. It is illustrated by the devastating consequences that isolated primitive human cultures have endured after suddenly being exposed to modern civilization.

That fact is well established, and it would seem that Fermi and other living scientists ought to be aware of the hard lessons learned from it.

Sagan was the exception. He urged the scientific community to investigate the histories of ancient civilizations. He was convinced that there was something to the so-called myths; too bad that his suggestions were not acted on.

The evidence of the existence of highly superior civilizations should not be obvious; in fact, we should expect it to be well camouflaged. Apparently it has been because even our smartest and most well-educated scientists cannot recognize it for what it is.

The Great Pyramid and the geometrical configurations of Earth's major rivers and land masses are like an *invisible elephant* standing in the room yet going unnoticed.

THE DRAKE EQUATION

The Fermi paradox is used as a kind of thought experiment to test any one of numerous theories about the possibility of there being intelligent life in the universe and whether an advanced civilization has ever existed, colonized planets, or made contact with humanity at any point in time.

The paradox involves what is referred to as the great silence, the fact that there is seemingly no hard evidence to support the statistical findings that always conclude that there must be intelligent life out there.

I have refuted the no-contact assumption; there is evidence of extraterrestrial contact on Earth, and there may be good reasons that extraterrestrial civilizations do not broadcast their presence.

The most closely related theoretical work to Fermi's was done by Professor Emeritus of Astronomy and Astrophysics Frank Drake, Ph.D., at the University of California, Santa Cruz. In 1961, he formulated a set of principles that have become known as *the Drake Equation.* The SETI project has based their research models on his work.

Drake formulated the equation a decade after Fermi raised his objections, in an attempt to find a systematic means to evaluate the numerous probabilities involved in the "alien life" debate. The equation is a mathematical formula used to estimate the number of detectable extraterrestrial civilizations in the Milky Way galaxy.[2]

The speculative equation factors in:

1. The rate of star formation in the galaxy
2. The fraction of stars with planets and the number of planets per star that are habitable
3. The fraction of those planets that develop life
4. The fraction of intelligent life and the further fraction of detectable technological intelligent life
5. The length of time such civilizations are detectable

In the final analysis, the equation is a close relative of the Fermi paradox. Drake suggested that a large number of extraterrestrial civilizations would form but that the lack of evidence of such civilizations (again presumed) suggests that technological civilizations tend to vanish rather quickly.

A central objection to the formula is that it assumes that civilizations arise and then die out within their original solar systems. If interstellar colonization is possible, this assumption is invalid, of course.

The equation has been used by both optimists and pessimists, who have arrived at opposite conclusions. Sagan, using optimistic numbers, suggested in 1966 that as many as one million communicating civilizations might have existed in the Milky Way. The number is inconsequential, as we shall see, confirming that the general principle is what counts.

Frank Tipler and John D. Barrow, both mathematicians and cosmologists, used pessimistic numbers and concluded that the average number of civilizations in a galaxy might be less than one. After penning the equation, Drake commented that it was unlikely to settle the Fermi paradox; instead, it was just a way of *organizing our ignorance* on the subject.

What are we "scientifically illiterate lay people" to make out of all of these contradictions and unsubstantiated speculations? One simple conclusion: *intelligent life exists in the universe beyond Earth.*

However small the number of advanced civilizations may be is irrelevant to our quest. We only need *one superadvanced civilization* to colonize the planet with life and then intervene much later to inject civilization into the process of human evolution.

Would it be too farfetched to conclude that at least one solar system—among hundreds of billions—produced an Earth-like planet that evolved a race of superintelligent beings? Unlike when Fermi and Drake were penning their theories, we now have the Kepler telescope reporting back to us that there are, indeed, many Earth-like planets out there.

Consider the alternative: Earth is so rare that it is the only planet in the entire universe to have spawned life. In essence, according to this view, we are alone, end of story. That position is the most extreme, completely homocentric perspective imaginable. It makes the notion that the sun revolves around the flat Earth seem enlightened by comparison.

The following is a refutation of the Fermi paradox and the Drake equation:

1. The central contention of the negative side of these equations is incorrect. There is evidence of technologically advanced, intelligent life-forms having visited and intervened in life on Earth.

2. The universe is a hostile place, and it is difficult for intelligent life-forms to create a lasting civilization, and almost none get a chance to gain a foothold before some catastrophic event wipes them out; however, that does not mean it has never been accomplished.

3. The very nature of technologically advanced cultures usually leads to global self-destruction before extrastellar space travel can be achieved; however, that also does not preclude the possibility of at least one civilization having achieved it.

4. Our existing SETI observations of the cosmos are based on erroneous assumptions that presume other civilizations would evolve as ours has; in fact, that is highly unlikely.

5. Lastly, an extraterrestrial race of beings would probably not want us, or any other "alien" civilization, to observe and monitor them. So they are actively preventing us from doing so. (See number 2 for the reasons this is likely the case.)

THE KARDASHEV SCALE

Regarding the last paragraph, in fact, we would be hard-pressed to find any scientist in any field who would admit to embracing the theory of the absolute *exceptional status of the earth*.

That said, it is time to move on to a more sophisticated view of the cosmos. The *Kardashev scale* is a system of measuring a civilization's level of technological advancement based on the amount of usable energy a civilization has at its disposal.

As our own civilization, for example, has progressed technologically, it has consumed more and more energy. While it is true that the scale is arbitrary—as it assumes that other advancing civilizations would also harness and consume energy—it is nonetheless useful as a benchmark for thought experiments concerning extraterrestrial life.

The scale has three designated categories: *Types I, II, and III.*

A Type I civilization has all the available energy impinging on its home planet, Type II has harnessed all of the available solar energy, and Type III all of its galaxy-wide energy. Of course, the scale is only theoretical, and in terms of an actual civilization highly speculative; nonetheless, it puts the energy consumption of an entire civilization in a cosmic perspective.

According to the Kardashev scheme we find:

- **Type I:** A technological level close to the level presently (referring to 1964) attained on Earth, with energy consumption at $\approx 4 \times 10^{19}$ erg/second (4×10^{12} watts). Argentine physicist Guillermo A. Lemarchand stated this as "a level near contemporary terrestrial civilization with an energy capability equivalent to the solar insolation on Earth, between 10^{16} and 10^{17} Watts."[3]

- **Type II:** OK, correct. A civilization capable of harnessing the energy radiated by its own star (for example, the stage of successful construction of a Dyson sphere), with energy consumption at $\approx 4 \times 10^{33}$ erg/second. Lemarchand stated this as "a civilization capable of utilizing and channeling the entire radiation output of its star. The energy utilization would then be comparable to the luminosity of our Sun, about 4×10^{26} Watts."[4]

- **Type III:** A civilization in possession of energy on the scale of its own galaxy, with energy consumption at $\approx 4 \times 10^{44}$ erg/second. Lemarchand stated this as "a civilization with access to the power comparable to the luminosity of the entire Milky Way galaxy, about 4×10^{37} Watts."[5]

From the above outline, we can see that our current civilization is a sub-Type I. A large-scale application of fusion power would vault us into that category and put us on the path toward a Type II. According to mass-energy equivalence formulas, Type I implies the conversion of about 2 kilograms of matter to energy per second.

While there is no known method to convert matter completely into energy, an equivalent energy release might be achieved by fusing approximately 280 kilograms of hydrogen into helium per second, a rate roughly equivalent to 8.9×10^9 kilograms/year. A cubic kilometer of water contains about 10^{11} kilograms of hydrogen, and Earth's oceans contain about 1.3×109 cubic kilometers of water, indicating that this rate of consumption could be sustained over geological time scales.

(We are not yet near that kind of energy output via any form of fusion power.)

An equally large-scale application of solar energy through converting sunlight into electricity—by either solar-cell technology or concentrating solar power indirectly through wind and hydroelectric means—would put us very close to Type I.

However, right now, there is no known way for human civilization to successfully harness the equivalent of Earth's total absorbed solar energy without completely covering the surface with artificial equipment, which is obviously not feasible, now or ever.

But if we put very large, space-based solar-powered satellites into orbit we might achieve Type I power levels someday.[6] Still, that possibility is not within reach now.

At present, we are nowhere near using the first two proposed methods.

Astrophysicist Michio Kaku suggested that our current civilization may attain Type I status in about two hundred years, Type II status in a few thousand years, and Type III status in about one hundred thousand to one million years (assuming it does not self-destruct or fall victim to natural catastrophes in the interim).

At present, we are on the course of harnessing hydroelectric, solar, and wind energy and turning them into electrical power. In fact, we only started with the hydroelectric method a little more than one hundred years ago when inventor Nikola Tesla invented AC power generation technologies. Additionally, the worldwide grid has become a reality within the last twenty-five years.

Solar cells and wind-turbine technologies have only recently become advanced enough to contribute to the grid in a significant, cost-effective way.

There are many historical examples of human civilization undergoing large-scale changes in a rapid manner, such as the Industrial Revolution. The transition between Kardashev scale levels could potentially represent even more dramatic periods of social chaos, as they do entail going beyond the hard limits of the resources available in a civilization's existing planetary environment.

Scientists studying these phenomena commonly speculate that the transition from Type 0 to Type I probably carries the risk of self-destruction. In a number of plausible scenarios, there would no longer be room for further expansion on the civilization's home planet as it neared the Type I threshold.

Excessive use of energy without adequate disposal of the carbon dioxide and heat (the greenhouse effect), for example, could make the planet of a civilization approaching Type I unsuitable to the biology of the dominant species and the production of its food sources; this is an actual looming threat today with a seven billion, and counting, human population currently on Earth.

Basing the level of a civilization's development on power consumption may seem arbitrary; however, it is a logical extension of our own civilization. We are compelled to go on revolutionizing our technologies because we are using up necessary natural resources at an ever-accelerating rate as we move forward.

We have largely reached the limit of harnessing hydroelectric power production now. With the industrialization of large countries like China, Brazil, and India, the prospect of using up the majority of fossil fuel resources is rapidly approaching.

The list of rapidly depleting resources is mounting each decade. Already, we are facing numerous man-made crises, such as global warming, nuclear warfare, environmental degradation, pollution, the extinction of plant and animal species, and so forth. It appears that advancing a technologically based civilization does come at a high cost.

It also seems evident that the prolonged advancement of a technological civilization appears like a slim possibility. As Drake noted, extraterrestrial civilizations would also have to face the same evolving crises that we do now, as well as all the natural disasters that we have always had to deal with as a species.[7]

It would seem that on this point we would have to agree with the Drake equation—most advanced civilizations do not last very long.

However, while that premise seems probable, some civilizations would overcome every challenge and continue to survive to reach the Type I level. At that point, they would probably colonize other planets, as our scientists are now considering, and create colonies, so the greenhouse issue would be averted, as the amount of waste heat could be distributed throughout the solar system.

Even fewer civilizations would make it to the Type II level, and only an infinitesimal fraction would survive long enough to reach Type III.

I would point out that there is a largely unconsidered limiting factor that would constrain the rise of a civilization to Type I status using our *electromagnetic methods* of power production, and that is the probability of eventual destruction by a *super solar storm*.

Happily, our sun is a relatively stable star, or so it has been up to now. However, stars that exhibit extremely explosive, unpredictable behaviors have been observed by astronomers.

We have unwittingly exposed ourselves to the possibility of a colossal disaster that would quickly destroy much of humanity—and fully wipe out civilization—though not cause species extinction.

Our current energy and food distribution systems and the entire global telecommunications infrastructure would not survive a massive, Earth-directed *solar storm*. Such an event would cause complete technological collapse and socioeconomic chaos, and perhaps the meltdown of the global economy.

The above points make it clear that as a civilization draws nearer to the full Type I status, the risks of destruction increase exponentially. This is why it seems very doubtful, if not impossible, for an advanced civilization to have reached the Type II or III status using our electromagnetic basis.

Kaku seems to have become highly aware of this problem. In recent years, he has issued numerous warnings about a coming super solar storm. He even went so far as to predict that it would occur in 2012 or 2013. Indeed, a solar storm did occur in July 2012, but the eruption was directed away from Earth; it missed us. However, just such a storm hit Earth in 1859, fortunately a half-century before the emergence of the electrical power grid.

We are already living with the sword of Damocles poised above our heads and ready to fall, though the average person has no awareness of this fact. For decades, the uncertain threats of nuclear destruction, earthquakes, tsunamis, meteor strikes, and so forth have preoccupied the mass media.

Yet the eventual and certain threat of *the solar destruction of the power grid* has gone unnoticed.

If any extraterrestrial civilization ever embarked on our power consumption methodology, it would have perished prior to reaching the interstellar contact and colonization levels. So will ours if we do not begin to find and deploy nonelectromagnetic methodologies of power distribution soon.

This is one reason we search the cosmos, in vain, for radio signals and other signs of intelligent civilizations that our astronomers (wrongly) believe would be transmitting electromagnetic radio signals. We may be exceptional in one way, the only civilization that has chosen this methodology to advance itself over a predictably very short time frame.

Given the above facts it does appear that the number of civilizations that have reached the Type II level is small, and it's even smaller for Type III. That fact puts added pressure on the directed panspermia theory.

However, in the vastness of space among the countless planets, we *only need one* to have reached the late Type II or early Type III level; we do not need a crowded universe full of advanced civilizations to support the Genesis Race theory.

So the Fermi paradox is wrong on at least two counts: (1) his assumption that there is no evidence that Earth was ever colonized and that humanity ever had contact with a superior race, and (2) the possibility that our electromagnetically based civilization would eventually evolve to the point of interstellar travel.

Interstellar travel turns out to be a hard time- and resource-consuming problem.

The proposed Genesis Race would have to come from a highly advanced, well-evolved Type II or Type III civilization. Given the above-outlined scenarios and facts, we can assume that the technologies they developed along their extended evolutionary path would bear very little or no resemblance to ours. The latter is probably the case.

CONCLUSION

The Fermi paradox fails to acknowledge the existence of contact and colonization anomalies in the historical record. However, it does support the conclusions of astronomers who project the existence of extraterrestrial civilizations.

The Drake equation also acknowledges the existence of cosmic civilizations, though it, too, fails to acknowledge the contact evidence already present on Earth. The SETI experiment is flawed because it assumes that extraterrestrial civilizations would have evolved as Earth's have.

In fact, it is probable that at least *one civilization* did overcome all obstacles and seeded life on Earth.

3
....
The Terraformed Earth

Perhaps the greatest evidence we have that proves the case for the involvement of an extraterrestrial civilization in the genesis of life on Earth is Earth itself. We are faced with a profound mystery when we carefully and objectively examine the geography of the planet.

To begin with I present a brief summary of plate tectonics and geographical data as an important first step to set up the paradigm-shifting scenarios that follow.

The theory of plate tectonics is nowadays generally accepted by geologists. The basic thrust of the theory is that instead of being permanent fixtures of Earth's surface, the continents and ocean basins undergo continuous change.

Both are parts of lithosphere plates that move against each other, and in the process new crust is created at midoceanic ridges (spreading centers), and old crust is consumed at convergent plate boundaries known as subduction zones.

Today, scientists have a good understanding of how the plates move and how such movements relate to earthquakes and volcanic activity. Most plate movement occurs along narrow zones between plates where the results of plate-tectonic forces are most evident. There are basically three different types of plate boundaries: divergent, convergent, and transform.

Scientists believe that the size of Earth has not changed significantly during the past six hundred million years and probably not much since shortly after its formation 4.6 billion years ago; Earth's unchanging size implies that the crust is being destroyed at about the same rate as it is being created.

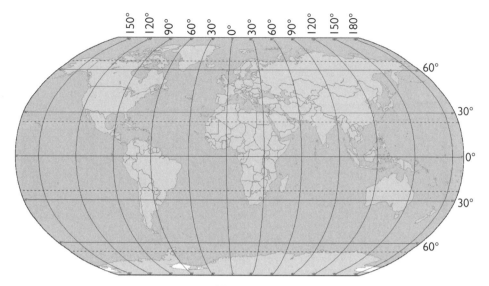

Fig. 3.1. World map with earth grid

Such destruction, or recycling, of the crust takes place along convergent boundaries where plates are moving toward each other, and one plate sinks (is subducted) under another in the subduction zone.

Regardless of these complex interactions, it is now a well-established fact that Earth's crust is broken into a dozen or so rigid slabs, called tectonic plates by geologists, that are moving relative to one another.

The various movements along differing plate boundaries cause coasts to form at the edges of a landmass and mountain ranges, plateaus, and valleys to form in the interior. For example, a collision between the Indian and Eurasian Plates pushed up the Himalayas, at the same time forming the Tibetan Plateau.

Off the coast of South America, along the Peru-Chile Trench, the oceanic Nazca Plate is pushing into and is being subducted under the continental part of the South American Plate. In turn, the overriding South American Plate is being lifted up, a process that created the towering Andes Mountains, the backbone of the continent.

Because continental crust is less dense than oceanic crust, the latter always slides under the continental crust. Strong, destructive earthquakes and the rapid uplift of mountain ranges are common outcomes of these types of movements.

The Himalayan mountain range demonstrates one of the most visible and spectacular consequences of plate tectonics. When two continents meet head-on, neither slides under the other because the continental rocks are relatively light, and they, like two colliding icebergs, resist downward motion. Instead, the crust tends to buckle and be pushed upward or sideways, actions that create mountain ranges.

As interesting and dramatic as mountain ranges are, most of Earth's surface is covered by oceans. We can think of the ocean bottom as a basin-and-range environment, very similar to, yet different from, the mountain-valley continental landmasses.

There are dramatic and very extensive ridges lying under the surface of the oceans. These are thought to be the youngest portions of the ocean basins, where new ocean crust is generated through mantle upwelling and plate divergence. Taken together, the oceanic ridge system of Earth extends about sixty-five thousand kilometers (forty thousand miles) around the globe.

The continental shelf is simply the flooded edges of the continents. Although the formations of coastal boundaries and mountain ranges are complex processes, they can be understood fairly easily.

Next, rivers obey the law of gravity and flow downhill from their mountain sources to their mouths at the flooded edges of continents (deltas) and empty into a gulf or sea. The sources of the world's major rivers are often in highly elevated or mountainous areas, but there are exceptions.

For example, the source of the Mississippi River is Lake Itasca, in Minnesota, which lies just 450 meters (1,475 feet) above sea level.

Although the world's major rivers flow through many different types of terrain, they exhibit similar physical characteristics and biological functions. As we have seen, tectonic processes result in the uplift and formation of major mountain chains, but then the world's major river systems help to erode those mountain ranges. They achieve this by transporting sediments from their basins to the sea through the processes of erosion, transport, and deposition.

For example, the Colorado River, located in the southwestern United States, flows through the Colorado Plateau region. The river's world-famous canyons were created over millions of years as the river carved out and eroded its way downward through the Colorado Plateau, which was being driven upward by tectonic forces.

A river's flow is halted when it reaches the sea, where the river deposits its sediments and creates a delta. River deltas commonly assume a triangular pattern that resembles the Greek letter *delta* (Δ)—a letter based on the shape of the Nile River Delta in northern Egypt. Fresh water and salt water meet in these deltas, creating some of the world's most biologically productive habitats.

All of the above presents a rough sketch of the logical and elegant scheme of geographical and geological formation, deformation, and recycling of materials. If you are wondering, dear readers, why you find yourself in a geography or geology class, I am quickly going to cut to the chase.

As pointed out above, the tectonic and river formation schemes are not too difficult to understand. However, the final result that you will not read about in any textbooks poses a very enigmatic problem that should be addressed and solved. What is that?

The continental landmasses, rivers, gulfs, and seas converge in a band around the globe at *30° north latitude*. Nothing in the plate tectonic scheme predicts that we would find this exact kind of configuration on a planetary-wide basis.

However, the Nile River flows northward from Lake Victoria to its delta and mouth at the 30° north latitude line to empty into the Mediterranean Sea. Across thousands of miles of ocean, the Mississippi River flows south from Lake Itasca to its delta, also at 30° north latitude, where it empties into the Gulf of Mexico.

East of the Nile, the Tigris-Euphrates River System flows from the Taurus Mountains south to its delta and empties into the Arabian Sea, also along the 30° north latitude line, and the Yangtze River flows from west to east and empties into the East China Sea at 30° north.

It is reassuring to appreciate the generalized, and quite logical, scheme of plate tectonics and how their actions generate events that create coastal boundaries, mountain ranges, and plateaus. However, being faced with the very precise relationships between the world's great river systems and the continental shelves is not comforting at all.

In fact, it is a wake-up call.

Why? It looks like Earth is the product of an intentional engineering program that is so sophisticated and vast that it has escaped our attention so far.

These geographical features present an astonishing reality, and that raises an almost shocking possibility at the same time. The exactitude of this global landmass-gulf relationship suggests that some kind of mathematical/geometrical force has been at work over the long, long period of the planet's geological and geographical evolution.

(If geographers and geologists have noted this startling convergence, and that seems very probable, they have kept very quiet about it.)

The next incredible aspect of this 30° north parallel land-river-sea convergence is the rapid appearance of civilization precisely at this global juncture. Is it purely by coincidence that the Egyptian civilization emerged at 30° north latitude?

We might conclude so, except that the Sumerian civilization, located in southern Mesopotamia, which is the present-day southern Iraq, was also positioned at the same latitude at the mouth of the Tigris-Euphrates, the Mayan and Olmec mound builder civilizations positioned at or near the 30° north latitude, and the most ancient Chinese civilization at the mouth of the Yangtze River.

Next, yet more fascinating and revealing aspects of the relationships between Earth's geometry and early civilizations are revealed if we switch the arbitrary Greenwich 0° latitude to 31° east longitude. This would include the Great Pyramid as well as Lake Victoria in southern Africa, which is the source of the Nile River.

Using this line as the prime meridian, a second startling reality becomes obvious: the Mississippi River Delta is exactly 120° west of the Nile River, and the Yangtze empties into the China Sea 90° east of the Nile.

Having three of the world's major river deltas located on a single meridian, each separated by significant and geometrically precise degrees of longitude, is a significant fact. Once again, can this really be the result of nothing more than a long series of random events?

Why would these great rivers—separated by thousands and thousands of miles—exhibit such geometrically precise relationships on a global scale?

This is not the end of the story, however. In fact, Lake Victoria, the key source of the Nile River, sits on the equator—the obvious 0° latitude base. Now, since we have shifted the 0° longitude base to the Great Pyramid–Lake Victoria meridian, this makes Lake Victoria the 0° base for both latitude and longitude.

We have both geographical and biological reasons to consider Lake Victoria the navel of Earth's surface and of its biodiversity. Why?

The lake sits in the middle of the region where the great apes and chimpanzees originated. Of course, they are considered our closest animal relatives. It is just west of the Great Rift Valley, which is home to many of Africa's animal species. The lake itself, the largest in Africa, contains an astounding two hundred different species of fish.

The globe reveals yet another landmass-river feature; the Amazon River flows in an easterly direction from the Andes to its mouth along an undulating course that straddles the equator.

Looking at a map we can see that the Amazon points to Lake Victoria, the Nile flows north and points to the Great Pyramid, and the Nile Delta sits on the Mediterranean Sea at 30° north latitude. while the Mississippi River flows in a southerly direction and empties into the Gulf of Mexico, exactly 120° west of the Great Pyramid.

In fact, the Nile and Mississippi Rivers appear to be inverted mirror images of each other. Scientists do not seem to have paid any attention to the above facts. In addition, I have not gathered and analyzed them based on the work of any other independent researcher.

Even if geologists investigated the foregoing data, it is doubtful that it would lead to any theoretical framework at present.

⌂

Considering all of the foregoing, we have the freedom to exercise both our logical capabilities and our imaginations and to consider how Earth's geology and geography may have come about. Given the high degree of precision—on a massive scale—we shall dismiss the idea that the geographical features were produced by an infinite series of random events.

Random events would not produce landmasses and rivers terminating at oceanic boundaries in a narrow band that encircles Earth along the thirtieth parallel. Billions of chance rolls of the geological dice simply could not create the exact geometrical features that we see on a global scale.

Just because we have no narrative capable of explaining these facts in any scientific way at present, this does not mean that there is no explanation. In addition, it also does not mean that we simply ignore these enigmas by resorting to unscientific "by chance" arguments.

The mountains, streams, rivers, valleys, deltas, gulfs, and seas are obeying an as yet unidentified set of rules, principles, and laws, just as plate tectonic movements are, that we simply neither perceive nor comprehend.

Water flows down mountainsides into valleys that gradually terminate in delta areas before emptying into a gulf or sea. However, gravity and plate tectonics together do not explain why the world's major rivers terminate along the same parallel.

For a moment, let us take a satellite position above Earth.

I shall now posit a radical scenario that involves the operations, knowledge, and technology of an extraterrestrial civilization. Our advanced civilization needs to have evolved hundreds of millions of years before our own to have created technologies that we cannot even begin to imagine. Our civilizations, according to current dogma, are only five thousand years old, and look how far we have come in such a short time.

Project our current rate of technological advancement forward a mere million years (a nanosecond in cosmic time scales), and what would human civilization be like on Earth?

We cannot even imagine that because no one even foresaw the emergence of cell phones, iPods, and the Internet fifty years ago, so how can we possibly project forward one thousand millennia? It would be an exercise in futility, and we know it.

So whatever limits we might put on any extraterrestrial civilization would be nothing more than a reflection of the limits of our own current level of knowledge and ignorance. Could there be a civilization out there that long ago mastered interstellar space travel? I will attempt to answer that question in subsequent chapters.

That said, our posited highly advanced civilization not only mastered space travel, they also mastered the science of planetary genesis. In fact, the main mission of their civilization might be to spread life throughout the universe. (Ultimately, that may be ours, too.) To succeed, they would first have to identify solar systems with planets that have the potential to evolve life once the seeds are planted.

Are we not doing that right now with the Kepler telescope?

Taking this scenario a quantum leap further we shall also ascribe an even greater and more incomprehensible power to them. They likely have the capability of terraforming and engineering entire solar systems. In other words, our cosmic civilization has evolved technologies capable of shaping geological and geographical conditions and the various features of planets.

Is this really such a sci-fi stretch? I think not.

Right now, our scientists are considering ways to reengineer the planets in our solar system. We could plant the seeds of life on Mars. In fact, our space probes have probably carried bacteria and viruses to the red planet already. It only takes an atmosphere with some oxygen and water to get the wheels of the bacterial and viral seeds in evolutionary motion.

In my first book, *The Genesis Race,* the first of this series, I argued that the cultural and archaeological evidence supported the intervention of an advanced race in human evolution. Furthermore, I also posited that the human race is, in fact, a hybrid species that was developed by this advanced genesis race.

The members of that interstellar race were referred to as "gods" by our remote ancestors.

We find references to them in virtually every culture around the globe. The Bible makes numerous references to them, whenever the singular God becomes the plural gods that are involved in the genesis, evolution, and behavior modification of early humans. (In Genesis 1:26, we see, "We shall make man, male and female, in Our image and likeness"); how much more specific did they have to be?

This advanced race could have created us to carry on their work. Are we not engaged, however slowly, in creating the technology to do just that? Another point I made in the first book was the idea that our DNA is embedded with their code, so our evolution must recapitulate theirs.

This advanced civilization is not an *alien* race in the way we normally think of that term. They are our ancestors, humans, or at least they were as human as we are during their early evolution. At this distant point, they may be quasi-material or holographic beings that are more light and intelligence than material substance.

They may have achieved the ability to shape-shift and appear and disappear at will. Possibly, they have also realized virtual immortality as well.

Nothing in the laws of physics prevents these possible developments.

The Bible tells us that the "gods" did not want mortal, earthly humans to gain access to the Tree of Life lest they become immortal. What is the Tree of Life they referred to? That tree was set beyond the Tree of the Knowledge of Good and Evil, which set humans apart from the other animals and which we did have access to.

We are long since past the garden and tasting the forbidden fruit and being barred from access to The Tree of Life (immortality). We are now in the throes of completely deciphering the genetic code: the structure of DNA and the genome (the complete set of genes or genetic material present in a cell or organism). We are learning the art of bioengineering and are exploring the solar system with our (primitive) space technologies.

One thing we should always keep in mind: there are no guarantees when it comes to the survival of a species in this universe. We are now facing the constant challenges that nature presents, as well as the constant challenges our own man-made civilization presents.

At this point, we are already fully committed to the continual acquisition of knowledge and to the constant development of new technologies. Can we meet all of the unforeseen challenges and consequences that the uncertain future holds? No one knows the answer to that question.

The geological and geographical features that I raised at the opening part of this chapter may need to be addressed and understood very soon. If Earth is the product of superadvanced engineering, then the sooner we realize it, the better off we will be.

CONCLUSION

The geology and geography of Earth exhibit a high degree of geometry, which is unaccounted for by science. It could be the result of terraforming operations conducted by an advanced, extraterrestrial race that possessed the science and technology to perform this feat. The convergence of rivers and landmasses on 30° north latitude is evidence of this operation, as are the precise distances between major rivers. In addition, the Great Pyramid appears to be a geodetic marker that points to the significance of that latitude.

SECTION II

· · · · · · · ·

THE GREAT PYRAMID
The Great Enigma

4
....
Alien Message in Stone

Are we to assume that the world's first civilizations arose along the same degree of latitude by a chance roll of the dice? In fact, our scholars and scientists have made, and continue to make, those assumptions without even attempting to conduct rigorous, scientific investigations into them.

The ancient civilizations spanning the globe pose many mysteries that have been heretofore documented in numerous books and articles by various authors. It would be redundant to go into the bulk of them.

However, I herein submit that we have a singular piece of evidence that Earth has been visited by an advanced race: the Great Pyramid, which sits on the Giza Plateau at 0° longitude.

It is very clear that the Great Pyramid was, among other things, built to be a very long-lasting geodetic marker. Its obvious relationship with Lake Victoria and the Nile River, the longest river in the world, is important. As was noted in the foregoing chapter, ascribing the 0° longitude point to Greenwich, England, was entirely an arbitrary and political matter made by the British when they were the global superpower.

In strictly geographic terms, the obvious point of 0° longitude and latitude is Lake Victoria, Africa, which sits near the Rift Valley, straddling the equator. Repositioning 0° longitude to Lake Victoria means that the Great Pyramid, which is due north of the lake, is also on the adjusted 0° longitude meridian. These features are easily identified by satellites.

Using that adjustment, it is easy to see that the mouth of the Mississippi River (which is 89° west of Greenwich) is 120° west of the Great Pyramid as well as the mouth of the Nile River. Next, the Yangtze River is 90° degrees east, as noted in the previous chapter.

Fig. 4.1. Original entrance to the Great Pyramid. Photo by Olaf Tausch.

As noted in chapter 3, the deltas and mouths of all of these rivers straddle the 30° north parallel, as does the delta of the Tigris-Euphrates River System. It stretches credulity past the breaking point to believe that these precise geographical relationships are purely the result of random events. (A supercomputer with the correct statistical software could confirm or reject this theory.)

One of the world's other great rivers, the Amazon, straddles the equator and runs from the Andes eastward to empty into the Atlantic, also at the equator, seemingly pointing toward Lake Victoria.

Now, considering the above facts, is it logical to assume that Earth's earliest civilizations emerged along the 30° north latitude, near these river deltas, ostensibly by chance? Next, this begs the following, persistent question, Why did early civilizations build pyramids and pyramidal-type structures on a massive scale around the globe?

No one can answer that question with any authority since none of us, scholars included, were alive and part of the planning process.

We must also face the fact that there is no evidence to support any gradual evolution of the social systems, knowledge, skills, and technologies needed to build pyramids in the late Neolithic era. There are no clearly discernable progressive series of developments that one can use to trace, and back engineer, the sudden rise of urban centers, metallurgy, advanced math, or writing in Sumer and the Indus Valley, or the construction of the Great Pyramid in Egypt. . . .

Before delving into the Great Pyramid, we must step back to gain a perspective on the real issues involved. It is instructive to begin by examining the technological progress that has occurred over the past several hundred years.

The Great Pyramid is forty-eight stories high; a similarly tall man-made structure with equal mass was not built until the twentieth century, when the Hoover Dam was constructed. That took place after a prolonged period of infrastructure, architectural, tool, and skill development that apparently took 4,500 years to accomplish.

Does it make any logical sense to find a structure at least 4,500 years old that was more sophisticated than any subsequent structure until the twentieth century?

Modern Egyptians did not build the Aswan Dam until Western civilization had advanced enough to provide them with the knowledge and technology to construct it. This suggests that Egypt devolved from the point when the Great Pyramid was constructed for the ensuing 4,500 years!

We know that technological innovation proceeds through a number of graduated steps. We are not at all surprised by the fact that the wheeled cart was turned into the horse and buggy and then the automobile. This advancement took place over a long period of time.

No problem; this is an entirely rational progression, in fact. The same is true of tools. There is no mystery in seeing the thousands of years of development from stone hammers and mallets to the modern iron and steel versions.

In addition, we know without even thinking about it that our modern power tools first required the invention of DC and then AC power. Crick and Watson had to discover the shape of the DNA molecule before the DNA genome sequence could be unraveled and bioengineering could be turned into a commercial enterprise.

All of that seems so obvious that it hardly needs mentioning. I bring this logical pattern up because we do not seem to apply similar logic to the artifacts we find in our earliest civilizations.

You cannot have computers or an electrical grid without first having an entire industrial infrastructure to produce the metals, circuitry, wires, cords, and such that go into computers and the delivery of electricity. For instance, AC power had to be developed before our current electromagnetic civilization could be put into place. We cannot separate technological advances from similar advances in social organization and education.

When we look at and carefully examine the Great Pyramid, we find the automobile preceding the wheeled cart. The same is true of the abrupt appearance of crop agriculture and large-scale flood irrigation techniques that we find in Egypt, Mesopotamia, and the Indus Valley.

There is no gradual step-by-step progression in the record that supports the notion that the ancient Egyptians possessed the knowledge, tools, skills, or level of social organization required to build the Great Pyramid. The same holds true for the genetic manipulation and sudden transformation of wild grass seeds into viable grain crops.

We do not find any antecedents because none were created by primitive human cultures back in the early Neolithic and late Paleolithic periods. We have not created any new major food crops because the ones we inherited already represented a high degree of advanced genetic engineering.

Wild grass seeds are minuscule and hardly worth the effort of harvesting, winnowing, and cooking; that is, until they have been genetically engineered, which they were more than five thousand years ago. Now we turn to the eternal mystery, the Great Pyramid.

TESTING THE HYPOTHESIS

An examination of the record of attempts at building pyramids that were conducted by Egyptologists, which was organized to show that the known Egyptian culture had the knowledge and technology to build the Great Pyramid, is revealing.

However, let us precede that examination by first establishing some facts and modern-day comparisons.

As noted above, the Great Pyramid is forty-eight stories tall. The base covers thirteen acres and was carved out of the solid limestone bedrock that forms the Giza Plateau. It has been estimated that the structure is composed of 2.5 million blocks, mostly limestone, each with an average weight of 2.5 tons. That gives us a mass of about six million tons.

Most of the limestone blocks were quarried near the site. However, there are large granite blocks, each weighing from fifty to seventy tons, positioned 175 vertical feet above the base. They frame in a room that is referred to as the King's Chamber by Egyptologists. These blocks were put in place with a high degree of precision. Above this room, the builders placed an additional forty-three blocks of granite, some weighing seventy tons.

The quarry where this particular type of rose granite is found is located near the Aswan Dam. That is a distance of about five hundred miles from the Giza Plateau. The pyramid was finished with an outer casing composed of Tura limestone that was quarried on the east side of the Nile, across the river from the Great Pyramid building site.

Just these barebones examples raise a number of thorny problems for the conventional interpretation of how the Great Pyramid was constructed using primitive tools and methods. First, while limestone is not a particularly hard rock, granite is an extremely hard stone to work with (7 of 9 on the Mohs hardness scale).

It has never been proven that the primitive methods proposed could be used to cut and chisel the blocks of granite we find in the King's Chamber to an extremely smooth finish. Remember that the Egyptians of the period not only lacked the wheel, they also lacked hardened metal tools made of iron or steel.

The method of carving the blocks out of the quarry proposed by Egyptologists is so primitive it is hard to believe they would even dare offer it. We are given to believe that the primary tool used was a round ball of granite. Could a hammer stone really produce the precision-cut, smoothly finished granite blocks found in the King's Chamber? In truth, the hammer stones of conventional history, which were supposed to have been used to quarry the blocks, could not quarry the granite blocks and never have been used to finish diorite statues to a smooth, polished finish.

Keep in mind that the Egyptian culture also did not possess the wheel or draft animals to help move the blocks at the time the Great Pyramid was constructed.

Fig. 4.2. Great Pyramid casing stones. Photo courtesy of Bill Alford.

The next thorny problem involves transporting thousands of limestone blocks across the Nile to the Giza Plateau. Although the outer casing is missing from most of the Great Pyramid today, we know that it once existed because four blocks remain intact on the northeastern corner of the lowest tier.

The casing blocks in question weigh an estimated fifteen tons; each is beveled at a precise 51:50° angle, and they were so accurately fitted together that there is almost no discernible space between them. However, in reality, the builders had applied a thin coat of mortar before fitting them into place.

An interesting fact about the mortar is that even though its chemical composition is known it cannot be exactly reproduced, and it is actually stronger than the limestone blocks it holds in place.

Tens of thousands of these precision-beveled blocks had to be cut, transported across the river, and then painstakingly fit into place. How? The shape and surfaces of the finished pyramid would have resembled a quartz crystal; that is the level of precision engineering embodied in the Great Pyramid.

Why would all this be necessary if it was nothing more than a tomb?

These are but several of the numerous challenges that the building of the Great Pyramid, using primitive tools and methods, poses, and they are not even the most severe at that.

THE JAPANESE FIASCO

Back in the 1970s, when the Japanese economy was riding high and national pride was at its peak, a Japanese team decided to show the world how the Great Pyramid was built.

First, they consulted with Egyptologists to ascertain the kinds of tools and methods that the ancient Egyptians had used to build the pyramid. They decided to construct an exact scale model. The enthusiastic team immediately ran into trouble when they tried to create the limestone blocks using primitive tools and methods. They simply could not pull it off.

Frustrated, they brought in modern jackhammers to do the job. Then they tried to ferry the blocks across the Nile on primitive barges but failed. They called in modern ferries. The next problem came when they attempted to drag the blocks, weighing less than two tons, on sleds across the sand. The blocks quickly sank, and the crew's efforts ground to a halt.

In all, the team had to resort to the use of jackhammers, bulldozers, trucks, and even a helicopter to get the blocks to the site and stacked up to form a pyramid. The final insult came when they discovered that it was not so easy to precisely position the blocks, even with the use of a helicopter. Their (small-scale) finished pyramid was so completely out of alignment that it could not form an apex at the top.

This was a serious effort that required investments of time and money (provided by Nissan). The Japanese are a proud people, and they are loath to lose face, but in this project they walked away deeply humbled. We must keep in mind that this attempt did not include any large granite blocks, facing stones, or complex interior architecture, which the Great Pyramid does possess.

THE OBELISK FIASCO

The next attempt to prove that the ancient Egyptians built the Great Pyramid using primitive tools and methods came in 1995. The PBS television show *NOVA* sponsored the project. The project was filmed and turned into a documentary, which can be viewed online at "This Old Pyramid"; www.youtube.com/watch?v=rfrXwBkzkeo (accessed March 20, 2017).

The American archaeologist and Egyptologist Mark Lehner brought in Roger Hopkins, an expert stonemason, to work with the granite using primitive tools. The late Aly el Gasab, one of Egypt's foremost specialists in moving heavy statues, was also brought onboard to tap into his vast experience.

The idea was to create and raise a thirty-five-ton granite obelisk using nothing more than the tools and methods that Egyptologists claim the ancient Egyptians had used. The project started with confidence, optimism, and enthusiasm.

However, that would soon change as they faced their first challenge.

According to the orthodox scenario, the ancients traditionally sculpted an obelisk from a single piece of granite carved from quarries in Aswan. Lehner sought hints about ancient quarrying at the so-called Unfinished Obelisk, a one-thousand-ton monolith that some unidentified, alleged "pharaoh" abandoned after structurally dangerous cracks appeared during its removal.

They proceeded under the assumption that ancient laborers pounded away the surrounding granite with round dolorite hammer stones. Even though Lehner had learned some hard lessons trying this method in front of the cameras, he was still convinced that ancient quarrymen spent months or even years chipping away at the hard granite. Wrong.

It was not long before the stonemason, Hopkins, realized that if the team wanted an obelisk anytime soon, it needed a shortcut. Like their Japanese forerunners, the crew soon requested bulldozers and other modern machinery, which, of course, was used to quickly quarry the obelisk.

Not only did they fail to make a dent in the granite quarry using primitive tools, they also could neither lift the block nor transport it across the sand—strikes one and two.

In truth, these initial failures were enough to discredit the ancient-tools-and-methods thesis. Being forced to resort to modern equipment served to show one thing: whoever did build the Great Pyramid used some form of advanced technology at least equal to modern machinery.

After using bulldozers to quarry the obelisk and a truck to transport it, the team was ready to demonstrate how the ancients raised their obelisks. In truth, a thirty-five-ton obelisk is a peewee compared to the majority of obelisks that dot the Egyptian landscape.

Imagine what would have happened if they had tried to quarry and raise the most massive obelisk, which weighs about 440 tons!

Before trying to raise their obelisk, the team examined a number of related issues surrounding these sculptural wonders that I have brought up already. For instance, how did the ancients transport them from the quarries at Aswan to Thebes and other New Kingdom capitals farther down the Nile?

Once again that only scratches the surface of unresolved problems. Whoever created the obelisks also polished the sides and painstakingly carved highly artistic hieroglyphs up and down their exposed surfaces. The NOVA team did not even try to duplicate that painstaking and time-consuming work.

After the team members traded theories and built model boats to demonstrate how the ancients ferried thirty-ton to one-hundred-ton obelisks (and even a 440-ton obelisk) down the Nile to various sites, the sculptor Martin Isler led them in successfully raising a smaller two-ton obelisk using a levering technique. With that accomplished, they thought they had the challenge of raising the obelisk licked.

Tensions mounted as the time neared to actually raise it. This caused further debates and discussions. Hopkins was convinced the answer lay in building a great earthen ramp up to a specially designed chamber that contained sand. In this scenario, laborers would carefully tip the base of the obelisk into the top of the chamber and then begin removing sand from a trapdoor in the chamber's base.

Then, as the obelisk reached a pedestal at the bottom of the chamber, team members would ease one edge of its base into a so-called turning groove, which would hold the obelisk in position as other laborers pulled it upright. The team agreed that his plan sounded like it would work, and they decided to use Hopkins's strategy.

At the last minute, the team decided that sand was not dependable. Instead, they chose to use an idea developed by Gasab. First, the crew would put the obelisk on a sled and haul it on rollers up the ramp. Once it began to pivot over the top edge of the ramp, workers yanking down on ropes fixed to its top would control its descent down another, steeper ramp into the turning groove.

That went as planned. The obelisk then rested at a 32° angle from the ground. Workers using levers quickly forced it up to about 40°—nearly halfway to success. Once at this angle, however, the team proved unable to get the leverage necessary to raise the obelisk the rest of the way.

The workers redoubled their efforts, pulling hard at ropes fixed to the obelisk's tip. But this simply forced the shaft's butt end deeper into the turning groove. As the sun set on the project, they realized they had to meet the challenge the following day.

Early the next morning, Hopkins set up a large A-frame and then ran the ropes tied to the tip of the obelisk over it. By adjusting the angle of the rope in this way, he hoped to give the pullers a mechanical advantage.

Now they were essentially pulling up rather than down. Nonetheless, this last-ditch effort proved futile. The ropes on the pullers' side of the A-frame angled down too steeply for enough workers to reach them. Another ramp was needed—one whose angle matched that of the rope—but time had run out on the project.

Strike three.

Even if they had succeeded in meeting the challenges posed by each step involved in raising a thirty-five-ton obelisk in this fashion, it would not have definitively solved the real problem. To truly test the primitive-tools-and-methods thesis, the team would have had to face the impossible task of quarrying, transporting, and raising a 440-ton obelisk, the heaviest one in Egypt. Why?

Just because you can lift one hundred pounds off the ground does not mean that you can lift one thousand pounds off the ground. We run into the problems of scales of magnitude and the limits of human labor and the structural integrity of wooden boats, beams, sleds, and so forth. A 440-ton obelisk is an extraordinarily massive chunk of granite equaling the combined weight of 220 average-size automobiles.

Again, to gain a realistic perspective we must turn to our modern equipment. A space shuttle weighs about four hundred tons. At the time it was being constructed, there was no crane that could lift that much weight. One was custom designed and built for the sole purpose of lifting the shuttle.

Our modern earthmovers—gigantic machines with thirteen-foot-tall tires and five-hundred-horsepower motors—are used at mines to haul large loads of rocks and ore. The largest of these has a capacity of about three hundred tons. Architects and engineers today simply do not use these massive-size structural stone components because they are unnecessary, expensive, and difficult to work with.

Given these indisputable facts, is it not *preposterous* to believe that a team of laborers could lift, transport, and raise a 440-ton obelisk? If much smaller objects posed an insurmountable task for modern teams, then the Great Pyramid presents the ultimate challenge to the primitive-tools-and-methods theory.

Before delving into the Great Pyramid further, it is instructive to read the following background quote written by forensic engineer Craig Smith:

> The logistics involved in the construction of this pyramid are staggering when one considers that the ancient Egyptians had no pulleys, no wheels, and no iron tools. Large blocks of limestone and granite—some weighing as much as 20 tons (18 Mg)—had to be cut at quarries and transported by boat across or down the Nile River. All of the interior rock was carved on the Giza Plateau, but the limestone used on the exterior facing of the pyramid came from Tura, which was situated across the Nile. Blocks of limestone weighing anywhere from 2.5 to 6 tons (2.3 to 5.4 Mg) made up the bulk of the structure. Estimates indicate that more than 2 million such blocks were used. Most of these were cut from a quarry at Giza; heavier blocks of granite from Aswan were used to construct the King's Chamber.
>
> The final dimensions of these stones were extremely accurate on the exterior faces of the pyramid: the joints were made within fractions of an inch—in some cases substantially less than 1/8 in. (3 mm). The pyramid was oriented with its major sides either north-south or east-west. This in itself was a remarkable

undertaking, given the accuracy to which it was done, because the Egyptians had to perform the work using astronomical or solar observations—the compass had not yet been invented.

The dimensions of the pyramid are extremely accurate and the site was leveled within a fraction of an inch over the entire base. This is comparable to the accuracy possible with modern construction methods and laser leveling.[1]

This quote is taken from an article, but Smith conducted the research as part of a team from the international engineering firm of Daniel Mann Johnson and Mendenhall that was hired to analyze the pyramid.

CONCLUSION

Though the archaeological record is littered with enigmas, the Great Pyramid stands as the most persuasive single piece of ancient evidence that supports the Genesis Race hypothesis. The key issue is the precision engineering achieved on a massive scale; the ancient Egyptians simply lacked the architectural knowledge, engineering skills, and technology required for the pyramid's construction. This nullifies the orthodox thesis. Ergo, an advanced extraterrestrial race built the Giza complex.

5

The Enigma of
Precision Engineering

The next issues we have to face when analyzing the technology required to build the Great Pyramid are

1. The precision-leveled base
2. The precise orientation to true north and the alignment with the cardinal directions
3. The sophisticated architectural design of the interior
4. The masterful engineering required to ensure that each of the 204 tiers was as flat as the base, so that the faces and edges of the pyramid would come together at the top to form a perfect apex

The base of the Great Pyramid is massive, covering about thirteen acres. As noted at the end of the last chapter, the engineering firm that analyzed the structure concluded that the base was so level that it would require modern laser technology to duplicate it.

Each side spans the distance of two and a half football fields in length. To say that this was a massive, extraordinarily complex undertaking would be a gross understatement.

Here again, we are given to believe that (a) workmen labored with granitic balls to hack the irregular surface of the limestone bedrock as flat as the bottom of a frying pan over a thirteen-acre area, (b) the surveyors—who were called rope stretchers—could survey a thirteen-acre base to the same accuracy today achieved with laser levels,

Fig. 5.1. Note the flat, fifty-ton, precision-cut-and-placed granite blocks that frame the King's Chamber

and (c) they knew how to accurately orient this massive edifice to the cardinal points and true north.

It is still the most precisely oriented building in the world.

The ancient Egyptian surveyors were called *rope stretchers* because that was the extent of their technology. Their architects and engineers would have possessed no more than rudimentary mathematics and very basic algebra.

As we saw, the modern Japanese team, who failed to reproduce a scale model (even one that lacked the complex interior spaces), found that they could not meet the many engineering challenges posed, even on a very small scale.

Perhaps if the obelisk team had succeeded at each stage of the process, we might be persuaded to consider the possibility that some kind of ramp system could have been used to build the Great Pyramid. However, if Egyptologists cannot duplicate the quarrying, lifting, transporting, and raising of a thirty-five-ton obelisk, then they certainly cannot account for the fifty- to seventy-ton blocks of granite that enclose the King's Chamber.

Additionally, it has never been shown that the types of boats found at the Giza Plateau could be used to transport the blocks from

Aswan to the site about five hundred miles up the Nile River.

The ramp debates have been going in circles for generations, and they are, in fact, meaningless. The quarry and transport problems of the largest blocks used in the pyramid's construction have to be solved first.

There is no point in trying to show how the millions of smaller blocks may have been lifted into place using a ramp system if you cannot first demonstrate that you can solve the greatest challenges. Those occur at the quarry and with the river transport of both the dozens of granite blocks used in the King's Chamber and the tens of thousands of casing blocks across the Nile.

The feasibility of hoisting the granite blocks out of the quarry, transporting them to the Nile, and then ferrying them down the river to Giza—using primitive tools and methods—has never been remotely tested, as noted in the prior chapter. (As we have seen, much smaller tests of the primitive-tools-and-methods thesis have failed.)

Since no one can demonstrate how these granite blocks even reached Giza, there is no point in speculating on how they were put in place to form the room referred to as the King's Chamber. That involved lifting them up 175 vertical feet, and no team of men pulling on ropes could achieve that feat.

The whole "how-the-pyramid-was-built exercise" is a dodge. It assumes that the blocks could be quarried and transported using primitive tools and methods; however, they could not. How many more generations are going to keep going in futile circles trying to prove this or that arbitrary, nonsensical thesis?

In fact, these issues can be scientifically resolved. It is quite possible to test and attempt to duplicate what Egyptologists claim occurred at the quarry. Every step can be performed using primitive tools and methods, as outlined by historians. This is one of the only areas of history and archaeology that can be tested using scientific methodology.

I propose that this simple "proof-of-concept" test be performed by an independent scientific body. This would definitively put the debate to rest, and "we" could move on to more productive lines of research. This is a critical point, and that is why it is being repeated here.

The next extreme challenge occurred during the actual construction project. As the engineers supervised the project, making sure that each tier was a flat plane, they had to take the interior design into account.

Their design includes passageways, a space (Grand Gallery) with a corbelled ceiling, two rooms (King's and Queen's Chambers), and a complex duct system that snakes from the inner chambers through multiple tiers.

In 1995, Christopher Dunn, an aerospace engineer and author of *The Giza Power Plant,* investigated the "sarcophagus" of the Great Pyramid. Using precision measuring instruments, he climbed inside to gauge the degree of precision used in creating the granitic object.

Dunn soon discovered that the box was so smooth and flat that a flashlight shone from behind a straight edge ruler* would not reveal any light passing through it. All the edges on the box were uniformly square and the surfaces completely flat.

Since Dunn couldn't find any significant deviation across the flat surfaces and square corners, Dunn eventually concluded that the level of precision achieved could only have been arrived at by using some type of advanced machinery.

Numerous other disinterested observers and researchers have noted these same high levels of precision that were achieved in the granite blocks that frame in the King's Chamber and the casing stones sitting on the lowest tier. These stones were planed and positioned with such precision that a piece of paper cannot be inserted between them.

A civilization can only produce high levels of precision on this kind of grand architectural level using sophisticated technology. In addition, the earliest civilizations to require precision building techniques were the ancient Greeks and Romans, the latter with the design of the Coliseum, but they built that sophisticated structure thousands of years after the Great Pyramid was constructed.

In order to justify the claim that the ancient Egyptians could produce such precision using primitive tools and methods, Egyptologists should have easily been able to quarry, lift, transport, and raise the thirty-five-ton obelisk. As we have previously noted, this challenge was, in fact, a very low-level test.

The same was true for the prior Japanese attempt to build a scale model of the Great Pyramid. In both cases, the primitive tools and methods failed, and the teams had to rely on modern equipment to get

---

*A straight edge is a type of ruler or gauge that engineers use. When placed on the surface of the wall it showed that it was completely flat since no light came through the straight edge.

the job done. Clearly, Dunn's conclusions agree with the facts, as they would predict the failures of the above-described tests.[1]

Very similar levels of precision had to be achieved to ensure that each tier was flat in order to create a true pyramidal shape. Precision on the scale of a forty-eight-story structure—composed of millions of blocks of stone—is simply unthinkable given granite hammer stones and primitive manipulation methods to achieve it.

(In actuality, it would be difficult to achieve today: this is considered in the next chapter.)

The objections to the orthodox scenarios are so strong, numerous, and rational that one can only wonder why Egyptologists tenaciously cling to them. The answer to that question is not as complicated or as irrational as it might seem on the surface. (This is addressed in the next section.)

THE GANTENBRINK SHAFT

The Gantenbrink shaft, named for the German robotics engineer Rudolf Gantenbrink, also displays that a high degree of precision

Fig. 5.2. The Gantenbrink shaft and door (approx. 8" × 8")

engineering was employed by the pyramid's builders. Egyptologists once considered this to be an "air shaft" and later thought that such shafts—the entrances to which are found in both chambers—might be "soul shafts," designed to direct souls to the afterlife, until a robot sent to explore the small eight-inch by eight-inch shaft ran into a small, copper-handled door that blocks passage.

No one knows the shaft's actual purpose.

THE SPHINX DATING CONTROVERSY

John Anthony West, an independent researcher, was inspired to investigate the Sphinx complex by an earlier investigator, R. A. Schwaller de Lubicz. The primary issue that West's mentor raised was the incongruity of the apparent erosion patterns evident in the complex with the views of orthodox Egyptologists concerning their chronology.

After carefully examining these weathering patterns, West became convinced that they were caused by a period of extensive rainfall.

Since the Giza Plateau is in a desert environment and there was not a period of extensive rainfall during the era following the assumed

Fig. 5.3. The Great Sphinx

building of the Sphinx in 2500 BCE, that conclusion came into direct conflict with the orthodox time line.

Of course, West was keenly aware of this mismatch. Not himself a geologist, he called in Robert Schoch, a credentialed geologist and an associate professor of natural sciences and mathematics at Boston University, to conduct a scientific investigation of the Sphinx complex.

After carrying out a thorough examination of the precinct using all of the knowledge and technological equipment commonly employed by geologists, Schoch concluded that the Sphinx erosion patterns were indeed caused by rainfall.

This prompted the geologist to find out when the last era of extensive rainfall had occurred in North Africa. Schoch discovered that that epoch had taken place about fifteen thousand years ago. When he announced his findings and redated the age of the Sphinx, it ignited a firestorm of controversy.

This often-bitter controversy has raged on for more than two decades, and it has not been resolved even at this late date. In truth, I am not that concerned with the outcome. What is important to the Genesis Race theory is what transpired at a conference held by the Geological Society of America in 1991.

The conference attendees heard Schoch's geological arguments for the redating. Then Lehner took the podium and gave the audience the results that contradicted Schoch's conclusions.

During his presentation, one key point that Lehner raised about the redating was the fact that there were *no human tribes or cultures identified in the region that were capable of building the complex at that early period.*

That point really had nothing to do with the science of geology, which was the focal point of the Sphinx controversy. Nonetheless, it did reveal why Egyptologists stubbornly hold on to their positions.

Stripped of the ancient Egyptians, circa 2500 BCE, using the established tools and methods of that period, they have no answer to the question of who constructed the Sphinx or the Great Pyramid and how those feats were accomplished.

Lehner's point was neither illogical nor was it incomprehensible; in fact, it was internally consistent with the logic used by the orthodoxy to this day. The problem is that the mounting evidence does not support the orthodox theories.

It simply does not matter that the attempts by Egyptologists to demonstrate their beliefs have failed; nor does it matter how many substantial objections have been raised by skeptics. They cling to their beliefs.

The time line and the efficacy of the primitive-tools-and-methods thesis constitute *central dogmas* that the orthodoxy simply cannot abandon, regardless of the evidence to the contrary. Though understandable in a broad cultural context, that position necessitates making the observable evidence fit their theories.

Of course, that position is entirely opposite to scientific methodology, which must make theories fit the evidence.

Archaeologists and historians can skirt around this issue because these disciplines are not within the purview of the hard sciences, such as geology. So introducing a geologist into the mix completely threw orthodox Egyptologists off-kilter. Suddenly, they had to meet the challenges posed by the supposedly hard science of geology.

There is more at stake in this controversy than the redating of the Sphinx complex.

Unfortunately, the contrary opinions of two credentialed geologists concerning the exact same geological features has revealed the fact that geology is not quite the hard science that the public has been led to believe it is. The facts it arrives at are also open to diverse interpretations.

In my view, the Sphinx controversy is not the central issue to resolve. The key objections to the orthodox theories involve (1) quarrying, transporting, and positioning the fifty- to seventy-ton blocks of granite 175 vertical feet above the base of the Great Pyramid, and (2) duplicating the high level of precision engineering evident in the overall construction of the Great Pyramid.

Given the total preponderance of the evidence, I am compelled to conclude that the primitive-tools-and-methods theory is untenable. Lacking any evidence that a technologically advanced human civilization existed at that time, we are then forced to consider other possibilities.

The Great Pyramid and the massive obelisks exist, and *someone, a reasoning body, had to put them there using some form of advanced technology.* There is a truth behind these mysteries, however well concealed it might appear to be.

I propose that an advanced Type II or III civilization constructed the complex, intentionally placing the Great Pyramid, as a geodetic marker, on the 30° north parallel latitude and the adjusted 0° longitude (rather than the Greenwich Prime Meridian). Long before that, they had seeded the planet, and prior to that event they had set planetwide engineering principles in motion.

ADDITIONAL EVIDENCE

The Great Pyramid was hermetically sealed at the time the caliph Mamun decided to bore through the limestone blocks to find the pharaoh's treasures he believed lay inside the massive complex. He used several simple yet ingenious means to penetrate through the limestone exterior: the applications of vinegar, fire, and hard labor.

After an extensive period of intense labors, his crew managed to bore through the exterior stones; they were fortunate in the fact that they ran right into a passageway. After combing through the interior using torches to light the pitch-dark passageway and Grand Gallery, they finally came to the room referred to as the King's Chamber.

Fig. 5.4. King's Chamber box

What did they find when they managed to get to this room? The caliph and his crew were crestfallen to be confronted by an empty room and an equally empty coffer. There were no valuable objects and no remains of any pharaoh.

No one had previously penetrated into the pyramid's interior, so no grave robbers had gotten there first and removed the hoped-for treasures.

Obviously, the above historical facts cast very serious doubts on the "tomb theory." If the caliph had found a mummy in the coffer, such would not be the case. We might dismiss this lack as representing an exceptional case if it did, in fact, not represent similar findings in the other 103 large pyramid complexes that dot the Egyptian landscape.

The traditional Egyptian burial sites found in the Valley of the Kings, for instance, did contain treasures and the remains of pharaohs when they were discovered. However, the massive pyramids did not.

These distinctions appear to have escaped the public, who often blindly accept the theories of Egyptologists that are routinely recited in history books and aired on TV specials.

However, the ever-growing database available on the Internet is changing that situation as the anomalous facts are presented on many websites.

King Tut's burial complex displayed the traditional features of an Egyptian tomb: colorful murals adorned the walls, treasures filled the chamber, and canopic jars were carefully set on the floor. None of that was present within the Great Pyramid. The walls were bare, the "coffers" empty, and the floors devoid of the usual objects associated with traditional Egyptian tombs.

Given this, how can Egyptologists assert that the pyramids are nothing more than giant mausoleums without any evidence to back up the claim? They cannot in any scientific way, but they do nonetheless, for reasons outlined above.

Next, the ancient Egyptians were devoted lovers of artwork. Their artists depicted every aspect of the environment and the culture. No one who has examined the extensive record of Egyptian murals and other works of art would deny this fact. Then why do we not find the most obvious features of the Egyptian landscape, the pyramids, especially the Great Pyramid, depicted in this extensive record?

The absence could be due to the fact that the artists did not consider the pyramids a part of their cultural record. Were they, even then, mysterious artifacts—attributed to a mysterious race of vanished gods—that triggered awe, fear, and wonderment, as they have for the millennia that have followed that remote era?

Egyptians of the 800 CE era typically informed travelers who came to visit the Great Pyramid that they called it "the house of terror." That does not sound like a cherished artifact made by the natives.

We have several other objections to the orthodox theories. The Great Pyramid displays neither any hieroglyphs nor any obvious attestations. These we would also expect to find associated with traditional tombs and other Egyptian edifices.

Ascribing responsibility to—and taking credit for—any feat is a very human characteristic, one exhibited by every advanced culture.

In addition, there are no ancient papyrus documents that contain references as to how or why the Great Pyramid was designed, engineered, and finished. We do not find any blueprints in this important record. Engineer Craig Smith, who was quoted in chapter 4, notes:

No records have been found that relate to the design of the Great Pyramid . . . they had no pulley.[2]

Does it not seem odd that this colossal accomplishment was not copiously documented and inscribed with dedications and inscriptions regarding Pharaoh Khufu, as other true Egyptian tombs in the King's Valley were?

If the Egyptians built it, they would have claimed it in **BOLD CAPS** in their papyrus records and in obvious hieroglyphic sequences. This is yet another piece of circumstantial evidence that argues against the Egyptians and for the Genesis Race having built the Great Pyramid and the other pyramids.

Despite all of this evidence to the contrary, Egyptologists continue to assert that the Great Pyramid is nothing more than a giant tomb. I have outlined the reasons already. They have to have a chronology and a history to justify their own existence as historians and scholars. To admit to any chinks in their armor would risk losing that battle and then the war.

But what about the apparent coffins in the King's and Queen's Chambers? Though they appear to be coffins, they did not contain any remains, so it appears that they were not ever used as coffins.

Then, if the Great Pyramid was not a tomb, what was its purpose?

(*Actually trying to answer that question needs to be preceded by the proof of concept testing that I proposed in the previous chapter.*)

THE NULL HYPOTHESIS

As noted in earlier chapters, we should not expect any advanced civilization to act in accordance with our logic and behaviors. The existence of apparent coffins absent of any remains may look like an insoluble paradox to us from our entirely homocentric view. Yet if we shift our perspective, we might just run into the reasoning behind this and other enigmas.

The lack of mummies, the lack of hieroglyphics and other kinds of attestations, and the existence of seemingly purposeless features in the interior—such as the three-hundred-foot-long descending passageway, the "air ducts" (do the dead breathe?), and the massive Grand Gallery—may actually represent clues that the builders left behind.

These clues seem to be based on *null* thought processes. If humans routinely bury their dead in coffins, then build a coffin but leave it empty. If they routinely ascribe credit to the achievements of individuals and groups, then leave the credits out. If they anticipate discovering hidden treasures within a hermetically sealed structure, they will eventually enter and find nothing.

The final null clue is the very massive, precision-engineered structure itself. If it was not a tomb, then what was its purpose? (Of course, that question vexes us to this day.) Build a sophisticated structure that has no obvious reason as to its end use and you leave it a perpetual mystery. Let the primitives stare in dumbfounded awe until they decipher the embedded code, if they ever do.

As was noted in prior chapters, we must assume that advanced extraterrestrial technology would be invisible to us. We should consider the possibility that what appear to be unsolvable mysteries are actually well-cloaked clues. Taken as single, isolated artifacts, they do, in fact, appear unfathomable. However, taken as a whole, they seem to embody a well-concealed yet potentially decipherable code.

The first step in understanding that code is to realize that the early Egyptian civilization did not build the Great Pyramid, but some as yet unidentified civilization surely did. At this point, we—the global human collective—do not seem to have arrived at that stage. After all is said and done, Egyptologists still embody our institutional position when it comes to the apparent mysteries that the Great Pyramid poses.

THE SECOND AND RED PYRAMIDS

Though the Great Pyramid commands the most attention, in fact, several other pyramids nearly equal it in size and would have required the same level of knowledge, the same engineering and project management skills as the larger pyramid.

The Red Pyramid is located at Dashur, not far from Giza, and is about the same size as the Pyramid of Cheops. It is the largest of three major pyramids located at this site, soaring 341 feet above the desert floor with a base that extends for 722 feet. Named for the rusty, reddish hue of its stones, it is also the third largest Egyptian pyramid, after the two described above. It contains a corbelled-arch gallery in the interior that resembles the one in the Great Pyramid.

This ancient site is thought to be older than the Giza complex, though there is no definitive proof to back up that assertion. At the time of its completion, the Red Pyramid was the tallest man-made structure in the world. It is also believed to be the world's first successful attempt at constructing a "true" smooth-sided pyramid. Local residents refer to the Red Pyramid as *el-harem el-wa-wa,* meaning the "Bat Pyramid."

Oddly, this pyramid was also finished with an outer layer of Tura limestone blocks, but only a few of these now *remain at a corner of the pyramid's base,* as with the Great Pyramid. This seems a strange coincidence. Supposedly, the outer casing was carried away during the Middle Ages, when, it is posited, much of the white Tura limestone was taken to rebuild Cairo.

The theory is that the locals took the trouble to dig through the fallen casing stones after a fourteenth-century earthquake knocked them loose. Though this scenario is at least feasible with the Great Pyramid, which lies at the edge of Cairo, the same cannot be said of the one at Dashur. There would not be any need to venture ten miles away to labor to break up limestone blocks and haul them to Cairo since there was an ample supply at Giza.

Additionally, why do the casing stones still exist on the so-called Bent Pyramid at Dashur if that single earthquake was powerful enough to dislodge the casing blocks from the other two huge pyramids?

There are many other pertinent questions that need to be answered about the missing casing stones at many of the sites, which seem to suggest the Egyptian pyramids were built in remote antiquity, not 4,500 years ago.

CONCLUSION

The Great Pyramid is not just a massive edifice; it also is a precision-engineered structure that exhibits features that could not have been built using the known primitive tools and methods that Egyptologists ascribe to its construction. Though test projects to build such structures using these primitive means have been conducted, they have repeatedly failed.

In spite of that fact, the orthodoxy still maintains that the ancient Egyptians built the complex, largely because they have no alternative builders to consider among established human cultures.

6

....

Building the
Great Pyramid Today

As long as there is strong institutional resistance to challenging and revising the orthodox theories, it is unlikely that the scientific community, as a whole, will get involved in the debate.

Therefore, I am not optimistic about the prospect of a concerted and rigorous scientific investigation into the Giza Plateau now or in the future.

That said, it is then incumbent on independent thinkers and researchers to conduct their own investigations despite the positions that various institutions embrace.

This, of course, means facing the accusations of members of the status quo who hurl charges of pseudoscience and fringe archaeology. This is a social hazard that all pioneers face.

Under the present rules of scholarship, the ruins of the ancient cities of Nineveh and Troy would not have been found by the men who did find them because they lacked academic pedigrees. What is an archaeologist, in the final analysis, but a pedantic grave robber with a college degree?

That barb is especially aimed at the forerunners of modern archaeology like Colonel Richard William Howard Vyse, who used dynamite to "investigate" the Great Pyramid.

Those issues aside, it is very tempting to try to answer the question as to the purpose and use of the Great Pyramid.

In fact, the speculative theories on this subject are so numerous

Fig. 6.1. Construction of Three Gorges Dam

that listing and describing them would require an entire book. It is not within the scope or intent of the present work to address, review, or analyze the plethora of theories.

My reasoning is simple: (1) none of the various theories can be tested, proved, or falsified, and (2) that being the case, it is more important to persuade the public and the scientific community that there are strong, viable, science-based objections to the orthodox scenario.

That said, Christopher Dunn's book *The Giza Power Plant* actually addresses the latter issue before presenting his plausible theory as to the Great Pyramid's end purpose.

His engineering background and experience lend a lot of weight to the objections he raises, as well as to the speculative conclusions he arrives at. That book and his articles are well worth reading.

Dunn concluded that the Great Pyramid could only have been constructed with the use of equipment at least equal to our modern machinery.

Could the pyramid have been built to function as a power-generation plant? Is it, in fact, a machine whose modus operandi remains invisible to us?

In general, I would answer *maybe* to the first question and *yes* to the second.

However, Dunn would also add that he has no idea as to how the Great Pyramid might have been used as some type of machine. It would seem to me that only an engineer can really pass judgment on Dunn's premise.

It is interesting to entertain various theories on that subject, but they remain in the realm of pure speculation. One thing is certain: *it was not a tomb.*

A more productive line of inquiry would appear to be summed up by the following question: Could we build the Great Pyramid today? We do have the possibility of answering that question through combining the knowledge and methods of a number of disciplines.

Unfortunately, the conclusions of any investigations will have to remain in the realm of logical inference and statistical probability. No one would take the proposal that we build an exact duplicate of the Great Pyramid seriously, and we have seen the results of smaller-scale projects.

The costs of doing so would be astronomical, and the project would probably grind to a halt as soon as time and budget constraints were exceeded. But there is another, more serious reason it will never be undertaken.

Nobody would see any economic utility in such a project.

Lacking any verifiable understanding of the end use of the structure, there is no apparent economic benefit to attempting such a massive project.

Proving definitively that we have the capability of building the Great Pyramid today is not in the cards. However, there is one little-known feature of the Great Pyramid that can only be appreciated from an aerial perspective. It reveals what few casual observers understand, that this pyramid is an engineer's nightmare.

The Great Pyramid is not a simple four-sided structure but a slightly concave, octagonal edifice, in fact. Each side is divided exactly in half by a seam that bends slightly inward (see fig. 6.2). That adds an almost alarming degree of difficulty to the engineering challenges.

Now, even though we have noted this previously, it bears repeating here that in order to ensure that the pyramid had true edges, was plumb, and could come together at the top to form a perfect apex, each tier had to be as level as the base.

Fig. 6.2. Aerial view of the Great Pyramid

That, of course, is why the base itself was precision engineered to the point where there is virtually no significant deviation over a thirteen-acre area.

To achieve the eventual seamless surface of the outer cladding required that the final blocks—which received the cladding stones—had to be arranged so that they maintained the 51:50° angle that the outer casing blocks were beveled at.

The Japanese team that tried to duplicate this engineering feat on a tiny scale model found they could not achieve it even with the aid of helicopters. Note that they did not include the additional concave features of the sides (shown in fig. 6.3) into their design.

The seam that divides each of the four sides in half is not apparent from the ground level, but it is obvious from an aerial perspective.

Of course, creating this added architectural twist complicated the engineering challenges greatly, as did the inclusion of the four interior ducts that had to snake through many tiers of the masonry from the King and Queen's Chambers.

Why the builders would have added this enigmatic feature remains a mystery. But there is no doubt that modern engineers faced with the challenge of duplicating the edifice would prefer to exclude the slightly concave sides.

Could they achieve it? I respond with a very qualified yes, but doing it would add much time to the construction process.

Many people are not aware of this concave feature. However, we

Fig. 6.3. The Great Pyramid (at top). Note the concave features.

have included it and now proceed to examine the evidence both for and against the prospect of its being within the current capabilities of modern architects and builders.

First, we do now have the capability of quarrying, lifting, transporting, and raising much larger obelisks than the *NOVA* team's thirty-five-ton granite obelisk. In fact, our modern machinery could handle the fifty- to seventy-ton blocks as well. In recent years, a massive mobile crane was built to lift an 850-ton bridge.

We have bulldozers to level the plateau and laser surveying equipment to ensure that the base is as flat as an iron frying pan. In addition, we also possess pulleys, hoists, steel guy wires, cables, and cranes capable of lifting and carefully positioning the blocks of limestone and granite.

But the Egyptians had none of this machinery.

Furthermore, modern architects and engineers have a century of experience designing and building skyscrapers, dams, and other large-scale structures.

Moreover, computer-aided-design technology (CAD) allows for the creation of models and statistical analysis as well as virtual simulations. In sum, we have the technology and the infrastructure to theoretically duplicate the project.

On the con side, most of our modern buildings are constructed out of wood, steel, and glass. Heavy blocks of limestone and granite are seldom used and never as the main components of skyscrapers.

There is little demand for fifty-ton blocks of granite; they are something that our construction crews rarely quarry, and stone-cutting and dressing operations are relatively unaccustomed to dealing with them.

Consider the following story:

Volga-Dnepr Airlines' new IL-76TD-90VD has carried its heaviest shipment to date; a 39 ton press for the paper industry transported from Finland to the United States. Loading and unloading of the 39-ton single piece of cargo required special equipment, including cranes and trailers, both in Jyvaeskylae in Finland and on its arrival at Rockford International Airport in Chicago. Organized in partnership between Procargo Ltd/Finland and Air Partner, the shipment—a replacement part for a paper machine—was destined for a pulp and paper plant.[1]

This random sample makes it abundantly clear that a thirty-nine-ton load is still considered heavy, even when using modern machinery to manipulate it. That proved true when Egyptologists failed to adequately manipulate the obelisk weighing thirty-five tons.

Modern buildings are mostly space that is enclosed by a rather lightweight shell composed of wooden or steel supports, beams, crossbeams, and windows. There are no forty-story almost-solid-stone modern structures.

In addition, though pyramidal-shaped structures have been built, none of these is remotely on the scale of the Great Pyramid and all are mostly internal space enclosed by a thin shell.

If any single firm on the planet could duplicate the Great Pyramid, it would be the Bechtel Corporation, which is a privately held company responsible for building some of the largest projects on the planet. They have the brainpower, machinery, skills, management, labor, infrastructure, and global resources that are perhaps equal to the task.

The firm was involved in the construction of the massive Hoover Dam project. Since a dam wall is a solid edifice, building one is a fair comparison to the construction of the Great Pyramid, though not at all an exact equivalent.

Work began on the Hoover Dam in 1931, during the Great Depression. The challenges that the engineers and workmen faced were prodigious. First, the Colorado River had to be diverted away from the dam construction site. To achieve that, tunnels—as wide as a four-lane highway—were blasted through the canyon walls.

At its base, the Hoover dam is 660 feet thick, 110 feet less than the sides of the Great Pyramid; it is 726 feet tall, more than 200 feet taller than the Great Pyramid. Though the dam did not require the quarrying, cutting, and transporting of millions of limestone blocks, it did require the making of huge blocks of concrete to shore up the base and millions of tons of concrete to build the dam's enormous wall.[2]

The project was put on a strict deadline that included the imposition of fees for any cost overruns or any failure to finish it on schedule; as a result, work on the project proceeded on a 24/7 basis.

It took an estimated eight thousand men using state-of-the-art equipment, machinery, and building techniques five years to complete the project, two years ahead of schedule.

The Hoover Dam serves as a good benchmark to use to establish whether our current civilization is capable of duplicating the Great Pyramid. On the basis of an objective analysis, I come down on the positive side with a few, but serious, reservations.

This conclusion differs from that of many independent investigators who think that the construction of the Great Pyramid still lies beyond our current capacity.

Given that the Hoover Dam was built more than eighty years ago and our machines and building techniques have improved since then, I am more or less convinced that we could build it today. The Chinese are currently constructing a much larger dam at Three Gorges.

Duplicating the Great Pyramid would still pose many challenges, but it is certainly feasible and within the realm of possibility, but only at this point in time.

While that tells us something about the progress our civilization has made, it also ought to make it very clear that no earlier civilization, including those of the Greeks or Romans, could have accomplished it. (We will examine that fact below.)

Now, if we can only claim that capability at this point, after thousands of years of continuous technological development, then it is a lead pipe cinch that the ancient Egyptians never built the Great Pyramid, any more than they could have built the Aswan Dam.

Every investigative pathway leads to the same conclusion: *some civilization built the Great Pyramid, but it certainly was not the ancient Egyptian culture that existed 4,500 years ago.*

To claim otherwise is to stand common sense and the whole notion of progress on their respective heads.

CONCLUSION

Though it may be possible, using modern equipment, to build the Great Pyramid today, the ancient Egyptians could not have done so. Modern architects and engineers have built dams that rival the size and mass of the ancient edifice; however, such dams still may not equal the overall complexity of the Great Pyramid.

Nonetheless, though no human culture could have built the Great Pyramid in the past, it may be possible to achieve that feat today or certainly in the future.

༼つ◕_◕༽つ

There are those who argue that the Greeks and Romans moved mega-lithic blocks of stone. They contend that this shows that the ancient Egyptian civilization surely could have achieved this feat.

The problem with that argument is that we are closer to the Roman Empire today than that empire was to ancient Egypt. Indeed, 2,500 years is a very long time in terms of the life of a human civilization. Most have lasted less than one thousand years.

Trying to imply that if the Romans could build the Coliseum and lift megalithic blocks of stone, then so could the Egyptians is a premise that simply will not fly.

It is like saying that since we build stadiums and so did the Romans, then they too could have sent rockets into space and deciphered the DNA code. That is a non sequitur.

A lot has happened over the last two thousand years since the time that ancient Rome collapsed. Well, a lot happened between the days of Rome's peak and 2,500 years earlier when the Great Pyramid was sup-posed to have been built.

There is such a thing as progress and technological development or there is not. If the ancient Egyptians built the pyramid, then progress is a falsehood.

We can examine another set of tests that were performed by the Romans two thousand years ago to better grasp what I am arguing.

At the height of Rome's imperial power, the leadership decided to show the world just how advanced the Roman Legion and its engineers were. How?

They decided that the best example would be to remove the ancient obelisks from Egypt, transport them down the Nile to Alexandria, and then ferry them, on ships, to Rome, where they would be reerected.

This would demonstrate to the citizens of the empire that Rome was indeed the global superpower. Who else would dare to accomplish the marvelous feats that the ancient Egyptians had accomplished? No one . . .

In fact, the Romans had a simple winch and even a basic crane appa-ratus. Their engineers had devised many sophisticated techniques and had constructed many very solid buildings, canals, walls, and so forth.

Roman architecture stands to this day in many parts of Europe.

They did manage to remove a number of obelisks from Egypt and to transport and erect them in Rome. But it proved to be a very difficult challenge that was not mishap-free.

Before going into that process a bit, I need to establish the exact nature of the challenge: the Romans never quarried an obelisk weighing two-hundred-plus tons, they did not try to carve hieroglyphics into them, and they did not have to plane down the obelisks so that they tapered, very symmetrically, from bottom to top.

All that the Roman engineers had to do was to take the obelisks down, ship them to Rome, and then reerect them there.

Though the Roman Legion had to keep records, we do not have details of exactly how they achieved their mission. However, we do know that to transport the largest obelisk ever attempted, they had to build the largest ship they had ever constructed. It was appropriately enough dubbed "the obelisk ship."

As I have noted previously, the real difficulty is not in the transport operation but in lifting the rock out of the quarry. This is why the Romans never tried to build granite obelisks from square one and inscribe them with Latin.

This clearly shows that even after several millennia, the Romans, at that time the most sophisticated, technically advanced civilization on Earth, could not have built the Great Pyramid. They never even imagined such an undertaking.

Moving sixteen centuries forward from Roman times, we find a detailed account of a successful attempt to reerect one of the obelisks.

7

Egypt

Civilization without Cities?

It was assumed that Sumer and Egypt were the first two human civilizations until the ruins of an equally old civilization that extend for nearly a thousand miles were discovered a century ago in the Indus Valley; this civilization is known as the Harappan culture, after the name of Harappa, its main city. This thriving, urban civilization existed at the same time as the Egyptian and Mesopotamian states—in an area twice each of their sizes.

As we have seen in the preceding chapters, the overwhelming preponderance of verifiable evidence comes down against the ancient Egyptians as the builders of the Great Pyramid.

However, there is yet more strong evidence for this conclusion presented in this chapter.

In fact, the actual situation in ancient Egypt begs the question of whether it was, in fact, a real civilization as we understand the term. The main reasons to support the civilization thesis revolve around the supposition that the Egyptians, circa 2500 BCE, built the Great Pyramid and other pyramids. That unconfirmed belief, once accepted, is then used to argue that they must have had a very advanced civilization.

It has the familiar ring of declarative, circular reasoning. Since, it is postulated, the Egyptians built the pyramids, they therefore must have had the advanced knowledge and building skills that allowed them to build one of the first civilizations since they had the tools and techniques to build the Great Pyramid, and so on, ad infinitum.

Fig. 7.1. Only a few artifacts remain in what was once the city of Memphis.

However, if we remove the pyramids from the list of Egyptian accomplishments, what do we find? They did not invent the wheel and did not even acquire it for a thousand years after the Sumerians. They did not invent metallurgy. They did not invent urban centers; the negative list goes on.

In fact, the fatal blow to the conventional theory comes from historians who have long called Egypt the "civilization without cities." That begs the question: *What characteristics define and constitute a civilization, and does ancient Egypt meet them?*

There is something entirely enigmatic about the artifacts that occupy the landscape of Upper Egypt. Among the enigmas, *one stands out by its absence: the ruins of ancient stone cities commensurate with the architecture and engineering evident in the monuments and temples.* Where are they?

In his website, historian Mike Anderson addresses this issue: "But there was one ancient civilization without a major city until the end of the second millennium B.C., a span of three thousand years . . . Egypt!"[1]

Equally as enigmatic are the things that we should find but that are, in fact, entirely missing from the landscape. Where are the ruins of the vast, sophisticated stone cities, governmental buildings, and royal palaces that should also occupy the landscape?

When and where did the ancient Egyptian stonemasons learn their knowledge and skills if not on the smaller governmental buildings, palaces, temples, and residences of its citizens? What we find are nothing but massive, overwhelming architectural wonders—stone temples, obelisks, pyramids—and little else of a more approachable stature that was built with similar, if smaller, cut-stone components.

A civilization is more than colossal monuments accompanied by primitive "worker and artisan" mud-brick villages, but that is what archaeologists have discovered in Egypt. Even though both the Sumer and Indus Valley civilizations lacked available stones to build with, they made brick structures out of standardized brick molds that still stand.

It is an artful dodger who claims that the Egyptian hierarchy was too humble to build massive palaces and government buildings to overwhelm the common folk. There is no good reason to ascribe a special status to ancient Egypt where human nature is concerned, though historians and archaeologists do just that.

The lack of not just cities but also of quarried, precision-cut stone buildings and sophisticated urban centers has been de-emphasized by tenured historians. Nonetheless, how are we to envision a civilization that would build cyclopean stone structures, but at the same time neglect to design and construct lasting stone cities, royal palaces, and governmental buildings?

In addition to the fact that by definition, a civilization builds urban centers, there is another, far more serious reason to insist we find them. The designing and building of stone cities replete with homes, palaces, and administrative buildings is needed to demonstrate where their supposed master architects, engineers, and stonemasons learned and plied their trades.

How can we possibly accept the premise that the Egyptians built the Great Pyramid without first seeing many generations of development exemplified in cities and towns?

That is exactly how we approach every other civilization on Earth. We examine them logically and reverse engineer their artifacts and justify them by looking for the technology and skills required to make them, but we don't do that with Egypt.

Consider the Greco-Roman civilizations, with Athens and Rome. Consider modern New York, London, and Beijing. Cities are the central features of civilizations, and only Egypt lacked them.

The Egyptians were not superhuman magicians, as today's scholars, including Mark Lehner and Zahi Hawass, would have us believe. The latter's motives, as Egypt's minister of antiquities, are obvious; he is a nationalist promoting his country, an understandable patriotic motivation.

But the ancient Egyptians were all too human, like the rest of us, and they were morbidly preoccupied by death and the afterlife. The tombs of the pharaohs in the King's Valley reveal that. On the other hand, they were superb artisans, and they loved their Nile River environs.

Strip the pyramids from the landscape and we see that the ancient Egyptians really were a simple, agrarian society borrowing knowledge and technology from other cultures.

Their tools were primitive, their domiciles modest at best; they lacked any knowledge of plumbing or civil engineering, sophisticated urban centers, and so on. Now, we must consider the fact that the ancient Egyptian civilization lasted for almost three thousand years, the Sumerian and the Indus Valley civilizations for less than one thousand.

Ancient Egypt was never a progressive society; it was a very conservative one. The technological innovation came out of Sumer, not Egypt. It is easy to examine the records and see that Mesopotamia and Sumer were the sources of intellectual output and social change; remove the pyramids, and Egypt is a very distant third place: (1) Mesopotamia, (2) Indus Valley, and (3) Egypt.

By the late fourth millennium BCE, the Sumerian civilization was already organized into about a dozen independent city-states, which were divided by canals and boundary stones. Each was centered on a temple dedicated to the particular patron god or goddess of the city, and they were ruled over by a priestly governor or by a king who was intimately tied to the city's religious rites.

Some of the cities, like Ur, are even mentioned in the Bible, as is Sumer (the land of Shinar). Even as early as 4100 to 2900 BCE, the Sumerians traded goods with other cultures that were transported along the canals and rivers of southern Mesopotamia. These operations facilitated the rise of many large, stratified, temple-centered cities (with populations of more than ten thousand people) where centralized governments employed specialized workers.

By the time the Egyptians were (allegedly) building the Great Pyramid, some Sumerian cities had populations approaching forty to fifty thousand residents. Egypt produced nothing of the sort. The remains of the Sumerian cities have been excavated extensively and studied intensively. Tens of thousands of cuneiform tablets have been unearthed and deciphered.

American anthropologist Robert McCormick Adams writes that irrigation development was associated with urbanization and that 89 percent of the Sumerian population lived in the cities. One of the more enigmatic features of Sumer is the fact that the Tigris-Euphrates Plain *lacked minable metals, rock quarries, and forests,* all essential resources in ancient Egypt. Sumerian structures were made of plano-convex–formed mud bricks that were not fixed with mortar or cement.

The cities were provided with towers and stood on artificial platforms; the houses also had a towerlike appearance. Each house was provided with a door that turned on a hinge and could be opened with a keylike device; each city also had a large entrance gate.

None of this extensive urbanization is evident in the ancient Egyptian record. There were semilarge villages but not true cities displaying any level of similar sophistication. The discoveries made during excavations of the Indus Valley over the past fifty years underscore how problematic the lack of Egyptian cities really is.

The people of this Indus Valley civilization did not build massive monuments like their contemporaries. Nor did they bury riches among their dead in golden tombs. There were no mummies, no emperors, and no violent wars or bloody battles in their territory.

Remarkably, the lack of all these is what makes the Indus Valley

Fig. 7.2. Typical Indus Valley urban center

civilization so compelling and unique, even more so because of the incredible level of sophistication archaeologists have found in the cities excavated since their discovery a mere one hundred years ago.

Examples: For protection from seasonal floods and polluted waters, the Sumerian settlements were built on giant platforms and elevated grounds. However, archaeologists tell us that Egypt's main city, Memphis, was reclaimed by Nile floods. If that is true, then it points up the fact that Egypt did not have civil engineers on a par with those of either Sumer or the Indus Valley.

On these Sumerian foundations, networks of streets were laid out in neat patterns of straight lines and right angles. The buildings along the roads were all constructed of bricks that were uniform in size, suggesting there were factories using molds to produce them.

The brick houses of all city dwellers were equipped with bathing areas supplied with water from neighborhood wells. Sophisticated drainage systems throughout the city carried dirty water and sewage outside of living spaces. Even the smallest houses on the edges of the towns were connected to the systems; the principles of personal and public hygiene were obviously well known and of great importance.

According to a report released by the Government of India's Archaeological Survey:

> The salient components of the full-grown cityscape consisted of a bipartite "citadel," a "middle town" and a "lower town," two "stadia," an "annexe," a series of reservoirs all set within an enormous fortification running on all four sides. Interestingly, inside the city, too, there was an intricate system of fortifications. The city was, perhaps, configured like a large parallelogram boldly outlined by massive walls with their longer axis being from the east to west. On the bases of their relative location, planning, defenses and architecture, the three principal divisions are designed tentatively as "citadel," "middle town," and '"lower town."
>
> The Harappans created about sixteen or more reservoir of varying sizes and designs and arranged them in a series practically on all four sides. A cursory estimate indicates that the water structures and relevant and related activities accounts for 10 hectares of area, in other words 10 percent of the total area that the city appropriated within its outer fortification. The 13 meters of gradient between high and low areas from east to west within the walls was ideally suited for creating cascading reservoirs which were separated from each other by enormous and broad bunds and yet connected through feeding drains.
>
> The citadel has yielded an intricate network of storm water drains, all connected to an arterial one and furnished with slopes, steps, cascades, manholes (air ducts/water relief ducts), paved flooring and capstones. The main drains were high enough for a tall man to walk through easily. The rainwater collected through these drains was stored in yet another reservoir that was carved out in the western half of the bailey.[2]

At the time that Egyptologists claim the Great Pyramid was built, the Indus Valley not only had cities, it also had carefully planned, intensively engineered urban centers that were organized in every detail; whether these facts fit our modern ideas of ancient history and progress or not, the Harappan cities were better planned than our own modern ones.

Nothing like these cities existed in Egypt, not even remotely, at any point in its very long life span—a very telling fact.

The hard truth is that much of modern India, Pakistan, and Afghanistan still lacks the indoor plumbing, street drainage, urban planning, and water-delivery systems that existed in Harappan cities four thousand years ago. How is this to be explained in the context of cultural evolution and the theory of human progress from the simple to the complex?

Of course, the sudden emergence of the Sumerian civilization, the cities of the Indus Valley, and the Giza complex do not fit into the framework of cultural evolution and progress.

The reason we refer to Earth's earliest civilizations in the context of history's mysteries is because of that paradoxical fact. The things described above should not exist at the point in time they were created because people were living in mud huts just a few generations before.

In addition, the rest of the world stayed in the late Stone Age or early Neolithic period for a very, very long time thereafter. In truth, the real Egyptian culture was not responsible for the Great Pyramid or the massive temple complexes. Those mysterious edifices were built by an advanced race. There were no cities in Egypt, and the pyramid had a different purpose.

I must leave that hanging for another book, as that lies outside the scope of this volume, which attempts to fully educate and inform readers about the theory of Cosmic Ancestry, which includes the integration of ancient mysteries and modern UFOs.

CONCLUSION

The lack of cut-stone urban centers in the ancient Egyptian record is strong evidence that casts a shadow across the orthodox scenarios invented by Egyptologists. There is no evidence showing that ancient Egypt, circa 2500 BCE, was a "civilization" that was in any way a match for the Sumerian or the Indus Valley civilizations. Remove the attribution of the Great Pyramid to the ancient Egyptians and the basis for claiming they were technologically advanced vanishes.

8

....

The Giza Pyramids
Represent the
Three Inner Planets

The notion that the pyramid builders designed the Giza Plateau layout to reflect the appearance of the Orion constellation was first proposed by Robert Bauval, the coauthor with Adrian Gilbert of *The Orion Mystery*. The theory has been a source of debate ever since.

However, even though that argument appears to hold water, I am going to propose that an equally or even more important set of relationships, earthbound ones, are embodied by the Giza pyramids.

If the three pyramids on the Giza Plateau were converted into spheres, it would be obvious that they would resemble the relative sizes of Earth, Venus, and Mercury to the naked eye.

But their pyramidal shape somewhat conceals this fact. The comparative astronomical data presented below, however, show that the dimensions of the pyramids do very closely approximate those of the inner planets.

The dimensions are so close, in fact, that in many cases the deviations are not significant enough to discredit the data, even on a strictly scientific basis. No such careful scrutiny is allowed by the nebulous, cosmic-based Orion theory. In fact, I see this not as an either-or choice, but as that of both-and . . .

The following dataset shows that various measurements of the three pyramids relate in ratios with the ratios between similar measurements of Earth, Venus, and Mercury, in a number of ways that far exceed chance.

Fig. 8.1. The pyramids of Giza

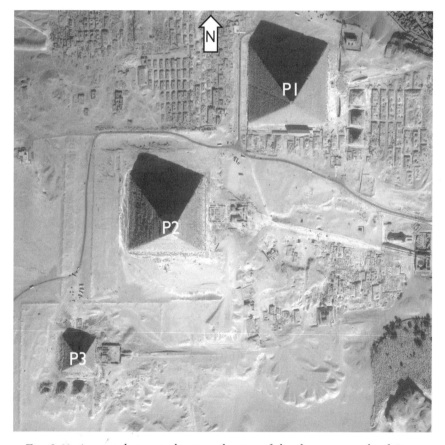

Fig. 8.2. An aerial view indicating the size of the three pyramids of Giza. P1 represents Earth, P2 is Venus, and P3 represents Mercury.

The Area of the First Pyramid vs. the Second Pyramid

- The area of the base of the first pyramid covers 13.6 acres.
- The area of the base of the second pyramid covers 11 acres.
- This shows that the second pyramid has 82 percent the area of the first.

The Mass of Earth vs. Venus

- The mass of Earth is 5.972×10^{24} kilograms.
- The mass of Venus is 4.8685×10^{24} kilograms.
- This shows that Venus has 81.5 percent the mass of Earth.

The Length of the Sides of the Second vs. the First Pyramid

- The length of each side of the second pyramid is 706 feet.
- The length of each side of the first pyramid is 755 feet.
- This shows that each side of the second pyramid is 95 percent the length of each side of the first pyramid.

The Diameter of Venus vs. Earth

- The diameter of Venus is 12,100 kilometers.
- The diameter of Earth is 12,752 kilometers.
- This shows that the diameter of Venus is 95 percent that of Earth.

The Height of the Second Pyramid vs. the First Pyramid

- The height of the second pyramid is 448 feet.
- The height of the first pyramid is 481 feet.
- This shows that the second pyramid has 93.13 percent of the height of the first pyramid.
- The Diameter of Venus vs. Earth
- The radius of Venus is 6,052 kilometers.
- The radius of Earth is 6,381 kilometers.
- This shows that Venus has 95 percent of the radius of Earth.

The Volume of the Second Pyramid vs. the First Pyramid

- The volume of the second pyramid is 15.417 million cubic royal cubits.

- The volume of the first pyramid is 18.023 million cubic royal cubits.
- This shows that the second pyramid has 85 percent of the volume of the first pyramid.

The Volume of Venus vs. Earth

- The volume of Venus is 9.28×10^{11} kilometers.
- The volume of Earth is 10.832×10^{11} kilometers.
- This shows that Venus has 85 percent of the volume of Earth.

The foregoing comparisons of the two pyramids' basic measurements with the two planets clearly reveal that the Great Pyramid represents Earth and the second pyramid represents Venus. In fact, there is extremely little deviation when the immense dimensions involved are factored in.

The orbital period of Venus is 225 days, which, compared with Earth's, which is 365, come out to 61.5 percent that of Earth, or 0.615, which is phi. This means that Venus revolves around the sun in 225 days, Earth in 365; the former then moves around the sun 1.6 times faster than Earth.

The matches between the measurements of the first and second pyramids and those of Earth and Venus are very precise. It is also clear that the phi approximations were intended, as all three pyramids display this feature.

The Area of the Base of the Third Pyramid vs. the First Pyramid

- The area of the base of the third pyramid is 5.2 acres.
- The area of the base of the first pyramid is 11 acres.
- This shows that the area of the base of the third pyramid is 47 percent of the area of the base of the first pyramid.

The Diameter of Mercury vs. Earth

- The diameter of Mercury is 4,879 kilometers.
- The diameter of Earth is 12,765 kilometers.
- This shows that the diameter of Mercury is 38 percent that of Earth.

The Length of the Third Pyramid
vs. the First Pyramid

- The length of each side of the third pyramid is 339 feet.
- The length of each side of the first pyramid is 755 feet.
- This shows that the length of the third pyramid is 44.9 percent of the length of the first pyramid.

The Radius of Mercury vs. Earth

- The radius of Mercury is 2,439.7 kilometers.
- The radius of Earth is 6,381 kilometers.
- This shows that Mercury's radius is 38 percent that of Earth's.

The Height of the First Pyramid vs. the Third Pyramid

- The height of the third pyramid is 215 feet.
- The height of the first pyramid is 481 feet.
- This shows that the third pyramid is 44.69 percent the height of the first pyramid.

The comparisons between Mercury and Earth and the third and first pyramids are admittedly not as exact as those between Earth and Venus and the second and Great Pyramid.

However, there is no question as to the overall effect of the Giza site; it looks like a pyramidal model of the three inner planets, and that effect is confirmed by comparing the measurements with the matching planetary data.

The base-to-height ratio of the third pyramid is also the same— 1.575—as the other two pyramids.

There is a vast amount of data contained within the Giza pyramids. How that portion presented above will be disputed and rejected by orthodox historians is fully anticipated by me. Their main objection will be to the notion that the ancient Egyptians possessed any knowledge of the specific planetary information given. That, of course, was only obtained in modern times using advanced technologies.

However true those points may be, they are simply not relevant to the theory presented in this series. The reason that the ancient artifacts of Egypt pose so many enigmas is that they are attributed to the Egyptian human culture that is known to have existed 2,000 to 4,500 years ago.

It is all but impossible to show how that culture, without the benefit of the wheel and horses, or pulleys, hoists, cranes, and front-end loaders could build a multimillion-ton, forty-eight-story high structure. That is a feat today's architects, engineers, and contractors with the aid of modern machinery would have difficulty duplicating now, at this late date in history.

But orthodox historians continue to try to fit this square peg into the round hole, and it never works; the enigmas persist, yet they try to pretend otherwise. The end result is a distortion of the facts, irrational theories, and outright disinformation.

Next, they will reject the notion that the Giza complex was based on a carefully thought out master plan. Their notion is that the precinct was developed haphazardly, in piecemeal fashion, by succeeding generations of pharaohs.

But we must ask, Why are the first and second pyramids so very close in size and the third is a dwarf by comparison? Did the alleged builder of the third, Pharaoh Menkaure, feel so dwarfed and overshadowed by his predecessors that all he could do was build a mere model of their immense structures?

Again, are the exact parallels between the first and second pyramids and Earth and Venus mere accidents? In fact, does it not make more sense to assume that the third pyramid is so small because it is a nearly exact model of Mercury's size relative to Venus and Earth?

Orthodox historians have to routinely resort to the concepts of "accidental" and "coincidental" when trying to explain many features of the Great Pyramid. How did the builders so precisely orient the base to the cardinal points? No ancient cultures were supposed to have knowledge of true north back then.

But as we saw in chapter 3, the builders knew a lot more about Earth's geography than true north. Of course, the fact that the pyramid sits on a meridian that just happens to be 120° from the Mississippi River and 90° from the Yangtze River will, no doubt, be dismissed as a mere coincidence.

In fact, orthodox historians have backed themselves into a corner, an intellectual reality that will be made very clear in the following chapters.

An advanced extraterrestrial civilization would have all this knowledge and far more. The expected objections are irrelevant. Historians are operating within the context of their own self-imposed limitations and preconceptions.

In truth, it is not outside the realms of physics or astronomy to consider the possibility that such a zero-point civilization designed and built the Giza complex. To dismiss the idea out of hand is to display an amazing degree of narrow-minded thinking. Are we not in the age of technological marvels and space exploration, after all?

In the preceding section, we saw that the pyramids display a very high degree of similarity to the three inner planets when considering their most basic three-dimensional measurements.

THE SITE PLAN AND THE DISTANCES BETWEEN THE INNER PLANETS

By placing the three Giza pyramids in exact predesignated locations and building each pyramid to a specific size of base and height, the builders constructed a representation of Earth, Venus, and Mercury, as well as making them the key geodetic marker.

In this context, we assume that the designers and engineers worked from a master blueprint. The precinct was not designed on the fly by succeeding pharaohs. The plan was fully created beforehand and then executed.

Now, turning to the relationship of the layout of the Giza site plan and the relative positions of the pyramids we find the following:

Sir William Flinders Petrie was a pioneering English Egyptologist who excavated many important ancient sites and was the author of the important text *The Pyramids and Temples of Gizeh*. Petrie took extensive measurements of nearly every feature of the pyramid, including the distances between them. Using Petrie's measurements,[1] John Legon, an independent Egyptologist and researcher, diagrammed the three main pyramids at Giza[2] as shown in figure 8.3.

Legon's diagram clearly shows that the original architects and engineers had a survey sight line. That line extends from the northwest corner of the Great Pyramid to the northwest corner of the second pyramid, then to the northwest corner of the third pyramid.

There was a generally accepted misconception (still accepted?) that the three pyramids were out of alignment. That notion was based on

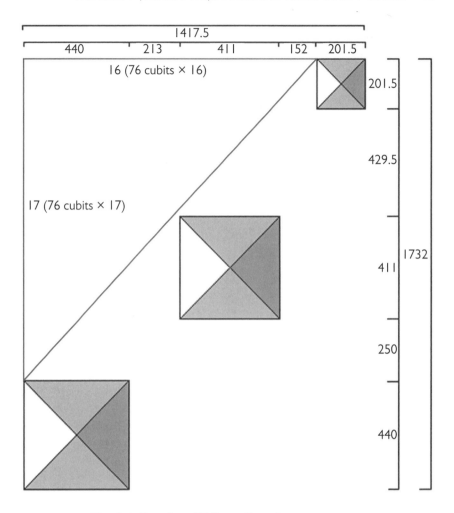

Fig. 8.3. Based on William Petrie's measurements,
John Legon diagrammed the three main pyramids of Giza.

the assumption that the centers of the three should be in alignment.

But who said that is what the builders wanted to achieve or should have achieved? The fact is that there is a straight-line alignment between the corners, as noted and shown above.

The next thing we note is that the first pyramid is closer to the second pyramid than the third is to the second pyramid. This is exactly what we would expect to find if the first pyramid represents Earth, the second, Venus, and the third, Mercury (see fig. 8.4).

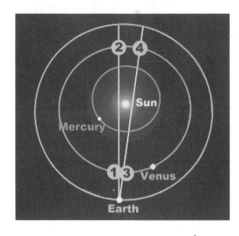

*Fig. 8.4. The orbital distances
of the inner planets*

Dear reader, I invite you to decide if the builders intended these relationships or if they are the result of random choices and chance.

The distance between the center of the second pyramid and the center of the first pyramid is 13,931 inches.

The distance between the center of the second pyramid and the center of the third pyramid is 15,170 inches.

In figure 8.3 a line is drawn connecting the apexes of each pyramid. This shows that while the builders used a straight sight line, they also wanted to convey curvature and movement. They achieved that by positing the third pyramid exactly where they did.

The top-down view suggests a curvature, which, of course, the orbits of the three planets follow.

The aerial photo of the Giza complex in figure 8.2 (where P1 is Earth, P2 is Venus, and P3 is Mercury) shows that the distances between the pyramids correlate with the relative average distances between the planets.

CONCLUSION

The three pyramids of the Giza complex reflect the ratios of the relative distances and sizes of the inner planets: Earth, Venus, and Mercury. This design feature adds greatly to the sophistication of the complex, which suggests that an advanced extraterrestrial civilization with accurate astronomical knowledge designed the complex.

9
....
The Earth Vortex

Cosmic Force. . . . Here is additional information for those who read my advertisement in The Miami Daily News, February 3rd, 1946. The North and South pole individual magnets are the cosmic force. They are the building blocks of nature's perpetual transformation of matter, and they are so small that they can pass through everything. They pass through the earth from pole to pole, and around the earth.

ED LEEDSKALNIN,
"DOUBLE HELICAL MAGNETIC INTERACTION"

This, the last chapter of the Egypt section, is related to the first chapter in this section, as it seeks to further explain why the Great Pyramid was positioned where it is and also seeks to examine and explore how and why the pyramids may have been constructed.

It is an odd and rather sad commentary on modern science that no scientists or engineers during the time that a man named Edward Leedskalnin was alive seemed the least bit curious as to how he moved megalithic blocks of coral without the aid of machinery.

Leedskalnin's theory of energy and magnetism was pooh-poohed then and would be even more derisively dismissed today. For years, he and his accomplishments were all but forgotten, until the Internet era took hold and interest in Coral Castle, which he built almost one hundred years ago, as well as interest in ancient mysteries and Nikola Tesla, skyrocketed.

Fig. 9.1. Coral Castle in Homestead, Florida

I bring attention to Leedskalnin and Coral Castle in this important chapter for several reasons. The first will become apparent after reading the following quote from the man himself:

> I have discovered the secrets of the pyramids, and have found out how the Egyptians and the ancient builders in Peru, Yucatan, and Asia, with only primitive tools, raised and set in place blocks of stone weighing many tons.[1]

Here, perhaps, we had a man who could solve the mystery of the ages; you would think that at least one scholar or scientist might have wanted to see if his boast was true.

What is it that the diminutive, five-foot-tall Edward Leedskalnin— who only weighed one hundred pounds—achieved that should have had engineers clamoring to his castle? If you do not already know, he managed to lift up, move, and carefully position large blocks of natural coral, some weighing sixteen to twenty-six tons, without the aid of any modern equipment.

His accomplishments can still be seen and inspected. Coral Castle is located north of Homestead, Florida, in Miami-Dade County, at the intersection of South Dixie Highway (U.S. 1) and SW 157th Avenue.

The structure comprises numerous megalithic stones (mostly limestone) formed from natural coral, each weighing, on average, several tons. The story of the site has become something of an urban legend, especially concerning issues revolving around exactly how Leedskalnin built it single-handedly by using magnetism and/or paranormal abilities.

He began building his coral home in 1920, but in 1936, when a planned subdivision threatened his privacy, Leedskalnin moved his entire operation ten miles to Homestead. He completed it there, and it still stands today and is a popular tourist attraction.

Within his castle walls, we find many curious and wonderful objects, including a twenty-two-ton obelisk, a twenty-two-ton coral moon, a twenty-three-ton coral Jupiter, a coral Saturn, and a nine-ton delicately poised gate that a child can push open.

How Leedskalnin managed this feat of engineering has remained a mystery because no one saw him do it. Apparently, he preferred to work at night by the soft light of a lantern. No credible witnesses ever saw

Fig. 9.2. The thirty-ton stone of Coral Castle

how this very frail man was able to move the huge blocks of solid rock.

Even when he relocated the entire structure to Homestead, neighbors never witnessed how he moved the coral blocks onto a borrowed truck that he used for the transport. Neither did anyone witness how he got them off the vehicle and then moved them to their present positions.

However, all the neighbors agreed that none had ever heard him use any machinery to achieve his feats. One story claimed that several curious neighbors did observe how Leedskalnin moved the stones. They said he placed his hands on the one to be lifted and then sang over it.

The above story, if true, suggests that Leedskalnin used resonant frequencies to somehow levitate the megalithic blocks by himself without the aid of any equipment.

According to an article in *FATE* magazine, "Some teenagers spying on him one evening claimed they saw him '*float coral blocks through the air like hydrogen balloons,*' [italics added] but no one took them seriously."[2]

Frank Joseph, the author of the *FATE* magazine article, also wrote, "Alternative science investigators suggest that Leedskalnin somehow learned the secret of the 'world grid,' an invisible pattern of energy lines surrounding the earth which concentrates points of telluric power where they intersect. It was here, at one of these intersections of Earth energy, that he was supposedly able to move his prodigious stone blocks using the unseen power of our planet."[3]

In fact, Leedskalnin did make mention of choosing Homestead because it was "in a vortex," as he described it. Could he have been alluding to this "unforeseen power" of Earth? The global grid and Leedskalnin's vortex, of course, at least in part, relate to the geodetic data given in the first chapter.

In chapter 3, we saw that the Great Pyramid was located at a site that was shown by Global Positioning System (GPS) to be 120° longitude from the Mississippi River and 90° longitude from the Yangtze River.

As noted, that reveals the underlying geometry of a number of the planet's key geological features. Additionally, we saw that the Nile, Mississippi, Tigris-Euphrates, and Yangtze River Deltas are all precisely located on the 30° north latitude. This latitude then demarcates the exact meeting point of the mouths of these great rivers and the ocean on a global basis.

I insert the Coral Castle story here not just because of Leedskalnin's claim of having discovered the ancient secret of moving megalithic blocks of stone, but also due to the foregoing assertion of why he chose Homestead specifically.

In his now famous booklet, *Magnetic Current,* which was ignored back in the day, Leedskalnin said that he had chosen Homestead because it was in a special place on the planet, *a vortex field* we shall call it.

This may be an intriguing allusion to some important underlying reality of nature, but what exactly was he referring to?

Leedskalnin built Coral Castle on a spot that he identified as having unusual properties. However, he did not publicly disclose any of the details of that feature. Nonetheless, we can examine the Homestead GPS coordinates and make our own deductions.

Coral Castle sits at 25°30' north latitude, 80°50' (adjusted 111°50') west longitude. We shall examine why this is, indeed, in the heart of a vortex. But first we need to clarify our terms.

How can we best describe the term *energy?* Energy is a very general concept that can mean many different things depending on the context.

But in this case, let's use several examples. Wind produces energy; we cannot see what we call "the wind," but we can feel it and also see its results in blowing sand, moving tree branches, and a rotating windmill. In addition, the Nile and Mississippi Rivers are constantly flowing *streams of energy* (in the form of water), as well, that we plainly see in constant motion.

Now let us consider here that there is a swirling current of energy out in the Atlantic Ocean called the Atlantic Gyre. In fact, it has a vortical (cyclonic) rotation. This gyre extends between the 20° and 30° north latitudes.

Let's use a specific example that might best illustrate the principles that Leedskalnin was using and tapping into.

On August 24, 1992, Hurricane Andrew hit the Bahamas, the southeastern end of Florida, and parts of Louisiana as it cut a path of widespread destruction. This devastating storm smashed into southern Miami-Dade County; in fact, Homestead took the brunt of the up-to-175-mile-per-hour winds, which quickly leveled much of the town.

Andrew was the most potent hurricane to ever hammer the United States until Katrina slammed New Orleans, another storm we will discuss later. It destroyed nearly everything that was standing directly in its path, and that included most of Homestead.

The damage was so severe that Homestead Air Reserve Base had to be shut down; 1,167 of the 1,176 of the city's mobile homes were completely destroyed; and the only thing in the city that seemed to remain standing (a water tower) was, nonetheless, not entirely spared because it was hit by a bolt of lightning.

When it was all over, Homestead looked like it had been obliterated by an atomic bomb. A whirling hurricane is a vortex; so are tornadoes. One thing other than the tower was left intact, and that was Coral Castle; it withstood Andrew's devastating blow.

The diminutive inventor was not talking about any occult or paranormal forces; by *vortex* he meant real, natural forces on a planetary scale of the kind that make hurricanes happen.

In addition, we have a well-known, enigmatic feature to include—the Bermuda Triangle, which has been identified as being located between

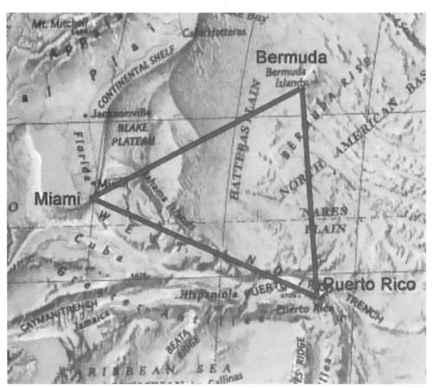

Fig. 9.3. The Bermuda Triangle

the 20° and 30° north latitudes with the tips of the triangle located south in Puerto Rico, west in Miami (Homestead), and north in Bermuda.

The Bermuda Triangle is located in a well-established magnetic vortex that produces erratic anomalies that include knocking out compasses and causing planes and boats to lose their bearings and disappear.

At this juncture we need to turn back to the importance of the 30° north latitude and the Great Pyramid as the geodetic lodestone set on Earth to mark and demarcate this critical feature of the planet.

There are other crucial features about this pivotal latitude that we must consider in order to comprehend Leedskalnin and, perhaps, the ancient pyramid builders.

From the equator to the 30° latitude (Great Pyramid), the prevailing wind currents are called the Hadley cell by meteorologists. The wind currents known as the Ferrel cell occur between 30° and 60° latitude. When the warm air rises from the equator and reaches the 30° latitude, it has cooled enough to sink and recirculate back to what is called the equatorial low pressure belt.

At 30° north latitude, however, there is an almost perpetual band of high pressure because this is the zone of major deserts around the world. The air sinks around 30° north and cycles back to the equator, where the water mainly originates from. The rain is squeezed out as the winds traverse the 0 to 30 meridians so that at the latter it is dry; 30° north is the terminus of this zone. It is at this latitude where the world's deserts are located, and it is warm to blazing hot and extremely dry. This, by no accident, is where the earliest pyramid-building civilizations emerged, right on this 30° north band where great river deltas meet the continental landmasses.

The equatorial region is hot, humid, and almost windless; a ring of clouds and mist hovers over the equator nearly all the time. While most lightning storms occur around this belt—and it rains there almost every day—most hurricanes occur between 20° and 30° latitude, whereas none happen within five degrees of the equator.

So now we put hurricanes alongside the Atlantic Gyre. In fact, they move over the gyre as they are growing and organizing. Note that Coral Castle was positioned inside the 20° to 30° latitude energy field.

In addition to being where the major rivers and landmasses meet, this latitude area was selected because it is a planetary *energy vector.* At this point, we shall delve more deeply into the global wind patterns and ocean currents because they are crucial to our discussion of energy and the biosphere (that is, life on the planet).

We do not feel it, but Earth is spinning on its axis, at about one thousand miles per hour, as it hurtles through space at seven hundred thousand miles per hour. Is it just a coincidence that the winds that flow in bands around the globe do so in 30° Hadley and Ferrel cells?

No, it has to do with some as yet unacknowledged planetary energy phenomenon. Why do I make this claim? Because these 30° bands also exist on the planet Mars.

Moreover, we can drill in the importance of the Great Pyramid geodetic marker by including the fact that at the onset of each eleven-year sunspot cycle, the first one *occurs on the 30° solar latitude*.

The patterns of the wind cells on Earth are worth a little further exploration here. Perhaps we could best picture these cells as wind tunnels in which each wind (30° cell) is blowing in the opposite direction to the one north or south of it.

The winds flow from the northeast in the 0° to 30° Hadley cell, then reverse and flow in a westerly direction in the 30° to 60° Ferrel cell, and reverse again in the polar cell.

I submit here that though we tend to think of the air as an insubstantial thing, air is made up of gaseous molecules of oxygen, nitrogen, and water vapor. These components create air pressure, which is exerted on every object on Earth, including humans.

With Earth spinning and roaring ahead like a spaceship, combined with the constant air pressure, cosmic rays, solar wind, and Leedskalnin's magnetism holding things together, do we really need the concept of gravity? (Christopher Dunn raised this issue in an article published in the magazine *Atlantis Rising*.)

At 30° north latitude, the air currents make a phase change, then again at 60°, and then again at the poles. Now we have to ask ourselves a basic question: What are the purposes of the troposphere (the lowest layer of Earth's atmosphere, where all of the weather takes place) and the ionosphere (a region of Earth's upper atmosphere, from about fifty to six hundred miles up)?

The fundamental answer is to produce thunder, lightning, and rain for the biosphere.

After all, those oxygen, water, and nitrogen molecules have work to do. There would be no biosphere without lightning, thunder, and rainstorms. The rotating winds are in constant motion as air from high-pressure areas moves toward low-pressure areas in each wind cell.

At this point, we shall pause and ask ourselves a simple question: Might not the earth be a gigantic vortex spinning in the solar system, an even larger vortex, which is also spinning in an ever larger vortex, the Milky Way? Yes, it is. Hurricanes and the ocean gyres reveal this fact.

In a sense, we can view the equator as a giant water pump. The constant sunshine hitting it lifts the moist air upward to form the nearly perpetual band of clouds that ring the equator.

The equatorial lightning storms are frequent, and it rains almost every day. However, the water quickly evaporates on the equator to reform as clouds. But the lightning storms that occur near the 30° latitudes are the most intense. That was made clear by Hurricanes Andrew and Katrina.

The 30° north vector, as signaled by the Great Pyramid, points to this energy field, but modern scientists do not see it. Leedskalnin did, however. It is like the elephant standing in the room that no one notices.

Note that hurricanes originate off the coast of Africa and whirl across the Atlantic, making landfall between 19.5° and 30° north. Katrina hit New Orleans, the mouth of the Mississippi River Delta, dead on at the 30° latitude.

At this juncture, we can appreciate that this latitude was selected as the site of the Great Pyramid because it is a planetary *energy vector,* a directional pointer showing the critical latitude on Earth's surface.

The pyramid was put in place as a geodetic marker that served many purposes. It pointed to not only the geometry of the planet but also to its geology, wind, and ocean circulation patterns.

If we take a top-down (polar) view of Earth, we can see that the wind and ocean currents are vortexes. In fact, in this context, Earth can be considered to be an electrical vortex.

What do I mean?

As noted above, the main function of the atmosphere is to produce thunder, lightning, and rain. Without freshwater, most life would cease to exist and the biosphere would collapse. But there is another important feature of the atmosphere—the ionosphere—that is also closely related to lightning.

It was Tesla who actually discovered that there was a layer of the upper atmosphere that contained an electrical charge. That charge produced a standing wave between itself and the earth, the ground in the circuit.

Lighting has a second function, which is to recharge the resonant cavity between the ground and the ionosphere, which is done by what are called the Schumann resonances, which are extremely low frequency (ELF) standing waves that occur at 7.8 Hertz; 7.8 is identified as the key frequency, and the others are resonances of the prime, standing wave, which is the time it takes light to circle the earth.

Here is where things ramp up and get truly intense and very profound for us. *The human brain is precisely tuned to these resonant standing waves.*

The 7.8 Hertz frequency is the peak of the alpha human brainwave, which goes from delta and theta to beta and gamma, extending from 2 to about 40 Hertz. There are roughly one hundred lightning strikes per second taking place on the planet at any given moment, keeping the standing waves continuously charged.

The brain is like a carefully tuned instrument resonating with Earth's electrical field. Tesla discovered the standing waves during his experiments in high frequency electricity at the Tesla Experimental Station in Colorado Springs, but he did not know that they related to human brainwaves.

At this point, we return to the Great Pyramid and Earth's river-landmass geometry. The ancient Maya built some of their major sites precisely at the 89° west longitude (adjusted 120° west longitude).

I discovered this in 1978 while studying an archaeological map. I was sitting in the Yucatán during an expedition. I just happened to notice that the sites of Dzibilchaltun, Uxmal, and others, all the way down to Tikal in Guatemala, were positioned exactly at 89° west longitude (adjusted 120° west).

I ran my finger up the map and found it landed on the mouth of the Mississippi River. My curiosity was piqued, but I did not know what to make of it.

(Do not confuse this essential Great Pyramid prime meridian with the alleged global grid system proffered by various researchers. This is the main geographical and geological pointer on the planet that must be used, at least by science, for a true picture of Earth. Moreover, you can draw a line from any point on a map to another point; so what?)

Of course, the Native American mound builders also constructed their pyramidal mounds on that same meridian as they lived along the Mississippi River. The vast Cahokia Mounds complex in Missouri sits exactly on the adjusted 120° west meridian.

When we examine the pyramid age, we must ask the following question: Are we looking at some kind of very sophisticated technological system that was based on a different set of principles that are invisible to us?

I submit that that is exactly what we are staring at but cannot see because the science behind it evades us. The Maya, for instance, were very astute astronomers who kept track of the planetary configurations assiduously.

In fact, they had seventeen different calendars, such was their apparent obsession with time.

But perhaps we have missed the real reason they practiced this discipline. The geographical positioning and alignments of the pyramids, as well as their geometry, could have been used to harvest scalar or other cosmic energy waves.

We know that Tesla discovered these freely available energies using his radiant energy receiver, which was patented, so it was proven viable. The problem with the Great Pyramid perhaps being such a receiver is that any apparatus that might have once existed inside of the Grand Gallery was removed.

But there are still features that suggest either sound or energy resonance might have been one of the key principles involved. It seems probable that the Maya used the planetary configurations as part of their technology as well. The planets also produce extremely low frequency waves that do impact Earth.

We can definitely assume that manipulating human consciousness was also a feature of the ancient technology. Some decades ago, investigators conducted an experiment in the cave beneath Mexico's Pyramid of the Sun using a native shaman who performed a traditional ritual. Further evidence of this supposition is the fact that archaeologists also discovered the complex had suffered through a massive conflagration at some point in time.

In addition, scientists recently conducted an investigation of a mound that is alleged to be a constructed pyramid in Bosnia and discovered that the mound was sending a high-frequency beam upward from its apex.

An even greater and admittedly shocking possibility arises when we note the importance of the Great Pyramid's geodetic position and Earth's river-landmass geometry. As noted in chapter 2, astrophysicist Michio Kaku brought up the possibility that we are living in a solar system, on a planet, fabricated by a Type II or III civilization.

(We are a type 0 civilization that might make it to Type I if we survive long enough. Kaku alluded to this fantastic possibility during an interview. According to the Kardashev scale, a Type IV civilization extracts energy, information, and raw materials from all possible galaxies; it's effectively immortal and omnipotent, with universal-scale influence, possessing the ability of theoretical time travel and instantaneous matter-energy transformation and teleportation.)

It is possible this is the message that the Great Pyramid and the other enigmatic sites and artifacts around the world are trying to tell us. We are not only the product of genetic engineering, but what we call "our" planet also was actually created and seeded by an advanced race.

If that is true, we stand almost no chance of comprehending their technology completely because it would be so advanced that their works would appear to be miracles to us.

We cannot dismiss this possibility now since our own planetary scientists are already planning operations to terraform another planet after a mere fifty years of space exploration.

SECTION III

· · · · · · · ·

Modern UFO Cases

Preface to
Modern UFO Cases

The phenomenon reported is something real and not visionary or fictitious. . . . There are objects probably approximating the shape of a disc, of such appreciable size as to appear to be as large as a man-made aircraft. . . . The reported operating characteristics such as extreme rates of climb, maneuverability (particularly in roll), and action which must be considered evasive when sighted or contacted by friendly aircraft and radar, lend belief to the possibility that some of the objects are controlled manually, automatically, or remotely.

LETTER TO THE COMMANDING GENERAL OF THE
U.S. ARMY AIR FORCES, SEPTEMBER 23, 1947,
FROM GENERAL NATHAN TWINING,
CHAIRMAN, JOINT CHIEFS OF STAFF

The above quote was the original, unfiltered assessment of the evidence gathered from the first official air force investigation into the UFO phenomenon.

Though I am going to present five major, very public cases, including the Roswell incident, in the next chapters, it is with reservations that I include a brief overview of the U.S. government's activities and positions regarding the history of the UFO phenomena in America.

It all began, innocently enough, when a UFO suddenly appeared in the skies over Los Angeles during World War II. The case has become known as the Battle over Los Angeles. Though it has barely received any attention, compared with Roswell, it is actually far more important (in my opinion).

No modern UFO event has been more thoroughly documented. It involved many tens of thousands of eyewitnesses, included a concerted artillery assault, was responded to by the police and fire departments, and appeared on the front page of the *Los Angeles Times* the next day.

(This case is presented in detail in the next chapter.)

What is of note at this point is the fact that the U.S. military could not and did not deny that it had fired on a UFO. The assault occurred over a half-hour period of time, and it produced a rain of spent shell casings and shrapnel that covered some of the nearby beaches.

This incident, which happened not quite three months after the attack on Pearl Harbor, was soon forgotten as the United States engaged the enemy in battle and the country became focused on winning the war. At that point in time, the U.S. military had no official position regarding UFOs, and the phenomenon was not a general mass media or public concern.

That would change radically soon after the war ended.

Not long after the atomic bombs were dropped on Hiroshima and Nagasaki, UFOs began appearing over the skies of New Mexico. It just so happens that the atomic bomb was developed in Los Alamos, New Mexico, and tested at the White Sands Proving Ground, located at Alamogordo, New Mexico.

The sudden appearance of UFOs over New Mexico in the postwar era does not seem like a mere coincidence. The Roswell incident represents the point where and when the U.S. military started to define a policy based on disinformation and denial.

Do not mistake the above assertion as being the first signal that I am about to launch into an antigovernment conspiracy rant. Neither I nor anyone else (except for the highest governmental officials involved) is privy to all the information that went into that decision.

Unfortunately, whether it was a correct call or not, it has produced a UFO history that has often bordered on the absurd. The American public has been told that even trained pilots did not witness a real UFO but had merely mistaken swamp gas for one.

In a long parade of succeeding cases, the mass media have been the conduit for such explanations as the following: a fighter pilot crashed and died because he chased a balloon he mistakenly thought was a UFO; credible observers had actually seen Venus and not a UFO; a combination of Venus and a weather balloon and even swamp gas had been mistaken for a UFO . . . and the list goes on, ad absurdum.

At times, the U.S. military has looked downright silly by changing their cover stories back and forth. Nonetheless, all of these maneuvers may be justified by national security concerns. Who can deny that possibility?

While that may be true in particular cases, I and most other independent investigators into the subject would argue that the U.S. government has the obligation to inform its citizens of the general truth. We shall see how other governments have handled this issue in later chapters.

After several waves of post–World War II UFO sightings were reported in the press, under public pressure a UFO study was launched by the air force.

The initial air force investigations into UFOs began on a small-scale under Project Sign at the end of 1947, following a host of highly publicized UFO sightings and the Roswell flap. Project Sign was launched specifically at the request of General Nathan Twining, chief of the Air Force Materiel Command at what is now Wright-Patterson Air Force Base.

Wright-Patterson was to become the home of Project Sign and all subsequent official U.S. Air Force public investigations. Ironically, this base was intimately involved in the Roswell case.

Sign's final report was inconclusive regarding the cause of the sightings. However, according to U.S. Air Force Captain Edward J. Ruppelt (who would become the first director of the subsequent Project Blue Book), Sign's initial intelligence estimate (the so-called Estimate of the Situation), written in the late summer of 1948, concluded that "flying saucers [UFOs] were real craft; were not made by either the Russians or the US; and were likely extraterrestrial in origin."

This estimate was forwarded to the Pentagon but subsequently ordered destroyed by General Hoyt Vandenberg, U.S. Air Force chief of staff, citing a lack of physical proof. Vandenberg subsequently dismantled Project Sign.

It was terminated at the end of 1948 but quickly reincarnated as Project Grudge, which was widely criticized as having a debunking mandate from the start. Ruppelt referred to the era of Project Grudge as the "dark ages" of early air force UFO investigation in his book *The Report on Unidentified Flying Objects,* published in 1956.

Grudge concluded that all UFOs were natural phenomena or other misperceptions, although contradictorily enough, it also stated that 23 percent of the reports could not be explained.

By the end of 1951, several high-ranking U.S. Air Force generals were so dissatisfied with the state of air force UFO investigations that they dismantled Project Grudge. It was turned into Project Blue Book in early 1952. One of the generals was William Garland, who was convinced that the UFO question deserved serious scrutiny because he had witnessed a UFO himself.

As noted above, Ruppelt was the first head of the project. He was a veteran and had been decorated for his service with the Army Air Corps during World War II. Ruppelt officially coined the term *unidentified flying object* to replace the many terms (flying saucer, flying disk, and so on) the military had previously used.

J. Allen Hynek, an astronomer, was the scientific consultant to the project, as he had been with Projects Sign and Grudge. He worked for Project Blue Book until the project was terminated in 1969.

The astronomer was an avowed skeptic when he signed on, but later said that his feelings changed to a more wavering skepticism; as the research progressed, he reviewed a number of UFO reports that he considered to be unexplainable (such as the Socorro, New Mexico, incident, which will be covered in chapter 13).

The project evaluated more than twelve thousand cases, most of which were readily dismissed for one reason or another. However, not all were, and this is an important fact.

Ruppelt resigned from the air force in the mid-1950s and wrote his book, which described the study of UFOs by the U.S. Air Force from 1947 to 1955.

Project Blue Book caused two very important developments: (1) Hynek became so convinced that there was a kernel of truth to the UFO phenomena that he launched an independent organization to study it (the Center for UFO Studies), which is still in operation, and (2) Ruppelt's work, which convinced his American readers that there was something to the UFO phenomenon that the air force was ignoring or lying to the public about.

However, as far as the air force was concerned, the UFO case was closed when Project Blue Book was terminated. The final conclusions:

1. No UFO reported, investigated, and evaluated by the air force was ever an indication of threat to our national security.
2. There was no evidence submitted to or discovered by the air force that sightings categorized as "unidentified" represented technological developments or principles beyond the range of modern scientific knowledge.
3. There was no evidence indicating that sightings categorized as "unidentified" were extraterrestrial vehicles.

Case closed?

More than forty years after the termination of Project Blue Book, air force personnel were still being told what to do in the event they observed a UFO. According to a recent *Huffington Post* article:

As recently as early September [2011], Air Force members who came across anything they didn't recognize were told to note "altitude, direction of travel, speed, description of flight path and maneuvers, what first called attention to the object, how long was the object visible and how did the object disappear?"[1]

The journalist who was investigating the situation, Lee Speigel, queried the air force about the UFO directives in light of the Project Blue Book conclusions made decades earlier. He was told that an interview would be arranged with an appropriate officer to go over the situation.

However, as he noted in his article, "but before the interview was set up, the 111-page instruction manual was revised on Sept. 6, and the

UFO instructions were deleted, as were other portions of the document, now shortened to 40 pages."[2]

This is why I began this preface by stating that I was reluctant to go over the history of UFOs in the United States. One soon finds oneself peering down a hall of mirrors and having a hard time distinguishing what is real from what is false.

Nonetheless, the most important UFO cases in the world have occurred in the United States. That fact makes it incumbent on any researcher to dig and dig deep, and to discern "spin" on any layer and get to the underlying facts.

10

....

The Battle over
Los Angeles

First, to set the record straight there was no "battle"; however, a U.S. artillery battery was ordered to launch a barrage at a suspected enemy target hovering over Los Angeles. There was no battle because the supposed enemy aircraft (a UFO) never returned fire nor did it drop any bombs. What follows is a brief summary of the bare-bones, established facts collected from military reports.

During the night of February 24 to 25, 1942, an unidentified object caused a succession of alerts in Southern California. This was not yet three months after the Japanese attack on Pearl Harbor. On the twenty-fourth, a warning issued by naval intelligence indicated that an attack could be expected within the next ten hours. That evening, a large number of flares and blinking lights were reported from the vicinity of defense plants.

An alert called at 7:18 p.m., Pacific time, was lifted at 10:23 p.m., and the mounting tension temporarily relaxed. But early in the morning of the twenty-fifth, renewed activity began. Radarscopes picked up an unidentified target 120 miles west of Los Angeles. Antiaircraft batteries were alerted at 2:15 a.m. and put on "green alert"—ready to fire—a few minutes later.

The air force kept its pursuit planes on the ground, choosing to wait for indications of the scale and direction of any attack before committing its limited fighter force. Radarscopes tracked the approaching target to within a few miles of the coast; then at 2:25 a.m. the regional

Fig. 10.1. Unidentified Flying Objects!
as shown on the front page of the Los Angeles Times, *1942*

controller ordered a blackout so that enemy planes could not find their targets.

Now what follows is a description of the events that happened above and on the ground, over and in greater Los Angeles.

Shortly after the blackout was ordered, air raid sirens shattered the peace and quiet of Culver City and Santa Monica; citizens of those towns scrambled to see what was going on, naturally assuming that the Japanese were mounting a second assault on U.S. soil.

Volunteer air raid wardens grabbed their gear and headed into the streets, going house to house, effecting a total blackout. The 37th Coast Artillery Brigade swung into action, and the sky was soon lit up by a swarm of searchlights. The beams converged on an object seemingly suspended in the sky.

Shock, surprise, and confusion swept through the observers, who were expecting to see enemy warplanes; instead, they saw a massive object (a UFO) that did not resemble any known type of aircraft.

The artillerymen were ordered to shell the object, and round after round of antiaircraft gunfire exploded repeatedly, with volley after volley aimed straight at the strange airship. Eyewitnesses later reported seeing the object take numerous direct hits, but they appeared to have no effect. This was an extremely serious event. The UFO never mounted any kind of counterattack.

However, the thirty-minute barrage sent shell fragments and casings raining down on homes, businesses, and even citizens who were watching it. Eyewitnesses later told reporters that the object was a "surreal, hanging, magic lantern."

Now what follows is the article (and my analysis of it) that appeared on the front page of the *Los Angeles Times* one day after the incident, on Thursday, February 26, 1942.

Los Angeles Times

FEBRUARY 26, 1942

Overshadowing a nation-wide maelstrom of rumors and conflicting reports, the Army's Western Defense Command insisted that Los Angeles' early morning blackout and anti-aircraft action were the result of unidentified aircraft sighted over the beach area.[1]

This is what the *Times* journalist got straight from the U.S. Army immediately following the "battle." It makes it very clear that the army had no idea what the object that the artillery battery was ordered to hit, with barrage after barrage, really was. There are skeptics who contend that the UFO was nothing but a balloon (the usual suspect). However, that is entirely at odds with the official army position.

Could a balloon withstand and stay in position while absorbing 1,400 rounds of artillery fire? The *Times* article also stated:

LOS ANGELES TIMES, FEBRUARY 26, 1942

The command in San Francisco confirmed and reconfirmed the presence over the Southland of unidentified planes; relayed by the Southern California sector office in Pasadena, the second statement read: "The aircraft which caused the blackout in the Los Angeles area for several hours this a.m. has not been identified."[2]

This was during the early stage of the war, so every effort to thoroughly identify the object was made and with great haste; if it had been a balloon or any type of known enemy plane, that fact would have been established right away.

The following article appeared in another local newspaper, the *Glendale News-Press,* on Wednesday, February 25, 1942:

Glendale News-Press

FEBRUARY 25, 1942

ANTI-AIRCRAFT GUNS BLAST AT L.A. MYSTERY INVADER

RAID SCARE BLACKS OUT SOUTHLAND, BUT KNOX CLAIMS "FALSE ALARM"

Washington (AP)—Secretary of the Navy Frank Knox said today that there were no planes over Los Angeles last night. "That's our understanding," he said. He added that "none have been found and a very wide reconnaissance has been carried on." He added, "It was just a false alarm."

Anti-aircraft guns thundered over the metropolitan area early today for the first time in the war, but hours later what they were shooting at remained a military secret. An unidentified object moving slowly down the coast from Santa Monica was variously reported as a balloon and an airplane.

"Cities in the Los Angeles area were blacked out at 2:25 a.m. today on orders from the fourth interceptor command when unidentified aircraft were reported in the area," the western defense command said.

Although reports are conflicting and every effort is being made to ascertain the facts, it is clear that no bombs were dropped and no planes were shot down.

There was a considerable amount of anti-aircraft firing. The all-clear signal came at 7:25 a.m. . . .

Wailing air raid sirens at 2:25 a.m. awakened most of the metropolitan area's three million citizens. A few minutes later they were treated to a gigantic Fourth-of-July-like display as huge searchlights flashed along a 10-mile front to the south, converging on a single spot high in the sky.

ANTI-AIRCRAFT GUNS OPEN FIRE

Moments later the anti-aircraft guns opened up, throwing a sheet of steel skyward.

Tracer bullets and exploding shells lit the heavens.[3]

All of the area's newspaper accounts agreed on the basic facts. A blackout was called, and air raid sirens woke up millions of Los Angeles–area residents at about 2:30 a.m. They observed the artillery battery launch barrage after barrage at the hovering, stationary object for half an hour.

Residents in a forty-mile arc along the coast watched from hills or rooftops as the play of guns and searchlights provided the first real drama of the war for citizens of the mainland.

The dawn, which ended the shooting and the "battle" fantasy, also proved that the only damage that resulted to the city was such as had been caused by the excitement (there was at least one death from heart failure), by traffic accidents in the blacked-out streets, or by shell fragments from the artillery barrage.

Attempts to arrive at an explanation of the incident quickly became as involved and mysterious as the battle itself. The navy immediately insisted that there was no evidence of the presence of enemy planes, and, as stated, Knox announced at a press conference on February 25 that the raid was just a false alarm.

At the same conference, he admitted that attacks were always possible and indicated that vital industries located along the coast ought to be moved inland.

The army had a hard time making up its mind on the cause of the alert. A report to Washington, made by the Western Defense Command shortly after the raid had ended, indicated that the credibility of reports of an attack had begun to be taken into account before the blackout was lifted. This message predicted that developments would prove "that most previous reports had been greatly exaggerated."[4]

The Fourth Air Force, then part of the army, had indicated its belief that there were no planes over Los Angeles, but the army did not publish these initial conclusions. Instead, it waited a day, until after a thorough examination of witnesses had been finished. On the basis of these hearings, local commanders altered their verdict and indicated a belief that from one to five unidentified airplanes had been over Los Angeles.

Secretary of War Henry L. Stimson announced this conclusion as the War Department version of the incident, and he advanced two theories to account for the mysterious craft: either they were commercial planes operated by an enemy from secret fields in California or Mexico, or they were light planes launched from Japanese submarines.

In either case, the enemy's purpose must have been to locate antiaircraft defenses in the area or to deliver a blow at civilian morale.

The spin came in shortly after the actual events, which were witnessed by tens of thousands of citizens, hundreds of military personnel, policemen, firemen, and so forth, all credible witnesses who reported what they had observed to the journalists on-site.

This was the first major, mass UFO sighting of the modern era. Yet surprisingly few people know that it even took place. Why? Since it occurred at the beginning of the war, it was never fully investigated.

Soon after that night, the incident was forgotten as attention turned to the prosecution of a real war. However, the documentation was and is in the public record. *No enemy planes were involved,* a fact that the defeated Japanese later confirmed. They never attacked Los Angeles.

CONCLUSION

This was the first mass UFO sighting that involved every kind of credible witness and social institution, including the military, the press, and law enforcement. Anyone skeptical of this heavily documented event is more concerned with his or her worldview, which does not permit UFOs, than with the facts.

11

. . . .

Roswell

The Smoking Gun

The Roswell incident probably would have quickly slipped into the realm of UFO cases that only hardcore UFOlogists study, if not for the alleged recovery of alien bodies. Unfortunately, the importance of this case—in the context of understanding the UFO phenomena—has been buried under that very sensational, single, overhyped aspect.

Who does not know about Roswell today? The name is now synonymous with the UFO phenomenon.

Fig. 11.1. Front-page article about the flying saucer of Roswell

First, in order to put this case in its proper context, it is important to get some background about the history, development, and testing of the atomic bomb during World War II.

It all zeroes in on one state: New Mexico.

In 1942, New Mexico was a little known, largely empty, sparsely populated state that only those born in the Southwest knew anything about. The Navajo, Zuni, and other Native American tribes lived in the northern plateaus, called mesas, as they do today. The southern desert country was largely uninhabited.

The fairly small, quiet town of Los Alamos is situated in northern New Mexico. It was virtually unknown in 1943, when the government hurriedly constructed buildings to house those serving in the top-secret Manhattan Project, which would eventually succeed in designing and manufacturing the first atomic bombs.

Why Los Alamos? Having determined the need for a centralized lab to conduct research in secret, General Leslie Groves of the Army Corp of Engineers wanted an isolated location for safety and to keep the scientists (the "brain trust") away from the prying media and curious populace. He reasoned that the lab should be at least two hundred miles from international boundaries and west of the Mississippi River.

Army Major John Dudley suggested Oak City, Utah, or Jemez Springs, New Mexico, but both were rejected. The Manhattan Project scientific director, J. Robert Oppenhemier, had spent a lot of time in his younger days in the northern New Mexico area, and he suggested the Los Alamos Ranch School on the mesa, and as soon as Groves saw it, he agreed.[1]

During the Manhattan Project, the Los Alamos site hosted thousands of employees, including many Nobel Prize–winning scientists. The location was a total secret. The lab's only mailing address was a P. O. box (number 1663) in Santa Fe, New Mexico. Though its contract with the University of California was initially intended to be temporary, the relationship was maintained long after the war.

The nature of the research was so carefully guarded that until the atomic bombs landed on Hiroshima and Nagasaki, Japan, University of California president Robert Sproul had no idea what the purpose of the lab was.

The only member of the University of California administration who knew the lab's true purpose—actually, the only one who knew its exact location—was Secretary-Treasurer Robert Underhill, who was in charge of wartime contracts and liabilities.

Work at the lab began in 1943 and culminated in the creation of several atomic bombs, one of which was used in the first nuclear test, near Alamogordo, New Mexico; code named Trinity, it was detonated on July 16, 1945. Thereby was the atomic age ushered in, all on the soil of one largely uninhabited state.

The White Sands Proving Ground, near Alamogordo, sits almost due south of Los Alamos in the south-central part of the state, in an isolated, desert locale. Roswell lies to the northeast of Alamogordo and the southeast of Los Alamos. A few hundred miles separate all of these locations.

Soon after the bombs were developed, tested, and used to end the war, UFOs of various descriptions began appearing over the skies of New Mexico.

With the historical background and geographical data in place, we have a context ready for the Roswell incident to be placed within.

Roswell is a small farming town in eastern New Mexico, as noted, slightly north and east of Alamogordo. In 1947, not long after the atomic bombs were dropped on Japan, Roswell was the home of the 509th Bombardment Group, stationed at Roswell Army Air Field. At that time, the 509th was the only atomic-bomb squadron in the world.

Other than perhaps a few small underlying jitters elicited by some of the top secret "nuke" operations conducted by the army at the Roswell base, the town was as relaxed as any other rural, largely agricultural community in the country. The civilian residents had their lives and work to do, and the military had theirs. In many ways, their lives were intertwined to the benefit of both sides.

The nukes had forced Japan to surrender (supposedly), and with the war over, Roswell was settling down into its normal prewar, peacetime routines.

That all changed the morning of July 8, 1947, when the citizens, civilian, and military alike woke up to the following article in the *Roswell Daily Record:*

Roswell Daily Record

JULY 8, 1947

RAAF CAPTURES FLYING SAUCER ON RANCH IN ROSWELL REGION

The intelligence office of the 509th Bombardment group at Roswell Army Air Field announced at noon today, that the field has come into possession of a flying saucer.

According to information released by the department, over authority of Maj. J. A. Marcel, intelligence officer, the disk was recovered on a ranch in the Roswell vicinity, after an unidentified rancher had notified Sheriff Geo. Wilcox here, that he had found the instrument on his premises.

Major Marcel and a detail from his department went to the ranch and recovered the disk, it was stated.

After the intelligence officer here had inspected the instrument it was flown to higher headquarters.

The intelligence officer stated that no details of the saucer's construction or its appearance had been revealed.

Mr. and Mrs. Dan Wilmot apparently were the only persons in Roswell who saw what they thought was a flying disk.

They were sitting on their porch at 105 South Penn. last Wednesday night at about ten o'clock when a large glowing object zoomed out of the sky from the southeast, going in a northwesterly direction at a high rate of speed.

Wilmot called Mrs. Wilmot's attention to it and both ran down into the yard to watch. It was in sight less than a minute, perhaps 40 or 50 seconds, Wilmot estimated.

Wilmot said that it appeared to him to be about 1,500 feet high and going fast. He estimated between 400 and 500 miles per hour.

In appearance it looked oval in shape like two inverted saucers, faced mouth to mouth, or like two old type washbowls placed together in the same fashion. The entire body glowed as though light were showing through from inside, though not like it would be if a light were underneath.

From where he stood Wilmot said that the object looked to be about 5 feet in size, and making allowance for the distance it was from town he figured that it must have been 15 to 20 feet in diameter, though this was just a guess.

Wilmot said that he heard no sound but that Mrs. Wilmot said she heard a swishing sound for a very short time.

The object came into view from the southeast and disappeared over the treetops in the general vicinity of six mile hill.

Wilmot, who is one of the most respected and reliable citizens in town, kept the story to himself hoping that someone else would come out and tell about having seen one, but finally today decided that he would go ahead and tell about it. The announcement that the RAAF was in possession of one came only a few minutes after he decided to release the details of what he had seen.[2]

Imagine waking up, slapping some cold water on your face, putting a pot of coffee on, filling a bowl with some Cheerios, and settling down to read the morning paper—only to be confronted with that improbable headline.

After that morning, neither Roswell nor the world would ever be the same. The story rocketed around the globe. The problem with the article was that while it suggested much, it revealed very few details, raising far more questions than it answered.

What really happened? Well, therein lies the rub.

Investigators came up with different conclusions more than thirty years after the event, and by then it was a very cold case. Three books were written by UFOlogists from 1980 to 1993. (We shall review them later in this chapter.)

First, the Wilmots witnessed the UFO's flight pattern, as was described in the article on July 8. They did so on July 2. All ensuing investigations agreed that the couple were beyond reproach, both being model citizens.

They claimed to have seen a UFO overhead, and we have no cause to doubt it. Mr. Wilmot gave a basic but good working description of it, and their testimony begins the Roswell story.

What about the rest of it?

During the first week of July, Mac Brazel, a local ranch manager, was riding with one of his children out to do a morning check on his sheep after a night of intense thunderstorms. This is typical stuff for a Western rancher. While scouting around, he ran into a curious pile of unusual debris apparently caused by a crash.

He noticed that something had hollowed out a shallow gouge several hundred feet long and that the debris was scattered over a large area.

He investigated the debris and noted that it had several strange physical properties. He decided to take a few samples—a large one he stored in a shed and a smaller piece to show his neighbors, Floyd and Loretta Proctor. After doing that, Brazel drove into Roswell and contacted the sheriff, George Wilcox.

Brazel was a typical no-nonsense, down-to-earth ranch hand and manager, not the kind of guy who sits on a hill waiting for a UFO to arrive and take him to a distant, utopian planet.

Following an eyewitness-testimony and chain-of-evidence approach, we find (1) on July 2, the Wilmots observed a UFO flying overhead; (2) on July 4, Brazel discovered strange debris scattered about, apparently caused by a crash landing that had gouged out a stretch of ground several hundred feet in length; (3) Brazel took samples of the debris, stored one larger sheet, and and showed a smaller sample to his neighbors; and (4) he then drove into town and notified the sheriff of his discovery.

On July 1 and 2, military radar and eyewitnesses had spotted fast-moving objects in the sky; this had actually become fairly commonplace from Los Alamos, in the far northern part of the state, to Alamogordo and the Roswell area, in the south-central southeastern parts. Most investigators claim that the crash took place on July 2. Brazel did not find the site until the fourth, and as soon as he did events moved extremely fast.

However, the July 2 date for the Wilmot sighting is a little suspicious; it seems possible that the date for the crash could have been third or fourth of July, when a violent thunderstorm hit the area. It has been speculated, quite logically, that the UFO was hit by a lightning strike, though this is not being claimed to be factual and must remain in the domain of speculation. The exact date is not as important as the incident itself.

A further point that needs clarification: the crash site Brazel discovered was actually midway between the towns of Corona and Roswell. Both towns are about seventy-five miles away from the site. The case is commonly called "the Roswell incident" because the debris and alleged alien bodies were taken to the Roswell Army Air Field.

Those are the facts as reported by the Wilmots and Brazel, and later confirmed by Brazel's children, the Proctors, and Wilcox.

Next, Wilcox notified authorities at Roswell Army Air Field. Following that, he took several deputies and went to the Foster ranch, which Brazel managed, to investigate the debris.

The air field's intelligence officer, Major Jesse Marcel, was dispatched to the site to conduct the initial investigation after the sheriff notified the authorities at the base. All who try to dismiss the Roswell case out of hand without thinking the facts and details through on a deep level should consider the following carefully.

Marcel was the intelligence officer of an elite atomic bomb group, the only one in the world. In addition, he was a career military officer and highly trained in his field. He would never have jeopardized his reputation and good standing by mistaking shards from an alleged air balloon for the debris of an extraterrestrial craft. He carefully examined the debris material and determined that it was *not of this earth*.

When he investigated the site, Marcel picked up pieces of the wreckage and noted that they were extremely light and very thin. Years later, when he decided to make his role in the Roswell case known to the public, Marcel stated, "It was not a weather balloon, nor was it an airplane or a missile." Of the character of the debris, he noted: "So, I tried to bend the stuff. It wouldn't bend."[3]

In other words, he stuck to his original findings, which formed the basis of the initial newspaper article.

After concluding his investigation, Marcel had the debris removed and transported to the Roswell base. The only people that were witness to the crash site and the debris were the Brazels, Wilcox and his deputies, Marcel, and the army mop-up detail.

Those are the key witnesses, and other than the military, only Brazel carried off some pieces of evidence, which his friends also examined. The main bulk of the evidence was hauled off by the mop-up detail and transported to the Roswell Army Air Field.

Thus far this is a simple, straightforward series of events, or so it seems on the surface anyway.

Now at this juncture we should pose a question: If the debris was nothing more than the remains of a shredded balloon (the final official report), why did the military take the time and expense to quickly ship it, via B-29 and C54 aircraft, to Texas, and then to the Army Air Force's Wright Field in Ohio?

If one accepts the balloon premise, then this question needs to be addressed. A shredded balloon would neither command any attention nor would it be shipped to distant military bases for follow-up examinations and storage. That logical supposition is simple and obvious.

Nonetheless, not long after Marcel had the material transported to Roswell, he got orders to ship it out to Fort Worth, Texas. Now we have to add another link in the chain of evidence: from the Brazel ranch, to Roswell Air Field, and then to Fort Worth.

If the debris pile was something other than a balloon, something that needed more examination because, as Brazel and Marcel suggested, it possessed unusual properties, then the scenario makes sense. Not only would the shipment to Wright Field be needed, so would the initial press release, which was obviously based on the conclusions of Marcel's investigation.

But no sooner had the *Roswell Daily Record* published an article based on the first press release than the editor received a follow-up release that was issued by General Roger Ramey, commander of the 8th Air Force, Fort Worth Army Air Field.

The first story was rescinded, and the blame was pinned on Marcel, who had mistakenly misidentified a weather balloon and its reflector for the wreckage of a "crashed disk," according to Ramey.

We are faced with an either-or choice because both versions cannot be true. How do we decide which one is real and which not?

The first press release was issued by Colonel William Blanchard, commander of the Roswell base. He trusted his intelligence officer to effectively handle his duties, and he examined the debris as well.

If Marcel had somehow failed to notice that the debris was really that of a balloon at the site, he certainly would have known for sure by the time it was taken to the base and shown to his commander.

MAJOR MARCEL AND COLONEL BLANCHARD

Coincidentally, it was reported that the day after the first and second press releases, Blanchard and his wife went on leave and left the Roswell area to go on a vacation (which was not completely true). So he was out of the loop and not available to respond to any questions that the second press release raised with the very fascinated and pestering mass media.

Given that the balloon scenario pins the blame for this whole fiasco on Marcel, we would naturally assume that such flagrant incompetence would hurt his future career. Wrong. Marcel continued with his duties and actually rose in rank to become a distinguished colonel. That simply does not pass the smell test.

It is these kinds of seemingly insignificant details that raise red flags that often add up and, taken together, point to the underlying truth. An officer does not get promoted to high levels of rank for being an incompetent fool who causes the Army Air Force (and the military in general) vast public embarrassment. Clearly, the army never considered Marcel to be either incompetent or foolish.

The same is true of Blanchard. If he had just rubber-stamped Marcel's report and also showed himself to be an incompetent fool, his career, too, would have been truncated. However, he also went on to eventually be promoted to a four-star general rank, the highest peacetime rank.

For a moment, let us consider the military career of then major Jesse Marcel up to the time of the Roswell incident.

He joined the army during World War II and performed well in intelligence school, so well that after his graduation he was assigned to be an instructor at the school. After a period of serving in that capacity, he requested a combat post, and the army granted it. In October 1943, First Lieutenant Marcel was assigned to the 5th Bomber Command in the Southwest Pacific theater.

For the next two years, he fought in the Pacific theater, initially as a squadron intelligence officer, and then as a group intelligence officer.

Marcel participated in several campaigns that were pivotal in retaking the Philippine Islands from the Japanese. During his combat tour, Marcel consistently showed that he was a stellar, highly competent officer. His commanders recognized his efforts by rewarding him with two Air Medals, the Bronze Star, a promotion to captain, and then one to major, in May 1945.

Does this sound like the type of man who would not be able to distinguish between the debris of a balloon and a UFO? I am not one to overlook these kinds of details because establishing credibility is of paramount concern in any UFO case. Marcel was not a sloppy, reckless investigator.

More proof? When Roswell was all over, he was transferred to the Strategic Air Command, where he was eventually put in charge of a Pentagon briefing room for the Air Force Office of Atomic Energy. There his responsibilities were to make sure that materials (charts, illustrations, and so forth) were ready on schedule for the chiefs of staff and to maintain the organization of the briefing room.

If Marcel concluded that the debris was not of this earth, I am convinced that he knew whereof he was speaking. If Marcel said that, following the second press release, he was under orders to never speak openly about what he had investigated at the crash site, rest assured, that was the case.

If any skeptics doubt that and would rather cast aspersions on his character, then give a reasonable explanation of why he would lie, based on his known character and military record.

In the end, the truth behind the Roswell incident can only be uncovered by establishing who might have lied and why he, she, or they felt compelled to do so. Remember, it is an either-or choice—a balloon or a UFO. The issue really revolves around who or what you believe: Marcel or Ramey, the first press release or the second. Marcel was an intelligence officer, which I clearly state; he did the on-site investigation and wrote up a report that was used for the first press release. Blanchard authorized the publication of that first press release. Ramey was at another base and above them in rank.

(Interestingly, Ramey, the point man in this case, will reappear in this book to debunk another major UFO case from five years later, which we shall go over in chapter 12.)

Let's delve further into the evidence. Returning first to the article based on the original press release that appeared in the *Roswell Daily Record,* we find an account given by the Wilmots, who said that prior to the press release being issued, they observed a disk flying northwest on July 2 (perhaps on the fourth), which Mr. Wilmot estimated to be fifteen to twenty feet in diameter. At the time they reported their sighting, the UFO crash story had not been published.

Later Brazel (and other citizens) reported that they had heard a loud explosion the night that the Wilmots observed the craft.

The object that the Wilmots observed and described in no way resembled a balloon. It was flying in the direction of the crash site. Their sighting and the subsequent explosion that was heard suggest the crash occurred on the second or third of July.*

Brazel found the debris field and showed some debris to the Proctors, and all agreed it was unlike anything they had ever seen. Then Brazel took his sample into Roswell, where he showed it to Sheriff Wilcox. The sheriff, in turn, called the base and reported Brazel's discovery to Major Marcel. The major then drove to the sheriff's office and inspected the sample. This all took place on July 6.

Marcel informed Blanchard, who ordered him to get someone from the Counter Intelligence Corps, proceed to the crash site with Brazel, and retrieve as much of the wreckage as possible. Shortly thereafter, the Military Police (MPs) showed up at the sheriff's office and confiscated Brazel's sample. (That accounts for what happened to that piece of the wreckage evidence.)

The MPs delivered that sample to Blanchard's office; it appeared that time was of the essence because the sample was immediately flown to the 8th Air Force Headquarters in Fort Worth and from there to Washington, D.C. In the meantime, Marcel accompanied Brazel to his car, and they headed to the debris field. Along the way, they stopped to examine the large sheet of debris that Brazel had stored in the shed.

On July 7, Marcel and Captain Sheridan Cavitt (the Counter Intelligence Corps investigator), dressed in civilian clothes, collected material from the debris field. Once they had filled the latter's car, Marcel told him to return to the base and said that he would continue to collect more pieces of debris, and then return to Roswell.

Finishing the job of filling up his own car, Marcel headed back to town, stopping at his home along the way. Marcel then showed his wife and son, Jesse Jr., some of the pieces he had collected and demonstrated the strange properties they possessed to his family.

About 4:00 p.m. that afternoon, a radio broadcaster at station

---

*Because the records are ambiguous, the exact date of the sighting is unknown. There was no investigation of this incident after it happened. It was forgotten for decades, so it is difficult to reconstruct.

KSWS began relaying a story (then unconfirmed) about a crashed flying saucer over the teletype machine. However, the message never got through because the FBI intercepted the transmission and demanded that she squelch the story or the station would face consequences.

Next, at 11:00 a.m. on July 8, Blanchard dictated the initial press release to First Lieutenant Walter Haut, the base's public information officer.

Haut immediately headed into town to deliver the release to the radio stations and newspapers. The first station was KGEL; he handed it to Frank Joyce.

At noon, the release hit the Associated Press news wire service.

Then the first flight in from Washington, D.C., arrived at the base, carrying a special team of photographers and Warrant Officer Robert Thomas. They were dispatched to Roswell by the Pentagon.

By this time, the army was already posting guards at all the roads that led to the Foster ranch (the crash site). When William Woody and his father, who had also witnessed the Wilmot sighting, tried to drive in that direction, MPs turned them back.

The response to the Associated Press wire release quickly overwhelmed the phone lines at the base, the local radio stations, and the newspapers; all were jammed up within hours.

Wilcox dispatched two deputies to the debris field for a second time, but MPs turned them back. Brazel was flown back to the debris field from the base. The impact site was observed from the air.

Base personnel told inquiring reporters that Blanchard had gone on leave; however, he actually went to the debris site.

Like Marcel, Blanchard was neither naive nor foolish. He verified Marcel's conclusions before issuing that press release. In addition, if Blanchard had committed any kind of incompetent blunder, could he have gone on to attain the highest peacetime rank the U.S. military offers, that of *four-star general*? No.

Why would the air force reward two officers for committing a monumental and quite embarrassing blunder?

The press release that Blanchard issued based on Marcel's assessment was accurate; the Roswell wreckage was of extraterrestrial origin. The retraction and subsequent replacement of a crashed UFO with a balloon was a cover story, pure and simple.

(But this assessment is as yet premature; I shall substantiate it much more before giving a final conclusion.)

Now the case was simple and straightforward when the first press release was issued. However, it soon got complicated when the evidence was shipped from Roswell to Texas. Then it got even more complex when the second press release fully retracted the information presented in the first one.

The case steadily grew in complexity when the planes arrived from Washington, D.C., and the ranch was cordoned off by the MPs. If, as Ramey insisted, there was nothing to look at but the pieces of a crashed balloon, why did a special team arrive from Washington to investigate the site? Furthermore, since a wrecked balloon is hardly a matter of national security, why post a military perimeter around the crash site?

As soon as Ramey invoked his "smoke-and-mirrors strategy," the case erupted with contradictions and absurdities.

All this, and I have yet to drag the poor, diminutive humanoids that were allegedly killed in the crash into the picture. Too much information too soon can overwhelm the analytical process. Roswell has too many witnesses, not too few; too much evidence, not too little; and too many years have passed since the incident occurred. It is, therefore, easy to get lost in the mass of complications and conflicting details.

STAYING FOCUSED ON THE SMOKING GUN

Just remember the initial press release and the early eyewitness reports, as well as the hands that held the evidence and how that evidence was transferred and to whom.

I am not presenting this case to try to prove that a UFO containing four aliens crashed near Roswell, a UFO that the U.S. government recovered and has kept hidden ever since. All I am really focusing on is the veracity of the first press release, the mass of evidence that supports its authenticity, and the reality it described.

With the general facts and general chronology, as well as the first-hand witnesses established, it is now time to add a higher resolution, and more details, to the picture.

Bessie Brazel was with her father when they discovered the debris at the crash site. She later gave this report:

> There were what appeared to be pieces of heavily waxed paper and a sort of aluminum-like foil. Some of these pieces had something like numbers and lettering on them, but there were no words that we were able to make out. Some of the metal-foil like pieces had a sort of tape stuck to them, and when these were held to the light they showed what looked like pastel flowers or designs. Even though the stuff looked like tape it could not be peeled off or removed at all. It was very light in weight but there sure was a lot of it.[4]

Mac Brazel passed away in 1963, long before UFO investigators started interviewing Roswell witnesses. However, he did give an interview to a *Roswell Daily Record* reporter at the time of the event; when asked about the debris he said that it was "bright wreckage made up of rubber strips, tinfoil, a rather tough paper and sticks."[5]

Marcel did not speak publicly about his investigations until 1978, thirty-one years after they took place. When asked about the debris he gave the following response:

> There was all kinds of stuff—small beams about three eighths or a half inch square with some sort of hieroglyphics on them that nobody could decipher. These looked something like balsa wood, and were about the same weight, except that they were not wood at all. They were very hard, although flexible, and would not burn. . . . One thing that impressed me about the debris was the fact that a lot of it looked like parchment. It had little numbers with symbols that we had to call hieroglyphics because I could not understand them. They could not be read, they were just like symbols, something that meant something, and they were not all the same, but the same general pattern, I would say.
>
> These little numbers could not be broken, could not be burned. I even took my cigarette lighter and tried to burn the material we found that resembled parchment and balsa, but it would not burn— wouldn't even smoke. But something that is even more astonishing is that the pieces of metal that we brought back were so thin, just like

tinfoil in a pack of cigarettes. I didn't pay too much attention to that at first, until one of the boys came to me and said: "You know that metal that was in there? I tried to bend the stuff and it won't bend. I even tried it with a sledgehammer. You can't make a dent on it."[6]

Clearly, the testimony from all three of the first eyewitnesses to inspect the debris at the site is in agreement as to its peculiar characteristics. In addition to these primary witnesses, their family members also had the chance to inspect the material that composed the debris. Brazel's son said that some of it was like balsa wood, only harder, and that he tried but was unable to scratch it.

Marcel had shown his son some of the debris material after he had filled his car with it and then returned to Roswell that night. His son, Jesse Jr. (who became a medical doctor), has given the following description:

> Foil-like stuff, very thin, metallic-like but not metal and very tough. There was also some structural-like material too—beams and so on. Also a quantity of black plastic material which looked organic in nature. . . . Imprinted along the edge of some of the beam remnants there were hieroglyphic-type characters.[7]

Also, Marcel claimed that, as ordered by Blanchard, he had been accompanied to the debris site by Cavitt. However, when Cavitt was interviewed by an air force investigator during hearings in 1992 to establish whether there had been a cover-up, Cavitt claimed that he could not recall meeting Marcel.

However, Cavitt did admit to inspecting the debris at the crash site with his assistant, Sergeant Lewis Rickett. The air force investigator then questioned Rickett.

Rickett said Cavitt took him to a debris area the following day. He described an extensive cleanup of a large area involving many men, heavily guarded by MPs. He was allowed to handle a remaining piece of debris.

> There was a slightly curved piece of metal, real light.
>   You could bend it but couldn't crease it.

It was about six inches by twelve or fourteen inches. Very light. I crouched down and tried to snap it. My boss [Cavitt] laughs and said, "Smart guy. He's trying to do what we couldn't do."

I asked, "What in the hell is this stuff made out of?"

It didn't feel like plastic and I never saw a piece of metal this thin that you couldn't break. This was the strangest material we had ever seen . . . there was talk about it not being from Earth.[8]

The above are the known, identified, first, and therefore primary group of eyewitnesses to have touched and inspected the "unknown" material. Most were also the first to visit and inspect the site with the debris still present.

All the eyewitness testimony was in agreement about the nature of the unique material. Clearly, it was not the stuff balloons are made of.

Now there are also numerous secondary witness reports to consider: Sergeant Robert Porter was a B-29 flight engineer. Porter helped load and then boarded the B-29 that flew from Roswell to Fort Worth, where Marcel was supposed to show some recovered material to General Ramey before proceeding on to Wright Field in Ohio. Porter told investigators:

I was involved in loading the B-29 with the material, which was wrapped in packages with wrapping paper. One of the pieces was triangle shaped, about 2½ feet across the bottom. The rest were in small packages about the size of a shoebox. The brown paper was held with tape. . . . The material was extremely lightweight. When I picked it up, it was just like picking up an empty package. We loaded the triangle-shaped package and three shoe box-sized packages into the plane. All of the packages could have fit into the trunk of a car.[9]

Sergeant Robert Smith, of the 1st Air Transport Unit at Roswell, said:

My involvement in the Roswell incident was to help load crates of debris on to the aircraft. . . . There was a lot of farm dirt on the hangar floor. . . . We loaded crates on to three or four C-54s. . . . One crate took up the entire plane; it wasn't that heavy, but it was a large volume. . . . All I saw was a little piece of material. The piece of debris I saw was two-to-three inches square. It was jagged. When you crumpled it up, it then laid back out; and when it did, it kind of crackled, making a sound like cellophane, and it crackled when it was let out. There were no creases. . . . The largest piece was roughly 20 feet long; four-to-five feet high, four-to-five feet wide. The rest were two-to-three feet long, two feet square or smaller.[10]

Lieutenant Robert Shirkey, the base's assistant operations officer, also witnessed debris being loaded onto the B-29. He said:

Standing only three feet from the passing procession, we saw boxes full of aluminum-looking metal pieces being carried to the B-29; Major Marcel came along carrying an open box full of what seemed to be scrap-metal. It obviously was not aluminum: it did not shine nor reflect like the aluminum on American military airplanes. And sticking up in one corner of the box being carried by Major Marcel was a small "I-beam" with hieroglyphic-like markings on the inner flange, in some kind of weird color, not black, not purple, but a close approximation of the two. . . . A man in civilian dress . . . was carrying a piece of metal under his left arm. . . . This piece was about the size of a poster drawing board—very smooth, almost glass-like, with torn edges.[11]

The above statements from supporting witnesses corroborate the observations of Marcel and the others and also establish that the material was not a mere balloon, since it was mysterious enough to transport it, posthaste, to military bases in Texas; Washington, D.C.; and Ohio.

If it had been a typical balloon, then would it have not been a lot cheaper and much less time consuming to simply have one team of forensic experts come to Roswell to definitively identify it?

But no, that debris was of such a unique character—and of such import to the Pentagon—that access to the crash site had to be blocked off by MPs, the first press release retracted, the debris material transported expeditiously to one, and then another distant military post, and a team dispatched from Washington to Roswell. One must logically ask, Why all the fuss over a few scraps of a crashed balloon?

In fact, as far as the objective of this book is concerned, the preponderance of evidence weighs heavily on the side of the first press release being the accurate and authentic one. That is really all I need to support the Genesis Race hypothesis.

One lone artifact, one piece of unknown metal associated with a crashed UFO, is enough to add yet another piece of evidence to the mounting ancient and modern compilation.

However, though this chapter could end here and be a satisfactory inclusion supporting the overall hypothesis of the book, there are reasons to extend the examination. Many UFO investigators, including the scientists behind the French COMETA Report from 1999, have serious misgivings about the way the U.S. government handled (and still handles) the Roswell incident.

Their concerns go beyond the cover-up aspect to much deeper and more disturbing scenarios. What if the cover-up was created to keep a very important strategy hidden for decades, at least, if not for good?

Is it possible that the U.S. Air Force recovered a UFO, reverse engineered its technology, and then developed whole new technologies from what they learned? Could this be why America has been the world's leader in military, scientific, and technological fields, in an ever-accelerating manner, since the early 1950s?

One method that can be used to attempt to answer these questions is examining any evidence that suggests the level of importance that the U.S. government placed on the Roswell crash materials. That includes any extreme measures taken to silence or coerce witness into changing their original testimonies.

We know that Marcel was ordered to Fort Worth to show Ramey recovered crash materials. Why did Ramey need Marcel to accompany the materials, since the second press release, which debunked Marcel's initial statement, had already been issued?

Marcel later addressed this question, explaining that in one interview conducted in Texas, under the direction of Ramey, a photo was taken of him with the real debris, but then everything was removed and other material from a balloon was then substituted for subsequent press photos.

The stuff in that one photo was pieces of the actual stuff we had found. It was not a staged photo. Later, they cleared out our wreckage and substituted some of their own. They then allowed more photos. Those photos were taken while the actual wreckage was on its way to Wright Field.[12]

The issue always comes to the question of why, if Ramey had already determined the material was that of a crashed balloon, would it need to be analyzed at several different bases? In fact, why not just hold a press conference at Roswell, let journalists examine and touch it, and then dispose of it? Logically, that would have been the case if the material had been from a balloon.

Brigadier General Thomas Dubose, chief of staff to Ramey, later confirmed Marcel's account, writing in a signed affidavit, "The material shown in the photographs taken in Maj. Gen. Ramey's office was a weather balloon. The weather balloon explanation for the material was a cover story to divert the attention of the press."[13]

We can use this complex transportation of the evidence as one gauge of the importance that the U.S. government put on the material, which was justified in Ramey's mind, anyway; it had to be kept secret. The decision to rescind the first press release and replace it with a radically revised version is another indication, and placing a no-entry perimeter around the crash site yet another.

Entirely removing the debris as expeditiously and quietly as possible is another. These are not run-of-the-mill operations that the U.S. military routinely uses on American soil.

All of these actions suggest that the Roswell debris material held a high value in the minds of the upper echelon in Washington, D.C.

Another way of measuring the value of the debris material is to assess the tactics used, if any, to silence or coerce witnesses to either stay quiet or to retract or publicly revise their stories to conform to the official version. Is there any evidence these tactics were used?

Decades after the incident, Marcel revealed that he had been ordered not to speak openly about his original findings; in the military, violating that kind of order is tantamount to career-ending suicide.

When it came time to pose with the balloon material, Marcel did. In fact, he went along with the program like a dutiful soldier and was later promoted. But after decades of keeping silent, he finally decided to tell all. By then he had been out of the military for some time.

⟨⟩

Now one thing has probably become apparent to you, dear readers, and that is my apparent failure to include the discovery of diminutive alien bodies at the crash site. Why have they been left out?

The first press release did not refer to any alien bodies, just a crashed flying saucer. Brazel did not mention them, nor did Marcel, though both discussed finding and examining the strange material at the debris site. None of the primary eyewitnesses referred to seeing alien bodies at the crash site on Foster's ranch.

The only mystery that the initial Roswell press release raised was that of the discovery of a crashed alien spacecraft. At the time, that was all that the media were focused on. The hubbub quickly died down when Ramey gave the (hopefully) reassuring order to rescind the initial press release not long after the first one had stirred the pot.

In fact, back in that era, in July 1947, Roswell was a blip on the mass media radarscope; however, that blip soon disappeared. Most journalists and members of the public were satisfied with the army's weather balloon explanation. The perception of the media or the public did not change for decades.

The incident was forgotten, like the Battle over Los Angeles had been.

The Roswell case, in general—and the discovery of alien bodies— did not become the source of controversy and public debate until several UFO researchers, in 1978, more than thirty years after the event, brought it back up.

THE ROSWELL BOOKS

In the late 1970s, Stanton T. Friedman, a physicist and UFOlogist, interviewed Marcel about what he found at the debris site. Marcel expressed his belief that the military had covered up the recovery of an alien spacecraft.

Marcel's story spread through UFO circles, being featured in some UFO documentaries at the time. That generated a small wave of interest. Then, in February 1980, the *National Enquirer* interviewed Marcel and published his account; that vaulted Roswell back into the national and worldwide spotlight.

Additional witnesses confirmed Marcel's claims, and they added significant new details as well. These included claims of a large-scale military operation taking place, which was mobilized for the recovery of (1) the alien craft, and (2) alien bodies at different crash sites.

By this point in time, Roswell was not only a cold case, it was an iceberg. As I noted previously, the preponderance of the evidence available to examine at the time of the event was enough to conclude that an alien craft had crashed and been recovered.

The problem at that time was that virtually everyone outside of the civilians and the military personnel who were eyewitnesses to the event accepted the official explanation. So there were no inquiries and examinations conducted by credentialed investigative reporters.

That said, while the information contained in the first press release is consistent with the body of evidence that surrounds the event (i.e., a crashed UFO was recovered), nothing in it alludes to alien bodies, nor does the established body of direct and strong circumstantial evidence. This is problematic.

Having witnesses step forward to give accounts after decades have passed opens the door for critics to totally dismiss the case.

For example: In 1989, former Roswell mortician Glenn Dennis made a detailed personal account of what had occurred. Dennis made the startling claim that alien autopsies were carried out at the Roswell base during the crash site flap.

Did he claim to have actually seen these alien corpses? No.

Dennis presented unverifiable circumstantial evidence to support his claim. He said that the base had contacted him and ordered four child-size coffins.

The next day, his curiosity got the best of him, and he went to the base to try to find out what was going on. However, he was summarily ordered to leave the facility. Prior to departing, he had a brief encounter with an unidentified nurse who spoke of strange odors and mysterious events that sounded like an autopsy was being performed.

This may sound like evidence, but is it? Dennis was not an actual eyewitness to an autopsy. The four coffins, in and of themselves, do not prove anything. The mysterious nurse, without a name, apparently vanished and was never located. So Dennis is a less than stellar witness.

The military did not have a difficult time disposing of the belated accounts that claimed the army had recovered alien bodies along with a crashed UFO.

In the concluding portion of a report released in 1997, they contended that the accounts of recovered alien bodies were likely a combination of innocently transformed memories of military accidents involving injured or killed personnel, innocently transformed memories of the recovery of anthropomorphic dummies in military programs like Project High Dive, which was conducted in the 1950s, and hoaxes perpetrated by various witnesses and UFO proponents.

The psychological effects of time compression and confusion about when events occurred explained the discrepancies with the years in question. This and other such reports were dismissed by UFO proponents as being either disinformation or simply implausible.

It is not hard to raise doubts about the veracity of accounts given by even highly credible witnesses when so much time had elapsed, and all the air force had to do was to raise plausible doubts.

However, had at least a few of the witnesses stepped forward at the time of the event and said they had seen alien bodies at the site, being removed from the site, or being transported from one base to another, the situation would have been much different. But that did not happen.

I can understand the reluctance of military personnel to go public while on active duty. That could end up with court martial proceedings and a less than honorable discharge. Such is not the case for civilian witnesses like Dennis, however.

Part of the difficulty of the belated research that attempted to link the July 8 press release to the recovery of dead aliens is that it blurred together the Foster ranch site and several other sites. As has been made crystal clear, the contents of the July 8 press release only referenced the debris site that Brazel had discovered and Marcel had investigated.

The first reference to alien bodies appeared in a 1980 book, *The Roswell Incident,* written by Charles Berlitz and William L. Moore. The book introduced an account by a Barney Barnett, who had died years earlier. Friends said he had on numerous occasions described the crash of a flying saucer and the recovery of alien corpses in the Socorro area (not Foster's ranch), about 150 miles (240 kilometers) west of the Foster ranch.

A second-hand account, given by friends, of events that Barnett may or may not have experienced and described is not good evidence. The book then describes a complicated story that includes Barnett and a mysterious group of archaeologists, who just happened to be there on the same day, and the military, who also showed up on time to lead them away from the crashed UFO they had allegedly all stumbled across on the same day.[14]

Personally, having conducted investigations into people and events that determined important legal outcomes, I would not even consider including this information as part of the Roswell case. The informant, Barnett, was dead when the research was conducted. No questions could be asked of him.

The book's authors even went so far as to construct a crash scenario that included various sites and ended up with the collected debris going to Muroc Army Airfield (now Edwards Air Force Base) in California.

What did that have to do with Roswell? Nothing?

To say that *The Roswell Incident* was flawed is being kind. It not only removes the reader from the actual evidence and the importance of the first *news release* and the debris, it also dallies off to distant sites with all sorts of loose speculations.

Along the way, a dead eyewitness is introduced as well as an unknown group of archaeologists, who supposedly get spirited away from a crash site by the MPs. All this has zip to do with Roswell. In fact, it has the smell of subtle disinformation designed to divert attention away from the real events.

Of course, none of those alleged events can be authenticated in any way. If the aliens were homicide victims, no detective could use that drivel as any level of evidence.

Another decade passed before the next book, *UFO Crash at Roswell* by Kevin D. Randle and Donald R. Schmitt, was published, in 1991.[15] The authors performed far more due diligence as concerns fact checking than their predecessors. Little attention, except in passing, was made of the claim found in *The Roswell Incident* that the aliens and their craft were shipped to Muroc Army Airfield.

The book showed a chain of events, with the alien corpses seen at a crash site, shipped to the Roswell base, as reported by Dennis, then flown to Fort Worth and finally to Wright Field in Dayton, Ohio, the last known location of the alleged bodies.

The problem here is that, as noted previously, Dennis is not a "smoking gun" eyewitness. How can he be used as a credible witness of an autopsy he never observed? Unfortunately, using Dennis as the key witness to the alleged alien bodies and autopsy would come to grief for the authors.

In 2010, *Discover* magazine published an article by a trained investigative reporter into the allegations that the authors made about the "missing" nurse. Dennis claimed that while he was at the base trying to find out what was going on, he ran into a nurse (name withheld) who gave him information. He then goes on to claim that she disappeared after that exchange.

The trained investigative reporter did not ask, What happened to the missing nurse, and can I find her? (The authors had used this approach.) He asked, Did this alleged nurse exist, and can I find her name in base personnel records?

Those are very different questions that lead to two widely divergent paths of investigation. Investigative reporters are on deadline, and time is their most precious commodity, so they know how to ask the right questions.

The reporter quickly located the five nurses that Randle and Schmitt claimed they had exhaustively searched for in vain. But he could not find any trace of Nurse X, who had allegedly talked to Dennis. (Dennis finally released her name to Randle.)

The question that I want answered is simple: Where were these alleged alien bodies found, and who claimed to have actually seen them? With the original Roswell incident, we know where the debris field was. We know the eyewitnesses who examined it. We know the chain of evidence and how it flowed from the debris site to Roswell, then to Texas, and finally to Wright Field.

But we do not know where these supposed alien bodies came from. Who found them?

As far as I am concerned, the alleged dead witness and the unidentified group of "archaeologists" are out of the picture (pure conjecture at best).

In another book, *Crash at Corona* by Stanton T. Friedman and Don Berliner, published in 1992, the authors suggested a high-level cover-up based on documents they obtained—*the infamous Majestic 12 archive.*[16]

These documents were anonymously dropped off at a UFO researcher's house (how convenient) in 1984 and were purported to be part of some 1952 briefing papers for incoming president Dwight Eisenhower.

At this point, we are hit by a whole new body of alleged documentation, obtained most unusually, that describes a high-level top-secret government agency. It sounds like the premise for a Hollywood spy thriller. Apparently, the agency's purpose was to investigate aliens recovered at Roswell and to keep that information concealed from public scrutiny.

Friedman had done a lot of the background research for *The Roswell Incident,* with Moore; and *Crash at Corona* simply built on that research. The title shifts the focus to Corona instead of Roswell, because Corona is closer to the Foster ranch crash site.

The chronology is largely the same as that offered in *The Roswell Incident,* and it includes Marcel and Cavitt, the counterintelligence agent, who was likely the "man in plain clothes" described by Brazel in 1947, visiting the ranch on Sunday, July 6.

The book claims that Brazel was "taken into custody for about a week" and escorted into the offices of the *Roswell Daily Record* on July 10, where he gave the account he was told to give by the government.

Friedman and Berliner included the Barnett account about the Socorro crash, and then went on to introduce a new eyewitness statement regarding the site. The next supposed eyewitness testimony came from a Gerald Anderson, who provided vivid descriptions of both a downed alien craft and four aliens.

The authors noted that much of their evidence had been rejected without a solid basis by Randle and Schmitt when they were writing *UFO Crash at Roswell* and that "a personality conflict between Anderson and Randle" meant that Friedman was the author who investigated his claim.

Friedman and Berliner's book, however, largely embraced the sequence of events from *UFO Crash at Roswell,* where aliens are seen at the Roswell Army Air Field, based on the Dennis account, and then shipped off to Fort Worth and after that to Wright Field.

The above books form the body of evidence presented to the public regarding the 1947 Roswell press release, which did not mention dead aliens. There would not be any *Roswell Incident* or any *Crash at Corona* without that press release.

Though the aforementioned books differ in many details, these last two agree on the general chronology of events and on one crucial detail: the dead aliens and their alleged autopsies *rest on the credibility of the account of one person—Glenn Dennis.*[17]

In my estimation, his testimony is not that of a credible eyewitness. He was a young man when it happened. He speculated about the four coffins but never actually saw anything (much less an autopsy). That story was supposed to have originated from a mystery nurse who does not appear to have ever served at the Roswell base.

What the introduction of the "dead aliens" did was (1) boost book sales, and (2) undermine the evidence that there was a real, and more important, cover-up of the *extraterrestrial debris* material, which was swept away by the sensationalism posed by four dead aliens being recovered and autopsied.

CONCLUSION

Following the detonation of the first atomic bomb, UFOs began to appear in the skies over New Mexico more frequently. At least one crashed near Roswell on the Foster ranch. A local ranch hand discovered the debris and reported his find to the sheriff. In turn, the sheriff informed the intelligence officer at the Roswell base. He investigated the material and concluded that it was "not of this earth."

The intelligence officer's findings resulted in a press release being issued on July 8, 1947. However, upon reflection, the higher echelon of the military retracted that release and claimed that the debris was that of an ordinary weather balloon. The evidence suggests that the second press release was a cover story aimed at concealing the truth from the public for reasons not yet established.

12

UFOs Buzz Washington, D.C., 1952

It probably came as a very unwanted shock to a number of high governmental officials. A crashed UFO found in the distant, isolated desert sands of New Mexico was one thing; having them buzz the White House quite another.

At 11:40 p.m. on Saturday, July 19, 1952, Edward Nugent, an air-traffic controller at Washington National Airport, spotted seven objects on his radarscope. He quickly calculated that the objects were located fifteen miles (twenty-four kilometers) south-southwest of the city; no known aircraft were in the area, and the objects were not following any established flight paths.

Nugent's superior, Harry Barnes, a senior air-traffic controller, watched the objects on Nugent's radarscope. He later described what he saw: "We knew immediately that a very strange situation existed . . . their movements were completely radical compared to those of ordinary aircraft."[1]

Barnes ordered two controllers to check Nugent's radar equipment; they found that it was working normally. Barnes then called National Airport's second radar center and talked to controller Howard Cocklin, who told Barnes that he was tracking the objects on his radarscope as well. Moreover, Cocklin said that he could see one of the objects through the window of the control tower: "A bright orange light. I can't tell what's behind it."[2]

At this point, more objects appeared on the radar screens of both

Fig. 12.1. UFOs at the U.S. Capitol, 1952

centers. They quickly headed in the direction of the White House and the Capitol Building; Barnes placed an urgent call to Andrews Air Force Base, located ten miles from National Airport. Although the controllers in the tower at Andrews first reported that they had no unusual objects on their radar, an airman soon reported sighting an unidentified object.

From the control tower, Airman William Brady saw an "object which appeared to be like an orange ball of fire, trailing a tail . . . [it was] unlike anything I had ever seen before." As Brady was trying to get the attention of other personnel in the tower, the object "took off at an unbelievable speed."[3]

At the same time, S. C. Pierman, a Capital Airlines pilot, was in the cockpit of his DC-4. After spotting what he believed to be a meteor, he was told that National Airport's control tower had picked up UFOs closing in on his position. Pierman observed six objects—"white, tail-less, fast-moving lights"—over a fourteen-minute period.[4]

Pierman was in radio contact with Barnes during his sighting, and

Barnes later related that "each sighting coincided with a pip we could see near his plane. When he reported that the light streaked off at a high speed, it disappeared on our scope."[5]

The control tower at Andrews continued to keep radar contact on the objects. Staff Sergeant Charles Davenport reported an orange-red light to the south; the light "would appear to stand still, then make an abrupt change in direction and altitude . . . this happened several times."[6]

The radar centers at the civilian airport and the military air force base were tracking an object hovering over a radio tower. The radar operators at both centers reported that the object vanished at the same time.[7]

By this point, the Air Force had launched an intercept operation. At 3 a.m., just as two jet fighters from Delaware's New Castle Air Force Base arrived over Washington, all of the objects vanished. However, when the inceptor jets ran low on fuel and had to return to base, the UFOs returned. This fact convinced Barnes that "the UFOs were monitoring radio traffic and behaving accordingly."[8]

The objects were last detected by radar at 5:30 a.m. Around sunrise, E. W. Chambers, a civilian radio engineer in Washington's suburbs, observed "five huge disks circling in a loose formation. They tilted upward and left on a steep ascent."[9]

It just so happened that Captain Edward J. Ruppelt, the head of Project Blue Book, was in Washington, D.C., that day. Nonetheless, Ruppelt did not learn about the sightings until Tuesday, July 22, when he read the headlines in a Washington-area newspaper. Of course, having a swarm of UFOs buzzing the nation's capital created quite a stir.

However, that sequence was only act one; act two would follow quickly on its heels.

At 8:15 p.m. on Saturday, July 26, 1952, a National Airlines pilot and stewardess on a Washington-bound flight observed several UFOs above their plane. Within minutes, radar centers at National Airport and Andrews Air Force Base reported tracking more unidentified objects.

A master sergeant at Andrews reported seeing the objects; he later described them as follows: "These lights did not have the characteristics of shooting stars. There was [sic] no trails. . . they traveled faster than any shooting star I have ever seen."[10]

Meanwhile, Albert M. Chop, the press spokesman for Project Blue

Book, arrived at National Airport and refused several reporters' requests to photograph the radar screens. He then joined the radar center personnel.[11] At 9:30 p.m., the radar center was picking up UFOs in every sector.

Reports reveal that the objects alternated speeds; they first traveled slowly, and then reversed direction and moved across the radarscope at speeds calculated at seven thousand miles per hour.

At 11:30 p.m., two jet fighters from New Castle Air Force Base flew over Washington. Captain John McHugo, the flight leader, was vectored toward the radar pips but made no visual contact, despite repeated attempts.[12] However, his wingman, Lieutenant William Patterson, did see four white "glows," which he pursued. As he was in hot pursuit, the "glows" turned on a dime and surrounded his fighter.

Patterson radioed the control tower at National Airport asking what he should do; according to Chop, the tower answered with a "stunned silence." The four objects then sped away from Patterson's jet and disappeared.[13]

On July 27, after midnight, Major Dewey Fournet, Project Blue Book's liaison at the Pentagon, and a Lieutenant Holcomb, an air force radar specialist, arrived at the radar center at National Airport. During the night, Holcomb received a call from the Washington National Weather Station.

They told him that a slight temperature inversion was present over the city. This is a weather pattern in which a layer of warm, moist air covers a layer of cool, dry air closer to the ground. This condition can cause radar signals to bend and give false returns. However, Holcomb felt that the inversion was not "nearly strong enough to explain the 'good and solid' returns on the radarscopes."[14]

Fournet relayed that all those present in the radar room were convinced that the targets were most likely caused by solid metallic objects. There had been weather-related targets on the scope, too, he said, but this was a common occurrence and the controllers "were paying no attention to them."[15]

Two more jets from Newcastle were scrambled during the night. One pilot saw nothing unusual; the other pilot moved toward a white light that "vanished" when he closed in. A Capital Airlines flight leaving Washington spotted "odd lights," which remained visible for about twelve minutes.[16] As they had on July 20, the sightings and unidentified radar returns ended at sunrise.

The foregoing account has been derived from completely confirmed military documents and the testimonies of military and a few civilian eyewitnesses. The fact that this UFO sighting occurred over the nation's capital created a massive public relations headache for the White House and the Pentagon.

President Harry S. Truman called Ruppelt and asked for an explanation of the sightings. Ruppelt, remembering a conversation he had with Captain Roy James, radar specialist, told the president that the sightings might have been caused by the temperature inversion.

However, at this point Ruppelt had not conducted any interviews of the witnesses nor had he even begun a formal investigation. He admitted his comments were made on the fly, so to speak.[17]

Nonetheless, the White House needed to allay the mounting anxieties and concerns of both the press and the public. Of course, all were worried about the security of the nation's capital. However, there was equal concern about an alleged "shoot-them-down" order that had been made public and confirmed by an air force public information officer, Lieutenant Colonel Moncel Monte.

Neither as nervous nor as irrational as officials assumed, the public sent telegrams and letters to the White House stating that the policy was dangerous. If extraterrestrial beings controlled the UFOs, they would obviously be much more technologically advanced than humans, people remarked.

Following these events, the government stated that no pilot had been able to get close enough to take a shot at a "flying saucer," as the objects would disappear or instantly accelerate as soon as an interceptor approached, sometimes out-maneuvering the pilot by "as much as a thousand miles an hour."

However, in seeming contradiction to the admitted "shoot-them-down" order, air force headquarters also put out statements claiming that the UFOs were no threat to the United States and were not controlled by "a reasoning body."

A press conference was called to combat contradictory stories, to assuage public anxiety, and perhaps to slow down the numbers of UFO reports being sent to Project Blue Book, which were clogging normal intelligence channels. Air force Major Generals John Samford, director of intelligence, and Roger Ramey, director of operations, held the press conference at the Pentagon on July 29, 1952.

(Yes, the same General Roger Ramey who debunked the Roswell case.)

It was the largest post–World War II Pentagon press conference to that point in time. The press reports characterized Samford and Ramey as the air force's two top UFO experts. Samford declared that the visual sightings over Washington could be explained as misidentified aerial phenomena (such as stars or meteors).

He also stated that the unidentified radar targets could be explained by temperature inversion, which was present in the air over Washington on both nights the radar returns were reported. (Uh huh . . . and Roswell was nothing but a weather balloon.)

That these remarks were concocted to explain the events away with a plausible cover story is obvious. We have to consider the gravity of the situation as well as the underlying inferences.

For a general to dismiss the radarscope data, which included the expert opinions of a number of trained operators, by claiming that the operators could not tell the difference between stars, meteors, and a squadron of UFOs is to suggest that our military personnel are highly incompetent.

In addition to radar operators, the above events were witnessed by numerous highly qualified pilots and other personnel. To simply wipe away their credibility with one fell blow seems incredible. If we cannot trust our military personnel to distinguish between a star and a potential enemy aircraft flying over our airspace, what are we to do?

I contend that this whole gambit, which began with Roswell, has had a very big backlash. The public does not really pay attention to what the air force has to say about UFOs, and the reputation of the armed services has suffered in general.

Do jet pilots know the difference between a star, light years away, and a squadron of UFOs suddenly encircling them? That is a purely rhetorical question that apparently escaped the mass media that are often dazzled by the ribbons that generals wear.

Of course, the reason that the press conference was convened at all was simply to deflect the press away from the story and defuse public interest, à la Roswell. Same General Ramey, same strategy, and it worked both times.

In response to a reporter's question asking whether the air force had recorded similar UFO radar contacts prior to the Washington incident, Samford replied that there had been "hundreds" of such contacts in which air force interceptors had been dispatched, but he added that they were all "fruitless."

Ruppelt later wrote that the conference proved to be successful "in getting the press off our backs."[18] Not everyone, especially some air force officers, bought Samford's explanation. Ruppelt noted that Fournet and Holcomb, who disagreed with the air force's explanation, were not in attendance at the press conference.

Ruppelt also observed that "hardly a night passed in June, July, and August in 1952 that there wasn't a [temperature] inversion in Washington, yet the slow-moving, solid radar targets appeared on only a few nights."[19]

The U.S. Weather Bureau, an entirely objective source and outside the military loop, also disagreed with the temperature inversion hypothesis; one official stated that such an inversion ordinarily would appear on a radar screen as a steady line rather than as single objects, as were sighted on the airport radarscope.

When Ruppelt, as the head of Project Blue Book, was able to interview the radar and control tower personnel at Washington National Airport, he found that not a single individual agreed with the air force explanation. The eyewitnesses stood their ground despite the Pentagon press conference.

However, the same was not the case when Ruppelt went to interview the eyewitness at Andrews Air Force Base. To a man, they agreed with Samford's interpretation. They told the military investigator they had mistaken a "bright star" for a "huge fiery-orange sphere," which is what they originally reported. Skeptical, Ruppelt checked an astronomical chart and found that there were no bright stars visible over the base that night.

Anything but naive, Ruppelt learned through a trusted source that the radar operators and other eyewitnesses had been "persuaded" by a superior officer that it was in their best interest to adopt Samford's position.

(Anyone who has been in the service will understand exactly how this kind of political maneuvering works.)

The above account is taken from military documents and from verified military eyewitnesses, radar operators, and pilots involved in the UFO sightings over Washington, D. C.

Now we turn to examine how the press handled the story. On July 28, 1952, the following headline appeared in the *Washington Post:* "'Saucer' Outran Jet, Pilot Reveals." The first two paragraphs of the article read as follows:

Washington Post

JULY 28, 1952

"SAUCER" OUTRAN JET, PILOT REVEALS.

Military secrecy veils an investigation of the mysterious, glowing aerial objects that showed up on radar screens in the Washington area Saturday night for the second consecutive week. A jet pilot sent up by the Air Defense Command to investigate the objects reported he was unable to overtake the glowing lights moving near Andrews Air Force Base.

The CAA reported the objects traveled at "predominantly lower levels"—about 1700 feet.[20]

In other words, the Pentagon began stonewalling the press right away. The reporter goes into some detail about his efforts to pry key facts out of a military spokesman, but it is clear that he had little success. The next cogent section reads:

WASHINGTON POST, JULY 28, 1952

A traffic control center spokesman said the nature of the signals on the radar screen ruled out any possibility they were from clouds or any other "weather" disturbance. "The returns we received from the unidentified objects were similar and analogous to targets representing aircraft in flight," he said. The objects, "flying saucer" or what have you, appeared on the radar scope at the airport center at 9:08 PM. Varying from 4 to 12 in number, the objects appeared on the screen until 3:00 AM., when they disappeared.[21]

From this report, we know that the top-down debriefing had not yet been established. It is entirely consistent with the original reports contained in the eyewitness accounts.

WASHINGTON POST, JULY 28, 1952

At 11:25 PM., two F-94 jet fighters from Air Defense Command squadron, at New Castle Delaware, capable of 600 hundred [sic] mph speeds, took off to investigate the objects. Airline, civil and military pilots described the objects as looking like the lit end of a cigarette or a cluster of orange and red lights.[22]

Here the reporter establishes that ground radar and military aviation personnel agreed on the nature of the objects; they were neither balloons nor "weather effects." The corroborating testimony gives a picture of a bright, reddish-orange squadron of UFOs moving in formation.

Next, the reporter makes a very good point:

WASHINGTON POST, JULY 28, 1952

Although "unidentified objects" have been picked up on radar before, the incidents of the last two Saturdays are believed to be the first time the objects have been picked up on radar-while visible to the human eye. Besides the pilots, who last Saturday saw the lights, a woman living on Mississippi Ave., told the Post she saw a very "bright light streaking across the sky towards Andrews Air Force Base about 11:45 PM."[23]

The article closes with a human-interest angle that leaves the reader with a wry smile.

WASHINGTON POST, JULY 28, 1952

One person who saw the lights when they first appeared in this area did not see them last night. He is E. W. Chambers, an engineer at Radio Station WRC, who spotted the lights while working early the morning of July 20 at station's Hyattsville tower. Chambers said he was sorry he had seen the lights because he had been skeptical about "flying saucers" before. Now he said, he sort of "wonders" and worries about the whole thing.[24]

CONCLUSION

The combination of radar contacts, civilian and military pilot observations, and eyewitness accounts from ground observers make this case unimpeachable. The Pentagon cooked up the weather-disturbance story based on Ruppelt's off-the-cuff remarks. However, after investigating the entire case, Ruppelt did not agree with the official Pentagon postulation, a fact he later published in his book.

These three major cases represent the strongest, most well-documented cases of mass sightings by highly credible witnesses, including military and civilian air controllers, radar operators, intelligence officers, and so forth. This ought to be of some concern to UFO researchers because they all occurred more than sixty years ago, at the dawn of the modern UFO era; nothing like them has occurred since.

13

The Socorro Incident

Socorro, New Mexico, is in the same part of the state, generally speaking, as Roswell, though west of it. This is home to one of the most important UFO sightings, which involved the observation of aliens and an alien craft on the ground by a police officer while on duty.

I have great respect for the late astronomer J. Allen Hynek, who served as the scientific consultant to various UFO investigations, including Project Blue Book. Hynek maintained a healthy scientific skepticism about the whole UFO phenomena.

However, this case made him reassess the hardened skepticism he came into his consultancy with. The Socorro incident shook up Hynek's perception of the UFO situation to the point that it forced him to conclude that he had no reasonable explanation for it.

Compared to the overly complicated Roswell incident, the Socorro incident is an investigator's dream come true. It only involves one key eyewitness, police officer Lonnie Zamora, and several backup witnesses, as well as the remnants of obvious physical trace evidence.

On Friday, April 24, 1964, Zamora was chasing a speeder driving due south of Socorro at about 5:45 p.m. During the pursuit he "heard a roar and saw a flame in the sky in the southwest some distance away—possibly 1/2 mile or a mile."[1] Thinking a local dynamite shack might have exploded, Zamora broke off the chase and went to investigate.

During interviews with Project Blue Book investigators, Zamora described the weather as being "clear, sunny sky otherwise—just a few clouds scattered over area."[2] In other words, it was a typical day in the

Fig. 13.1. Artist rendering of the Socorro incident

sun-drenched state of New Mexico; therefore, visibility was excellent.

During his Project Blue Book interview, Zamora went at some length to describe his initial observations. The report reads:

> Flame was bluish and sort of orange too. I could not tell size of flame . . . sort of motionless flame, slowly descending. Was still driving car and could not pay too much attention to the flame. It was a narrow type of flame. It was like a "stream down"—a funnel type—narrower at top than at bottom. Flame possibly 3 degrees or so in width—not wide.[3]

He also described the explosion he heard as being a roar, similar to yet different from a jet's. He added that it "changed from high frequency to low frequency and then stopped. Roar lasted possibly 10 seconds."[4]

Zamora drove to the gravel road turnoff that led to the dynamite shack he suspected had caused the explosion and flames. The road angled steeply uphill, and Zamora had to make several attempts to get his patrol car to navigate it. During his first two attempts, the roar was continuing. When he finally managed to get the car up the hill, it had stopped.

According to the Project Blue Book report:

> After I got to the top, traveled slowly on the gravel road westward. Noted nothing for a while . . . for possibly 10 or 15 seconds, went slow, looking around for the shack—did not recall exactly where the dynamite shack was.
>
> Suddenly I noted a shiny type object to south about 150 to 200 yards. It was off the road. At first glance, I stopped. It looked, at first, like a car turned upside down. Thought some kids might have turned over. Saw two people in white coveralls very close to the object. One of these persons seemed to turn and look straight at my [Zamora's] car and seemed startled—seemed to jump quickly.[5]

From Zamora's account, we can ascertain that his mind did not, at first, register what his eyes were reporting to him. It was no car overturned by reckless teens who were standing by it, but as he drove toward the object he kept filtering what he was seeing through the lens of that concept. The investigator entered Zamora's account into his report:

> Object was like aluminum—it was whitish against the mesa background, but not chrome. Seemed like O in shape and I at first glance took it to be overturned white car. Car appeared to be up on radiator or on trunk, this first glance.
>
> The only time I saw these two persons was when I had stopped, for possibly two seconds or so, to glance at the object. I don't recall noting any particular shape or possibly any hats, or headgear. These persons appeared normal in shape—but possibly they were small adults or large kids.[6]

At this point, Zamora radioed to the sheriff's office: "Socorro 2 to Socorro, possible 10-44 [accident], I'll be 10-6 [busy] out of the car, checking the car down in the arroyo."[7]

He stopped his cruiser while talking on the radio and started to get out; then his mike fell down, and he reached to put it back up. Next, the patrolman shoved the mike in its slot, got out of his car, and started to go down to where the object (which he still thought was a car) was sitting.

At this instant, he heard the roar start up again, "very loud roar—at that close was real loud."[8] At the same time as the roar began, he saw a flame shooting out from the underside of the object. Next, the craft started to lift off the ground going straight up—slowly up.

He noted that "the flame was light blue and at bottom was sort of orange color."[9] From his new angle, he saw the side of the object, not the end, as was his first angle. He thought that it might blow up because the roar was so loud. "No smoke, except dust in immediate area."[10]

At this point, the full reality of the situation hit Zamora, and he knew he had not been observing an overturned car. He turned away from it and scrambled, losing his prescription sunglasses and bumping into the back fender of his car as he tried to run from the UFO. According to the Project Blue Book report:

> I glanced back couple of times. Noted object to rise to about level of car, about 20 to 25 feet guess—took I guess about six seconds when object started to rise and I glanced back. I ran I guess about halfway to where I ducked down—about fifty feet from the car is where I ducked down, just over edge of hill. I guess I had run about 25 feet when I glanced back and saw the object level with the car and it appeared about directly over the place where it rose from.[11]

Clearly, Zamora was scared as he realized the gravity and strangeness of the situation. However, he struggled to keep his professional composure even as he acted on his self-preservation instincts.

> Being that there was no roar, I looked up, and I saw the object going away from me. It did not come any closer to me. It appeared to go in straight line and at same height—possibly 10 to 15 feet from ground, and it cleared the dynamite shack by about three feet. Shack about eight feet high.[12]

The shaken officer ran back to his patrol car, keeping an eye on the object as he did. He picked up his glasses and got into the car. It was at this point that he decided to radio to Nep Lopez, the station radio operator; once connected, he asked Lopez to "look out of the window, to see if you could see an object."[13] However, Zamora failed to give the radio operator enough information to carry out the task. He stated:

> As I was calling Nep, I could still see the object. The object seemed to lift up slowly, and to "get small" in the distance very fast. It seemed to just clear the Box Canyon or Six Mile Canyon Mountain. It disappeared as it went over the mountain. It had no flame what-soever as it was traveling over the ground, and no smoke or noise.[14]

After this sequence, Zamora made a sharp, professional decision. Despite the trauma and case of nerves the incident had generated, he drove down to inspect the landing site.

> Noted the brush was burning in several places. At that time I heard Sgt. Chavez (New Mexico State Police at Socorro) calling me on radio for my location, and I returned to my car.
>   . . . Then Sgt. Chavez came up, asked me what the trouble was, because I was sweating and he told me I was white, very pale. I asked the Sgt. to see what I saw, and that was the burning brush. Then Sgt. Chavez and I went to the spot, and Sgt. Chavez pointed out the tracks.[15]

The landing gear of the UFO had left imprints in the ground that both officers observed. That narrative sums up the crux of the case; however, more would come to light during ensuing investigations.

Several independent witnesses reported either an "egg"-shaped craft or a bluish flame at roughly the same time and in the same area—some of them within minutes of Zamora's encounter, before word of it had spread.

Two tourists, Paul Kies and Larry Kratzer, who were approaching Socorro in their car from the southwest, less than a mile from the landing site, said they had witnessed either the landing or takeoff and reported seeing the flame. They reported it when they went back home to Iowa, and their story appeared in the Dubuque *Telegraph Herald* a few days after their return.

Several other stories appeared in New Mexico newspapers in succeeding days. They included reports of sightings of oval-shaped objects, including another landing case with burned soil near La Madera, in northern New Mexico.

Citing points that were similar to those in the Socorro incident, the FBI report on the La Madera case noted the witness reporting a blue-white flame associated with the object; four rectangular, V-shaped landing marks; and several circular marks about four inches in diameter.

(Skeptics who claim there is no hard evidence to support the alien spacecraft theory are wrong. Apparently, they have not examined the rather large collection of such evidence compiled since the Roswell debris was examined by Marcel.)

In addition, there were a large number of witnesses who reported hearing the loud roar during takeoff and landing. One member of the Socorro sheriff's office told Ray Stanford, author of *Socorro "Saucer" in a Pentagon Pantry*, that "hundreds of persons" on the south side of town had heard it.[16]

Multiple policemen arrived shortly after Chavez to help investigate the scene, including Ted Jordan and James Luckie. All noted fresh burning at the site. Luckie and Chavez were quoted in the Socorro newspaper, saying that clumps of grass and burned greasewood bushes were "still hot" when they arrived.

Chavez said that dry grass was still "smoldering" as were the greasewood plants. Jordan later filled out a sworn statement, saying, "When I arrived, greasewood branches were still smoking."[17]

The FBI field report, written by the agent on the scene within two hours, similarly stated that all first responders noted "four irregularly shaped smoldering areas."[18]

Chavez was again quoted in an air force report written two days later about the smoking brush. According to the report, "[Chavez] went to the area where the craft was supposedly sighted and found four fresh indentations in the ground and several charred or burned bushes. Smoke appeared to come from the bush and he assumed it was burning, however no coals were visible and the charred portions of the bush were cold to the touch."[19]

(It sounds more like some kind of radiation effect, perhaps microwaves?)

Similarly, several policemen later told Stanford that wedge-shaped landing traces appeared to have penetrated into the moist subsoil, suggesting that the traces were freshly made.

Hynek also commented on the freshness of the soil impressions in a letter to fellow astronomer Donald Menzel: "I have the word of nine witnesses who saw the marks within hours of the incident who tell me the center of the marks were moist as though the topsoil had been freshly pushed aside."[20]

The FBI investigator had also observed that the rectangular marks "seemed to have been made by an object going into the earth at an angle from a center line pushing some earth to the far side."[21] Also observed were "three circular marks in the earth which were small, approximately four inches in diameter and penetrated in the sandy earth approximately one-eighth of an inch."[22]

The evening of the encounter, army Captain Richard T. Holder and FBI agent Arthur Byrnes Jr. together interviewed Zamora. However, for reasons that remain unclear, at the time the FBI asked that their presence at the scene be kept quiet.[23]

Holder took a telephone call from a colonel at the Joint Chiefs of Staff. He was a young captain and was surprised and unnerved to be speaking to such an important, high-ranking officer. At the colonel's command, Holder gave a report of his investigation over a secure, scrambled line.

Long after the event, Holder would wonder about such important U. S. military officials; "Why in the world were they so interested?"

Hynek quickly went to Socorro, arriving on Tuesday, April 28, in an official capacity to investigate the case. He met with Zamora and Chavez and interviewed them about the encounter. He and air force Major Hector Quintanilla, director of Project Blue Book, initially thought the sighting might be explained as a test of a lunar excursion module.

However, after some investigation, Hynek determined that this definitely could be ruled out as an explanation for what Zamora saw.[24]

In a memorandum, Hynek wrote that "Zamora & Chavez were very anti-AF [air force]."[25] The air force was suggesting that the event was a hoax, but Zamora was "pretty sore at being regarded as a romancer,"[26] and it took more than half an hour for Hynek to "thaw him out"[27] so he could hear the account from the only eyewitnesses.

Hynek also wrote that "the AF is in a spot over Socorro"[28]: they were suggesting that the encounter could be attributed to Zamora having seen an unidentified military craft, though no craft could be matched to Zamora's report. Hynek agreed with many others that this explanation "won't go down" as plausible.

He also wrote, "I think this case may be the Rosetta Stone. There's never been a strong case with so unimpeachable a witness."[29] Also noting his growing frustration with Project Blue Book, Hynek wrote, "The AF doesn't know what science is."[30]

In 1968, physicist and UFO researcher James E. McDonald located Mary G. Mayes, who asserted that when she was a University of Arizona doctoral student in radiation biology, she had been asked "to analyze plant material from the Socorro site. Afterwards, she was to turn in all records and samples, and heard no more about it."[31]

When interviewed by McDonald, Mayes reported that she and two others had worked on studying physical evidence from the Socorro site, but she could not remember the names of the others. According to Mayes, she had examined the site the day after the event and had gathered plant samples for analysis.

Mayes later determined that the plants, which had allegedly been burned by the UFO's flames, were unusually "completely dried out."[32] Mayes also found no evidence of radiation but found "two organic substances" she was unable to identify.

Mayes also reported to McDonald about an area of apparently "fused sand" where the sand had taken on a glassy appearance, near where the object had allegedly landed and then departed.

The area of glassy sand was roughly triangular, measuring about twenty-five to thirty inches (760 millimeters) at its widest, though it gradually tapered down to about one inch wide; it seemed about a quarter of an inch thick. Mayes thought the glassy areas looked as if a "hot jet hit it."

The evidence in this case is beyond strong; it is overwhelming. It takes more than skepticism to doubt it. You have to have an absolute belief that UFOs do not exist, so that you don't want to be presented with evidence to the contrary. As the old saying goes, "My mind is made up, so don't trouble me with the facts."

In a secret report prepared for the CIA, Quintanilla offered further details regarding the Zamora case.

There is no doubt that Lonnie Zamora saw an object which left quite an impression on him. There is also no question about Zamora's reliability. He is a serious police officer, a pillar of his church, and a man well versed in recognizing airborne vehicles in his area. He is puzzled by what he saw and frankly, so are we. This is the best-documented case on record, and still we have been unable, in spite of thorough investigation, to find the vehicle or other stimulus that scared Zamora to the point of panic.[33]

CONCLUSION

I agree with the above assessment. If Project Blue Book, not known to be lenient in either UFO investigations or their conclusions of them, considered this an unsolved, open case, who can argue with them? In my estimation, Zamora saw an extraterrestrial craft at the Socorro site, and along with the craft, he observed several small humanoid aliens, which he mistook for teenagers.

Final Note: Any skeptic or debunker who screams "hoax" or "misidentification" (in the usual hysterical tone) needs to stop frothing at the mouth for a moment and consider the following: no serious government investigator ever once impugned Zamora's integrity or character. Furthermore, he grew so tired of being badgered by the air force (and UFOlogists and skeptics) that he eventually dodged interviews, resigned from the police force, and took a job at a gas station.

To imagine that the individuals who have these kinds of intense UFO experiences invent them for publicity or personal gain is to exhibit little factual awareness of the social reality. They all suffer various traumas during and after the experience, both psychologically and socially.

14
Policeman Escorted
Aboard the Ship

Date: December 3, 1967
Location: Ashland, Nebraska, United States
Police sergeant Herbert Schirmer, age twenty-two and an honorably discharged Vietnam veteran, was on patrol when he encountered something hovering above the road; the object had a flashing red light. Surprised and unsure of what it was, the patrolman flashed his high beams at it.

For an instant, he thought it might be a truck having engine trouble, but as his eyes focused he could see it was nothing of this Earth.

Instead, a disk-shaped object displaying a shiny, polished aluminum surface hovered before his disbelieving eyes. The blinking red lights were shining out from portholes on the sides of the craft. The UFO was hovering six to eight feet above the ground on Highway 63. It was 2:30 a.m. when the incident occurred.

As he fixed his gaze on it, the craft began to slowly ascend; at the same time, he noticed a siren-like sound accompanying the ascent while a flame shot out from the underside. He later remembered sticking his head out of the window and watching the UFO depart, quickly shooting up into the night sky.

Shaken but still rational, he got out of the car, carrying his flashlight to inspect the surface of the road where the UFO had hovered, almost hugging the ground. After this, he drove to the police station and wrote the following terse description in the logbook: "Saw a flying saucer at the junction of highways 6 and 63; Believe it or not!"

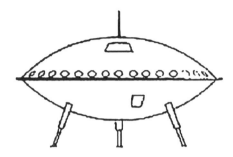

Fig. 14.1. Spaceship sketch by Sgt. Herbert Schirmer

He was puzzled to notice that it was 3 a.m., as the sighting seemingly lasted no more than ten minutes.

As the morning wore on, Schirmer contracted a headache and a "weird buzzing" in his head, and he discovered that he had a "red welt" on his neck. It was about two inches long and approximately half an inch wide, located on the "nerve cord" below one of his ears. A few hours later, Chief Bill Wlaskin visited the alleged encounter site and found a small metallic artifact.

Troubled by the lingering feeling that he had "lost" some time, Schirmer agreed to undergo hypnotic regression therapy. He was to find out that the short sequence of events that he could consciously recall was not all there was to the event.

The sessions revealed that the occupants of the landed craft came and took him aboard the craft. They were able to communicate with him through some form of mental telepathy. The aliens told him that they would visit him twice more and that one day he would "see the universe."

Under hypnosis, Schirmer recalled how humanoid beings between four and one-half to five feet tall escorted him from his car and into the ship. Once inside, the "leader" gave him a tour and explained various things about themselves and their mission on Earth.

He described the entities as having slightly slanted "catlike" eyes; with gray-white skin; and long, thin heads with flat noses and slitlike mouths. They wore silver-gray uniforms, gloves, and helmets (which had a small antenna on the left side around their ear), and at the left breast of each suit, they had the emblem of *a winged serpent*. Schirmer had the impression that the small antennas were somehow a part of their communication process with him.

The young patrolman said that he was given an extensive amount of unsolicited information by one of the crew. Schirmer described the alien's voice as seeming to come from deep within him, but he says he also simultaneously received input that must have been through telepathy. Though there is more, I am going to focus on three aspects of Schirmer's memories.[1]

First, when asked by the hypnotist to describe the craft's interior and its propulsion system, Schirmer replied, "The ship is operated through reversible electro-magnetism. . . . A crystal-like rotor in the center of the ship is linked to two large columns . . . those were the reactors. . . . Reversing magnetic and electrical energy allows them to control matter and overcome the forces of gravity."[2]

Though the rookie patrolman was young, he was also a veteran and a reasonable, serious-minded individual. No evidence has ever been presented showing that he had ever paid any attention to the subject of UFOs, and Schirmer made statements to that effect.

At one point during the interview, the interviewer decided to test Schirmer's knowledge of the field. He was asked whether he had heard of Barney and Betty Hill (a couple who had been abducted by a UFO years earlier in a famous case). Schirmer paused for a moment, obviously thinking, and then replied, "Oh, yeah, they were those outlaws in that movie."

He must have been one of a minority who had not heard of the continuing publicity concerning that abduction just six years previously.

No one who treated or spoke with Schirmer thought he was prevaricating. Nonetheless, when the skeptics crawled out of their dark holes, Schirmer was said to have hallucinated the events. That is a serious accusation that could cost a rookie policeman his job.

But those who are quick to cast aspersions on the character of good, honest people who happen to encounter UFOs have no concern about anything but their own cherished worldview (or perhaps they are simply doing their jobs as paid disinformation specialists).

That view does not permit extraterrestrials to fly through Earth's skies in advanced spacecraft. How do they know this to be true? They do not; that is just their belief. In fact, there is *no scientific principle of physics* that forbids a civilization that is technologically advanced enough from visiting our planet. None.

But those with a dogmatic worldview could care less about the facts or other people's experiences of them. All that matters is their personal belief system.

Skepticism is warranted in any scientific or legal enterprise where the facts have to be determined and explained using the best available evidence. However, there are limits to human perceptions and to the ability to establish "the truth" in any endeavor that involves complex circumstances. Invariably, different witnesses give contradictory testimonies in court when describing the same series of events.

How are the facts established? By the way the preponderance of the evidence comes down, how logical the arguments are, what the character of the key witnesses is established to be, and so forth. It is easy for anyone to trash a UFO witness and for government officials to trash their own military personnel.

However, what if we put the spotlight on them and ask how they know what they claim to know about a situation that they themselves were not witness to? Am I going to accept the testimony of a fighter pilot who reports a UFO sighting or that of his superior officer who "knows" that UFOs do not exist?

Schirmer had a job to do, and he was carrying out his duties. His sheriff confirmed his good standing.

Actually, the alleged abductees' credibility problem was not *just* the fault of the government or civilian debunkers; it also involved the UFOlogy community itself. Though they were well intentioned, in the early days of UFO research, the organizations were concerned about being taken seriously by scientists and the general public.

In that context, a mass sighting over Washington, D.C., verified by military personnel was credible, but an individual claiming to have been abducted and talked with aliens face-to-face—that was over the edge.

Schirmer had been on the police force for seven months when the incident occurred. He had served a tour in the navy and was ready to settle down in Ashland. Unlike his father, he did not plan to make the military his career, though he described himself as a military brat.

He was later described as a stolid, unimaginative, no-nonsense kind of person by people in Ashland. In fact, he was the exact type that makes a good cop. Add to that the fact that he was six feet, three inches tall and weighed 220 pounds.

Ashland was a small community, and Schirmer was one of only three officers on the force. He came on duty that night at 5 p.m. The rookie followed his usual routine, patrolling the back streets and alleys of the town. Around 1:30 a.m., he started to get an uneasy feeling. Dogs were barking and howling. The cattle were making a lot of noise, bawling and bellowing. He told an interviewer, "There was big bull in a corral. He sure was upset. He was kicking and charging the gate. I made sure the gate would hold. I scanned the area with my spotlight. There was nothing out of the ordinary."[3]

He decided to continue his patrol route and checked a couple of gas stations along U.S. Highway 6. At 2:20 a.m., he continued southwest. He drove on, and when he neared the intersection with Highway 63, he spotted the flashing red lights he mistook for a truck. The details clarify why he originally had difficulty identifying it. When he first saw the lights, a small ridge partially obstructed his full view.

The lights were coming from his right; he drove past the source and then swung around on a loop road. At that point, he checked his watch and noted it was 2:30 a.m. He later described the UFO as being football-shaped and at least as wide as the road. The craft was hovering just above the level of the top of his head.

The portholes were about two feet in diameter. Beneath the craft, he noticed a catwalk that encircled it. He did not notice any odors, smoke, or exhaust. Curiously, the young cop never mentioned being frightened by the alarming, unearthly events. At least he did not do so consciously. That changed under hypnosis.

Schirmer calculated that the entire event had lasted no more than five minutes. When he drove back to the station, which took another five minutes, it was 3:00 a.m.; he had lost twenty minutes from his memory. This is not unusual in abduction cases, as we shall see in chapter 17, which discusses the abduction of Kelly Cahill.

When Wlaskin read Schirmer's terse report, he went straight to his house. Wlaskin later told a reporter at the *Lincoln* (Neb.) *Journal*, "I put the question right to him. And he told me what he saw. . . . I don't doubt him . . . he saw something and reported it the way he saw it."[4]

Even though the chief was willing to back him up all the way, Schirmer wanted to take a polygraph to prove his story. He did and passed with flying colors. However, at the same time, he was experiencing some symptoms similar to post-traumatic stress disorder.

He had felt ill right after the incident and was continuing to get headaches and to hear a buzzing sound before going to sleep. At that point in time, Schirmer had not retrieved the lost twenty minutes.

Of course, the mass media picked up the event, and in short order Schirmer received visits from representatives of the Condon Committee.[5] This was the informal name for the University of Colorado UFO Project, which was funded by the U.S. Air Force from 1966 to 1968 and was under the direction of physicist Edward Condon. The Condon Committee itself has since been debunked as having an anti-UFO bias embedded in it.

After interviewing Schirmer, the committee decided to review his case since it was compelling and he was a credible witness. Thinking that he was a naive young cop from the sticks, they invited him to come to Colorado to appear before a study group.

They baited the hook by telling him that Condon would be in attendance. However, they knew that he would not be. A very interesting and embarrassing scene developed when the Condon cons tried to pass off a stand-in to Schirmer. However, he had learned Condon's first name was Edward prior to the interview.

Veteran UFO investigator Jacques Vallée was in attendance, and he tells the story this way:

When Sergeant Schirmer arrived in Boulder for a series of psychological tests he asked to see Professor Condon; he had been induced to make the trip because of its potential scientific significance. He had been assured that serious interest in his sighting existed and that professor Condon, the well-known physicist would attend the session in person.

Unfortunately, Dr. Condon was not on campus at the time, and the scientific committee realized that the trick they used to get the officer to come and to be tested threatened to be exposed. So Sergeant Schirmer told me they introduced someone else to him as Professor Condon.

Schirmer was no fool. During the ensuing conversation, some-body came into the room and addressed "Professor Condon" by a first name which had no resemblance to Edward or Ed. Schirmer confronted the scientist. "You're not Condon," he cried, and a very embarrassing scene followed.[6]

Schirmer underwent a hypnosis session at that time with Leo Sprinkle, Ph.D., author of *Soul Samples: Personal Explorations in Reincarnation and UFO Experiences* and founder of the annual Rocky Mountain UFO Conference. Under hypnosis, he painted a slightly dif-ferent picture of the "abduction" event, as the below list indicates:

1. The police car stalled or stopped.
2. The headlights went off during the sighting.
3. Schirmer was "prevented" from taking his gun out.
4. He was "prevented" from using his radio.
5. A bright light was emitted and shone into his squad car.
6. Schirmer observed a blurred white object sent from the UFO; the object approached the car and appeared to be intelligent.
7. Some sort of conversation occurred between him and the object.
8. Communication with someone in the craft occurred at the time of the UFO sighting, and a feeling of direct mental contact with someone was occurring at the time of the interview with the study group.
9. Information was obtained that indicated that the craft was pro-pelled by some type of electrical and magnetic force that could control the force of gravity.

One wonders whether Sprinkle ever paused to consider the damage done to people in Schirmer's shoes. This is a very significant sociologi-cal issue, especially here in the United States.

For instance, back in Ashland, an effigy of Schirmer was hanged from a tree near the north gate of the Ashland cemetery. He had become the object of ridicule and scorn to some of the townsfolk. He also received an anonymous phone call telling him that his car had been bombed, which was untrue.

Schirmer later confessed to having been disturbed by the ridicule and accusations that were soon directed his way, but for a time, he shrugged them off.

Still, Wlaskin had confidence in his rookie cop. Two months after the Condon trip, the sheriff resigned and Schirmer was appointed chief of police of Ashland. However, by then he was having trouble concentrating and was bothered by the social side effects of public disclosure, and several months later he resigned. (This is also what happened in the Zamora case.)

The Condon Committee released its findings a year later. Schirmer's case was rejected out of hand for lack of evidence and because he apparently did not pass their "psychological" evaluation.

However, the case was yet to be closed as far as Schirmer was concerned. He contacted a writer with experience in UFO investigations by the name of Warren Smith. He told Smith that he was plagued by headaches and insomnia.

Smith arranged for him to meet author Brad Steiger, an investigator into paranormal topics. After that meeting took place, Smith suggested that Schirmer undergo another series of hypnosis sessions.

Loring Williams, a professional hypnotist, put Schirmer under and regressed him back to the events. What follows is his account of what happened that night, given while under hypnosis.

Schirmer said that he drove up the hill and into a field above a road known as a local lovers' lane and beer party site. He tried his radio, but it would not work. The engine of his squad car died, and the lights went out as well. Three telescoping legs descended from the bottom of the UFO, and it settled on the ground.

Then physical entities emerged from the ship and came to his car. Schirmer tried to draw his revolver but could not. One entity stood in front of the car holding something that was emitting a green gaseous substance, which enveloped the car. A second entity pulled out some kind of device from a holster and pointed it at Schirmer's car; then a blast of light hit him, and he lost consciousness momentarily.

Here we must pause to consider this version's departure from Schirmer's earlier accounts. In this session he stated that the UFO actually landed. Now, as with the Zamora case, that should have left some trace depressions in the ground along with flattened, desiccated patches of grass. However, none of that kind of evidence was found at the site by the Condon investigators.

Smith claimed to have found such evidence when he conducted his own investigations, but his findings are suspect because he failed to take any supporting photos. That alone makes him a shoddy investigator.

The way this case kept evolving and changing brings up two points about UFO investigations and investigators: (1) professionally trained investigative journalists are almost never involved, and (2) as seen in the Roswell case (where a science fiction author, Kevin D. Randle, conducted an investigation), the lack of a professional methodology for establishing the credibility of potential witnesses undermines the results of the investigation.

Bringing hypnotists into early UFO cases was standard practice at the time. However, in retrospect, the results of hypnotic regression are always open to skepticism. Each time Schirmer was regressed, he provided yet more sensational details about the craft and its occupants. These included the following statements:

- The ship drew power from electrical lines and from water.
- The craft was powered by some kind of reverse electromagnetic engine.
- The aliens had mother ships located beyond detection as well as bases on Earth and Venus.
- The aliens said they were not hostile toward human beings.
- Their purpose involved monitoring Earth.

CONCLUSION

The Schirmer case is of great interest as much for what it reveals about how early investigations were conducted—by scientists and UFOlogists—as for the UFO sighting itself. While there is a kernel of objective truth to it (as the sheriff states, "He saw something"), no one can establish whether Schirmer's accounts beyond the initial stages of the sighting are real or not. This case lacks the corroborating witnesses and trace evidence that the Zamora case contained, so it is not as strong. However, he was a credible witness who had a close encounter.

SECTION IV
· · · · · · · · · ·

CLOSE ENCOUNTERS
AND
ALIEN ABDUCTION
CASES

Preface to
Close Encounters and
Alien Abduction Cases

This is the most controversial, emotional, and problematical area of modern UFO research. First, why have the vast majority of these cases occurred in the United States?

Yes, there are a few that have taken place in other countries (several are presented herein), but they are the exceptions. Additionally, why was there such a huge wave of reports in the 1980s and fewer and fewer in the decades that followed?

Most researchers currently agree that the abduction phenomenon is largely a thing of the past. As to why it was mostly an American phenomenon, the answer probably has cultural roots. Several huge movies, such as *Close Encounters of the Third Kind* and *ET,* preceded the 1980s wave of abduction cases. The history of UFOs suggests that close encounters of the third kind are rare and abductions extremely rare.

Moreover, abductions and all the detailed information that abductees are given about the alien culture and home planet do not add up. Why would the UFO occupants, so intent on remaining elusive in 99.99 percent of the cases, suddenly want to tell all?

In the vast majority of cases, the occupants of UFOs make every effort to remain unidentified. In addition, they seem to want to observe rather than interfere or make full contact.

Last, in the Travis Walton case, the most heavily documented and verified, I am convinced that the events—as described by the seven loggers, including Walton—leading up to his being zapped by a beam of energy, are true.

However, I am also equally convinced that Walton's accounts once inside the UFO are not true or rather not an accurate portrayal of what occurred. I am not saying that I think Walton has intentionally lied about them.

It appears that he was so critically injured that his mind came up with the bizarre account while he was in a comalike state. Furthermore, it seems clear that the UFO occupants did not really want to make physical contact with anyone.

However, when Walton triggered a security device, probably automatic, he either died or was critically injured. That necessitated the aliens rescuing and medically treating him. I will give my reasoned assessment of the abduction portion of *Fire in the Sky,* the book Walton wrote about his experience, in the next chapter. Walton has recently stated that he now believes that he was not abducted but actually rescued.

15
The Travis Walton Case

Note: Unless otherwise indicated, all quotes in chapter 15 are from Walton's book *Fire in the Sky*.

It was fall when Travis Walton went to work with his logging crew in the Apache-Sitgreaves National Forest in northern Arizona. In Walton's own words:

> It was the morning of Wednesday, November 5, 1975. To us, the seven men working in Apache-Sitgreaves National Forest, it was an ordinary workday. There was nothing in that sunny fall morning to foreshadow the tremendous fear, shock, and confusion we would be feeling as darkness fell.

The crew had the job of thinning a thick stand of small trees that were spaced together too tightly to allow them to grow at a fast rate. That particular day they were cutting, as Walton describes "a fuel-reduction strip up the crest of a ridge running south through the contract. Fuel reduction is the process of cutting the thinning slash into lengths and piling it up to be burned in the wet season."

This was a no-nonsense group of working men, not prone to sit around and speculate about whether life existed in outer space. Logging is hard, demanding work, and it leaves no time for fooling around. This was a young team; the boss, Mike Rogers, was twenty-eight, and Walton was just twenty-two.

The workday proceeded as usual, without any mishaps or seri-

Fig. 15.1. Travis Walton in 1975

ous personal conflicts. Injuries, arguments, and even fisticuffs are not unknown among logging crews.

Most people have the impression that Arizona is nothing but wide-open desert and unending sunshine and warmth. That is largely true of the southern portion of the state but not of the north, which is a combination of canyons (e.g., Grand Canyon) and forested mountains.

By midautumn, the nights are cold, and the mornings and afternoons are chilly. As Walton describes it:

> The afternoon sun was starting to cool as it began angling steeper down in the west. In the mountains, sundown comes early. . . . The gathering chill was beginning to numb my nose. With summer ending, it was starting to get down to five or ten degrees at night. I worked a little faster to ward off the chill, eagerly anticipating the reprieve of the day's conclusion. Not long to go before we could head for home.

Sundown came, but the crew continued working. Walton looked at his watch and noticed that it was six o'clock. He signaled the crew to stop. The harsh, deafening sound of buzzing chain saws died down. Darkness began to sink in as they loaded their gear into the bed of the pickup truck. They piled in, eager to get home. Walton describes the seating arrangement:

> Dwayne by the left rear door, John and Steve in the middle, and Allen by the right rear door. In the front, I sat by the door, riding shotgun. Ken sat in the middle, and of course Mike was driving. The seven of us usually sat in the same place every day. Nonsmokers in front, smokers in back.

The truck bounced along the logging road for a short distance, and then Walton noticed something out of the corner of his eye, a light that was coming through the trees on his right side, about three hundred feet ahead. For a moment, he dismissed it as the glow of the setting sun, but he quickly realized that it was already well into twilight and darkening fast.

His next thought turned to the possibility of a hunter's campsite, headlights, or a fire blazing. He noticed that some of the guys seemed to be sharing his thoughts because they had fallen silent as if mulling over the situation as he was.

At this point, the truck was heading toward the light. Then it quickly passed by it.

During that instant Allen yelled, "Son of a . . ."

Next, Walton blurted out, "What the hell was that?"

He struggled to focus and make sense out of what he was seeing. But all that was visible was a bright, glowing light because a thicket of dense trees was obstructing his view.

Mike, fully engaged in driving the truck, asked them what they were looking at.

Dwayne replied, "I don't know—but it looked like a crashed plane hanging in a tree!"

By this time, the truck was struggling to climb an uphill stretch. The adrenalin was pumping through the crew, and Mike put the pedal to the metal trying to squeeze out whatever speed the pickup had left.

They finally bounced past the tree thicket to a point where they had an unobstructed view of the light source. All were immediately dumbstruck.

"Stop!" John yelled. "Stop the truck!"

Mike hit the brakes, and they skidded to a halt. Walton pushed the door open to get a clear view.

"My God!" Allen yelled. "It's a flying saucer!"

Travis Walton did not know it then, but his next, impulsive decisions would forever change the course of his life.

Mike turned the engine off.

The crew silently stared at the object that hovered about twenty feet above the ground. Walton describes it as "a strange, golden disc"; it sat motionless, not making a sound. Walton gives a striking portrayal of the scene:

> The craft was stationary, hovering well below the treetops near the crest of the ridge. The hard, mechanical precision of the luminous vehicle was in sharp contrast to the primitive ruggedness of the dark surroundings. Its edges were clearly defined. The golden machine was starkly outlined against the deepening blue of the clear evening sky.

Walton's mind automatically began to analyze the craft. He calculated the object to have an overall diameter of fifteen to twenty feet and to be about ten feet thick. He describes the disc as having a "shape like that of two gigantic pie-pans placed lip to lip, with a small round bowl turned upside down on the top."

He searched for any signs of antennas, portholes, protrusions, or anything that resembled a window or hatch. However, he saw nothing of the sort. He turned toward his crew members, and "I glanced from one to another stricken face."

Then he turned back to further study the craft, which was still hovering silently in the air. It was at this critical point that he made his fateful decision. "I was suddenly seized with the urgency to see the craft at close range."

He jumped out of the truck and headed for the hovering craft. His abrupt, inexplicable action startled the rest of the crew.

"What do you think you're doing?" Mike asked in an urgent, harsh whisper.

Walton ignored him; determined to stay the course and satisfy his curiosity, he moved closer to the craft.

At this point, the other men tried to warn him off, but to no avail. Though he struggled with doubts for a moment, he shook them off. He describes the conclusion of this sequence the following way: "Finally I reassured myself with: I can always run away."

As determined as he was, he nonetheless approached the craft slowly and cautiously, adopting a half-crouch as he neared it. About six feet from being directly below the machine, he stared up at it and was amazed by its smooth, curving hull. His momentary fears had given way to an overwhelming sense of awe and a mounting curiosity about what might be inside of it.

In a few fleeting moments, he heard a strange mixture of sounds, and then the machine began wobbling erratically on its axis. The craft was still in the same position, and it was still hovering "at approximately the same height while it wobbled." He instinctively tucked tighter into his crouch.

At that instant, a bright, blue-green ray shot from the bottom of the craft, but Walton neither saw nor heard anything. "All I felt was the numbing force of a blow that felt like a high-voltage electrocution. . . . [The] beam struck me full in the head and chest. My mind sank quickly into unfeeling blackness."

His crew members watched in horror as Walton's body arched backward, arms and legs outstretched, the force of the blow lifting him off the ground. They saw him then being hurled backward through the air about ten feet. Finally, he landed and lay motionless, for all appearances dead on the ground.

Panic immediately gripped the crew. Paralysis and awe quickly turned to fear and self-preservation. Mike frantically cranked the ignition and gunned the engine. Hell bent for leather, they had one purpose, to leave the scene and to do so as quickly as possible.

There was only thing on Mike's mind as they sped off; he shouted, "Is it following us?" The rest of the crew stared ahead blankly in silence.

Terrified, Mike drove recklessly, bumping over the dirt logging road at speeds far in excess of what he would normally drive. The truck careened down the road, crashing into a boulder, and then a tree limb bent the rearview mirror backward. The situation was going from bad to worse with each passing minute.

THE ABDUCTION

Oblivious to what had just happened, Walton came to and was quickly overcome by excruciating pain. In his words, "I felt badly burned, all over, even inside me."

He was lying on his back motionless, eyes closed; his mouth was filled with a bitter, metallic taste that was accompanied by an intense thirst. Walton wrote that he felt completely spent to the point of being ill. "The trembling felt odd, like a strange mixture of exertion and illness. Something was terribly wrong."

Walton continued to struggle through a period of turmoil during which he shifted between mental disorientation, physical pain, and blurred vision. Slowly, his mind and vision began to clear enough so that he could make out the features of a light and ceiling.

Realizing that he was hurt, he wondered what had happened. Then it all came rushing back. His next thought was that he must be in the hospital.

Then I felt something pressing down lightly on my chest. It felt cool and smooth. A strange device curved across my body. . . . I could feel that it extended from my armpits to a few inches above my belt. It curved down to the middle of each side of my rib cage. It appeared to be made of shiny, dark gray metal or plastic.

Still suffering from shock, Walton was as yet unable to appreciate the reality of the situation.

I looked past the upper edge of the device. I could see the blurry figures of the doctors, leaning over me with their white masks and caps. They were wearing unusual, orange-colored surgical gowns. I could not make out their faces clearly.

At this point, it appears that he actually perceived the situation with some clarity, but his mind hesitated to accept what his eyes were reporting (like Zamora). That state quickly changed.

Abruptly my vision cleared. The sudden horror of what I saw rocked me as I realized that I was definitely not in a hospital. . . . I was looking squarely into the face of a horrible creature! It looked steadily back at me with huge, luminous brown eyes the size of quarters.

No sooner did Walton realize that he was being examined by three alien doctors than he flew into an aggressive rage. He hit one of them, who fell into another. The situation steadily deteriorated as Walton grew increasingly desperate. Finally, the aliens left the room, and he found himself alone.

Though he had succeeded in getting rid of his tormenters, his mind was not entirely rational: "I've got to get out of here, I thought frantically with a surge of determination."

How he imagined that he could escape a spaceship in flight is hard to comprehend, unless he still did not fully understand where he was and just how little control he had over the situation. Nonetheless, he reports that he ventured out of the room and into a passageway. Suddenly overcome by anxiety, he started running.

Charging past one door, he suddenly realized that it could have led to an exit, but another one soon appeared. "I slowed down to a walk as I neared it. . . . Maybe this would be my way out."

There are elements of the Travis Walton case that need further critical analysis. In this investigator's opinion, there are good reasons to suspect that the abduction segment, as Walton has characterized it taking place in the interior of the craft, did not occur as Walton has described it.

Before presenting the evidence to back up the above assertion, a very important issue needs to be addressed. I am not a skeptic nor am I in any way a debunker. I am convinced that Walton and the rest of the logging crew did experience the events involving the observation of a UFO hovering in the Apache-Sitgreaves National Forest, which they have individually and collectively given an accurate account of.

PROBLEM

The account of the events that led up to the direct observation of the UFO have the gritty, earthy feel of the reality experienced by loggers during actual logging operations. I have lived in logging communities in Northern

California, and I am well aware of the attitudes and behaviors that loggers exhibit as well as what challenges they encounter in the woods.

Every aspect of the account given of the crew's experiences leading up to and including the UFO observation are consistent with what one would expect of a logging crew. As presented in Walton's book, *Fire in the Sky,* the literary style and tone reflect a reportage approach, and it sounds like Walton is simply reporting his experiences (mostly in his own words) to a journalist who is acting as an unbiased literary conduit.

By the time the crew packs up the logging gear and climbs in the truck and they leave, the reader is bouncing along with them down the bumpy logging road, twilight is approaching, and the forest shadows are deepening into dark blotches that will soon unify into pitch blackness.

To this point, there is nothing to suggest the account contains, in any way, fictional devices used to increase the drama or embellish and color the story. When they encounter the UFO, the men act as one would expect them to in such a situation. They are so shocked and ter-rified by the sight of an otherworldly object hovering soundlessly before them that each is riveted to his seat.

However, Walton alone is compelled by a profound curiosity to overcome his fears and approach the object. The emotional tension and drama of the scene seem quite real and authentic as the rest of the crew urge him to get back in the truck. Consider the following account:

> I ducked into a crouch when a tremendously bright, blue-green ray shot from the bottom of the craft. I saw and heard nothing. All I felt was the numbing force of a blow that felt like a high-voltage electro-cution. The intense bolt made a sharp cracking or popping sound. The stunning concussion of the foot-wide beam struck me full in the head and chest. My mind sank quickly into unfeeling blackness. I didn't even see what hit me; but from the instant I felt that para-lyzing blow, I did not see, hear, or feel anything more.

This too seems as real as it is terrifying.

> The men in the truck saw my body arch backward, arms and legs outstretched, as the force of the blow lifted me off the ground. I was hurled backward through the air ten feet.

It is at this point that we need to stop and intently focus on the gravity of the event described. Walton has been hit by a bolt of unknown energy so powerful that it lifts his body off the ground, tossing it ten feet through the air like a rag doll. The very impact is so intense that he instantly blacks out (and seemingly dies).

Following this event, the crew panics and flees the scene as fast as possible. As they are driving, the following heated conversation takes place:

Mike anxiously asked: "I saw him falling back, but what happened to him?"

"Man, a blue ray just shot out of the bottom of that thing and hit him all over! It just seemed to engulf him." Ken's voice was solemn with awe.

"Good hell! It looked like he disintegrated!" Dwayne exclaimed.

"No, he was in one piece," Steve contradicted. "I saw him hit the ground."

"I do know one thing. It sure looked like he got hit by lightning or something!" Dwayne returned. "I heard a zap—like as if he touched a live wire!"

That raises an issue: a charge with the intensity described—enough to render a person immediately unconscious, lift the body off the ground, and hurl it about ten feet through the air—should have killed Walton. People are critically injured and killed in accidents when contact is made with live wires that do not carry the high-voltage current described by Walton and the crew observing the event.

For example, the amount of electricity used to execute someone sentenced to die via the electric chair only causes spasms and convulsions prior to death. Even if the restraints were removed, the body of the condemned individual would not fly up ten or even five feet off the chair.

The scenario suggests that Walton was killed or at least critically injured to the point of near death, as evidenced by the fact that he lay limp and motionless on the ground as his cohorts sped off.

This assertion is supported by the radical shift in the tone, style, and content that characterizes the abduction chapters when Walton finds he is in the interior of the craft.

The narrative resumes with Walton regaining consciousness in slow, painful stages. He seems to be in a supine, motionless position with his eyes closed; then he notes that his body is wracked with excruciating aches and pains. Next, he claims to be so fatigued and weak that he feels ill.

The narrative is outside of time, in that the reader is not given any sense of when these perceptions and events occurred in relation to his being zapped and then lying on the forest floor. We read:

> My mouth was dry and I was very thirsty. Oddly, the weakness in my muscles did not seem to come from hunger. The trembling felt odd, like a strange mixture of exertion and illness. Something was terribly wrong.

Then the situation changes, so dramatically and so radically, in such a quick succession of events that they seem to have no connection with all that he has just described. No sooner has he realized that he has been badly injured, is exhausted, and is barely able to open his eyes and clearly focus than he is in combat with three diminutive, horrid-looking aliens.

In one moment, he cannot move and his vision is entirely blurred; in the next, he describes the aliens and the objects around him in great detail. The net effect on the reader is jarring.

> Their thin bones were covered with white, marshmallow-looking flesh. They had on single-piece coverall-type suits made of soft, suede-like material, orange brown in color. I could not see any grain in the material, such as cloth has. In fact, their clothes did not appear even to have any seams. I saw no buttons, zippers, or snaps. They wore no belts. The loose billowy garments were gathered at the wrists and perhaps the ankles. They didn't have any kind of raised collar at the neck. They wore simple pinkish tan footwear. I could not make out the details of their shoes, but they had very small feet, about a size four by our measure.

Too much detail is included in a chaotic scene that has Walton aggressively attacking these entities after barely being able to open his eyes and move. (It reads like a Hollywood script insert used to describe what the aliens look like so that the prop crew gets the general idea.)

I submit that the sequence does not at all seem either real or logical. Whereas the forest narrative seemed like a naturally flowing account of the facts, the abduction narrative has the pronounced hallmarks of literary construction. The language is obviously the ghostwriter's (not Walton's), and the descriptions of the sequence of events do not fit into the context of the prior events already established.

In fact, the abduction chapters read like *literary surrealism;* they have an ongoing dreamlike quality. Walton continues to act in ways, and to describe his surroundings in ways, that do not conform to the logic of the situation.

For example, if he had attacked the alien doctors, would we be incorrect to assume that the ship would include a security detail that would have been alerted? The narrative does not mention that. Yet among established patterns, UFOlogists have noted that alien crews act in a very strict, military manner. We read:

> Afraid of the aliens' return, I looked toward the door. No sign of anyone. I needed something better to defend myself with.

Walton has just regained consciousness, is recovering from fatigue, is in pain, and has described his vision as being out of focus, yet he is able to give a vivid description of the alien's oversized "bald heads" and such other details.

> Those glistening orbs had brown irises twice the size of those of a normal human's eye, nearly an inch in diameter! The iris was so large that even parts of the pupils were hidden by the lids, giving the eyes a certain catlike appearance. There was very little of the white part of the eye showing. They had no lashes and no eyebrows.

(Travis Walton was an unpretentious logger, and I doubt that he has ever used the word *orbs* [instead of *eyes*] in his life and especially not in his early twenties.)

It is odd that he is able to note all of the foregoing minutiae during the throes of a fight prompted by an increasingly desperate feeling that is urging him (irrationally) to try to escape from the situation. (How can one escape a spaceship in flight?)

(Being a veteran journalist who has written reports based on investigations that I conducted that were later used to persuade a grand jury that they needed to indict someone, I strongly note that the literary mind of the ghostwriter grows increasingly dominant as the abduction scenario unfolds.)

Not only is there is no security detail when Walton ventures out of the room and into the passageway, he also reports it as being completely empty. This, too, seems highly improbable and out of synch with logic.

However, it is when he stumbles into a room and describes himself as being alone in a control room that the situation turns totally unreal.

> Glancing apprehensively toward the open door, I slowly went toward the chair. As I gradually approached it, a very curious thing began to happen. The closer I got to it, the darker the room became! Small points of light became visible on, or through, the walls, even the floor. I stepped back and the effect diminished.

Now he is describing himself alone in a room that appears to contain some high-tech equipment.

> I looked at the controls on the chair. On the left arm, there was a single short thick lever with an oddly shaped molded handle atop some dark brown material. On the right arm, there was an illuminated, lime-green screen about five inches square with a lot of black lines on it that intersected each other at all angles.

At this point, I submit that the narrative has assumed a completely fictional tone, style, technique, and content. A captive onboard an alien craft, who recently assaulted the crew, is now wandering the premises alone and has discovered a room with equipment that he is tampering with. Seriously?

Let us come down to Earth for a moment. No sci-fi writer would stretch credulity that far.

Our corner convenience stores contain video surveillance cameras that record the entry, movement, and exit of every patron. But in the abduction account, the UFO does not include a security detail or, apparently, any advanced surveillance devices. Once again, that seems extraordinarily improbable.

Did the UFO not zap him when he approached too close to it? This suggests a high-level security orientation. The abduction narrative simply does not hold up to a forensic type of close scrutiny of every available piece of evidence down to seemingly unimportant details.

I am not suggesting that Walton was not aboard the craft that he and the others observed in the forest. Neither am I implying that he deliberately faked the account of what occurred while he was aboard the craft. What is being suggested is the probability that his account is more dream than reality, more fragmented impressions than facts.

How so? Since he was unconscious, and perhaps even deceased, when he was taken aboard, Walton would have gone through a period of convalescence under the care of a medical staff, during which time he may have been in a comalike state (or even in a true coma).

As he emerged slowly from that state in stages, he alternated between becoming slightly aware of himself and his surroundings and slipping back into unconsciousness.

In this light, the abduction scenario (as portrayed by Walton) makes sense. The events he claims occurred are so improbable that, in my opinion, they could not represent a true account. For instance, Walton asserts the following:

> Trembling, I sat down on the hard surface of the chair. I put my hand onto the molded T-grip of the lever. The handle was slightly small for my hand. The whole chair seemed a little too small. I rotated the handle of the lever forward, feeling the slow, fluid resistance of it. I felt suddenly disoriented as the stars began moving downward in front of me, in unison. Quickly I pulled my hand off the lever. . . .
>
> I whirled around and looked at the door. There, standing in the open doorway, was a human being!

Now we are presented with an entity, apparently human in appearance, that is quite the opposite of the demonic-looking little aliens. He is described as large, muscular, and well proportioned. In all, Walton seems to allude back to an earlier era of UFOlogy, when space brothers and sisters who inhabited some distant, utopian paradise visited Earth, bringing messages of cosmic brotherhood to contactees such as George Adamski. Walton continues:

> Two men and a woman were standing around the table. They were all wearing velvety blue uniforms like the first man's, except that they had no helmets. The two men had the same muscularity and the same masculine good looks as the first man. The woman also had a face and figure that was the epitome of her gender. They were smooth-skinned and blemishless. No moles, freckles, wrinkles, or scars marked their skin. The striking good looks of the man I had first met became more obvious on seeing them all together. They shared a family-like resemblance, although they were not identical.

Immaculate specimens of ideal (if extraterrestrial) *Homo sapiens*!

The aura of timelessness still permeates the narrative. What happened to the excruciating pain, dizziness, blurred vision, lack of mental clarity, fatigue, dysfunctionality, and so forth? He has apparently completely recovered over the course of no chronologically established time frame. Walton seems to float from one sequence to another without pausing to sleep or eat.

Returning to the event that immediately preceded the abduction sequence, it is clear that Walton would have suffered extensive burns, shock, paralysis, and other symptoms of major trauma from the beam's blast. Under normal Earth hospital conditions, his recovery would have taken some time, not the few days that Walton had aboard the ship.

Typical victims of lightning strikes either die or survive; however, the survivors suffer extensive burns that often result in permanent scars.

Certain elements of the Walton case described above depart from the body of evidence accumulated from contactee and abduction cases. Specifically, in all the well-documented cases where the credibility of the contactee has been ascertained, the alien entities closely monitor the contactee and tightly control the events. This definitely is not the case where the Walton abduction is concerned.

In fact, in recent years, after having a protracted period to reflect on the event, Walton's view of it has changed. He is now of the opinion that it was *not so much an abduction as it was a medical intervention.*

I would concur emphatically with Walton on this point. What remains to be seen is whether he will entertain the possible interpretation of his abduction narrative offered herein.

CONCLUSION

Walton and his crew gave an accurate account of true events that ended in the observation of a hovering UFO over the forest in northern Arizona in 1975. However, the abduction events that followed Walton's exposure to an intense energy beam neither conform to the norms of alien behavior established by UFOlogists, nor do they agree with the logic of the situation. Therefore, it appears likely that Walton's recollections of what happened aboard the craft are the product of dreams and hallucinations triggered by trauma he experienced during his convalescence onboard the craft.

16
Young Pilot
Vanishes in Flight

The following information is from the front-page article of the *Australian,* October 23, 1978 (see fig. 16.1).

On the twenty-first of October, 1978, twenty-year-old Frederick Valentich was flying a Cessna 182L aircraft. His flight plan was to take him from the Moorabbin Airport to Bass Strait, off King Island in Australia.

Visibility was good, and the prevailing winds were light. He left Moorabbin at 6:19 p.m. Less than an hour later (at 7:06 p.m.), he contacted Melbourne air traffic control and asked if any aircraft was flying in the immediate airspace.

Flight Service Officer Steve Robey replied in the negative. He reported seeing nothing else on his radar. Valentich told Robey that he could see an unknown aircraft that was "long" and had what appeared to be four bright landing lights.

Valentich reported that it was moving too fast for him to make out any greater details. However, he noted that it had passed at high speed about one thousand feet above him.

Robey then asked for an estimate of the craft's size. Thirty seconds of silence ensued before Valentich came back, stating, "It's orbiting me."

Next, he described that it had a shiny metallic surface and a green light. Twenty-eight seconds of silence then followed his radio message

THE AUSTRALIAN

NUMBER 4433   MONDAY OCTOBER 23 1978   20 CENTS

'It's a long shape ... coming for me right now ... hovering on top of me'

UFO MYSTERY

Plane vanishes after 'loud metallic noise'

By ROBIN SOUTHEY

A MASSIVE sea and air search was continuing last night for a light aircraft which vanished over Bass Strait seconds after the pilot reported he was being followed by an unidentified flying object.

The pilot, Mr Frederick Valentich, 20, of Avondale Heights, a Melbourne suburb, was on a flight from Melbourne to King Island on Saturday night when radio contact was lost at 7.12 pm.

The plane, a $43,000 single-engined Cessna 182, owned by Southern Air Services, of Moorabbin, On the pilot was on board.

In his last minutes of radio contact near Cape Otway, Mr Valentich told Melbourne control he was being followed by a large aircraft with four bright lights traveling

Fig. 16.1. The Australian, *October 23, 1978*

before Valentich reported that the craft had vanished. After twenty-five more seconds elapsed, Valentich radioed again, asking Robey if a military inceptor could be what buzzed him.

Robey requested more information on the craft; Valentich said that it had returned and was heading toward him from the southwest. At 7:12 p.m., he reported that his engine was not running properly and that he was heading for King Island.

There was a brief silence before he returned to say, "It is hovering— and it's not an aircraft!"

Apparently, Valentich kept holding the radio transmit button in the send position as seventeen seconds of metallic scraping sounds were recorded by the tower. After that, all contact was lost.

A search-and-rescue alert was issued immediately. The air and sea search effort, however, failed to find any trace of Valentich or his aircraft. An official Australian Department of Transport investigation into the disappearance was also launched, but it, too, failed to find the young pilot or any trace of the Cessna.

The Department of Transport's findings concluded, "The reason for the disappearance of the aircraft has not been determined"; the flight had been "presumed fatal" for Valentich.

After Valentich's disappearance, twenty people came forward to say they had seen an "erratic" green light in the night sky; a few claimed to have witnessed it buzzing a plane, presumably Valentich's. Skeptics scoffed at this, claiming that these reports came from publicity hounds.

What the skeptics didn't seem to have accounted for was the fact that the transcripts of the conversations between Valentich and Robey were not made public until sometime after the event.

The alleged publicity hounds could not have known about Valentich's "green light" since it had not been made public at the time the UFO sighting reports were given.

An unedited transcript of the radio conversation follows: DSJ is Valentich. FS is Robey in the control tower.

19:06:14 DSJ: Melbourne, this is Delta Sierra Juliet. Is there any known traffic below five thousand?

FS: Delta Sierra Juliet, no known traffic.

DSJ: Delta Sierra Juliet, I am, seems to be a large aircraft below five thousand.

19:06:44 FS: Delta Sierra Juliet, What type of aircraft is it?

DSJ: Delta Sierra Juliet, I cannot affirm, it is four bright, and it seems to me like landing lights.

FS: Delta Sierra Juliet.

19:07:31 DSJ: Melbourne, this is Delta Sierra Juliet; the aircraft has just passed over me at least a thousand feet above.

FS: Delta Sierra Juliet, roger, and it is a large aircraft, confirmed?

DSJ: Er—unknown, due to the speed it's traveling, is there any air force aircraft in the vicinity?

FS: Delta Sierra Juliet, no known aircraft in the vicinity.

19:08:18 DSJ: Melbourne, it's approaching now from due east towards me.

FS: Delta Sierra Juliet.

19:08:41 DSJ: (open microphone for two seconds.)

19:08:48 DSJ: Delta Sierra Juliet, it seems to me that he's playing some sort of game, he's flying over me two, three times at speeds I could not identify.

FS: Delta Sierra Juliet, roger, what is your actual level?

DSJ: My level is four and a half thousand, four five zero.

FS: Delta Sierra Juliet and you confirm you cannot identify the aircraft?

DSJ: Affirmative.

FS: Delta Sierra Juliet, roger, stand by.

19:09:27 DSJ: Melbourne, Delta Sierra Juliet, it's not an aircraft it is (open microphone for two seconds).

19:09:42 FS: Delta Sierra Juliet, can you describe the—er—aircraft?

DSJ: Delta Sierra Juliet, as it's flying past it's a long shape (open microphone for three seconds) cannot identify more than it has such speed (open microphone for three seconds). It's before me right now, Melbourne.

19:10 FS: Delta Sierra Juliet, roger and how large would the—er—object be?

19:10:19 DSJ: Delta Sierra Juliet, Melbourne, it seems like it's stationary. What I'm doing right now is orbiting and the thing is just orbiting on top of me also. It's got a green light and sort of metallic like; it's all shiny on the outside.

FS: Delta Sierra Juliet.

19:10:46 DSJ: Delta Sierra Juliet (open microphone for three seconds). It's just vanished.

FS: Delta Sierra Juliet.

19:11:00 DSJ: Melbourne, would you know what kind of aircraft I've got? Is it a military aircraft?

FS: Delta Sierra Juliet, confirm the—er—aircraft just vanished.

DSJ: Say again.

FS: Delta Sierra Juliet, is the aircraft still with you?

DSJ: Delta Sierra Juliet; it's (open microphone for two seconds) now approaching from the southwest.

FS: Delta Sierra Juliet.

19:11:50 DSJ: Delta Sierra Juliet, the engine is rough-idling. I've got it set at twenty-three twenty-four and the thing is (coughing).

FS: Delta Sierra Juliet, roger, what are your intentions?

DSJ: My intentions are—ah—to go to King Island—ah—Melbourne. That strange aircraft is hovering on top of me again (open microphone for two seconds). It is hovering, and it's not an aircraft.

FS: Delta Sierra Juliet.

19:12:28 DSJ: Delta Sierra Juliet. Melbourne (open microphone for seventeen seconds).

[An unexplained metallic sound abruptly terminated the voice communications.]

CONCLUSION

This thoroughly documented case was probed by government authorities. This is only one of a few cases where a close encounter resulted in the disappearance of the witness.

17
The Kelly Cahill Abduction
Australia

On October 4, 1993, Kelly Cahill was sitting in the family car as her husband was driving. They were heading to her friend's home in the mountains to celebrate her daughter's birthday. It was just after dark, and they were nearing their destination, still about a half-hour drive away.

It was just after 7:00 p.m.

Cahill was busy looking out the window when she peered across a field; as they were driving past it, she noticed a ring of orange lights. According to Cahill, "It was the first time I ever thought I had seen something that wasn't normal. . . . I was going to shut my mouth. I thought, No, he's just going to have a go at me. But a couple of minutes up the road I said,

'I swear I saw a UFO.'"[1]

Her husband dismissed that idea immediately, saying, "Don't be stupid! It was probably a helicopter."

She retorted, "It wasn't making any noise. It was just sitting on the ground."[2] After a brief exchange, they dropped it, and soon arrived at her friend's residence.

The party turned out to be a bit of a dud because the daughter had just broken up with her boyfriend and wasn't in the mood for a celebration. They decided to leave early, retracing the same route they had followed to get there.

As they were driving back down the road in the same stretch where Cahill had witnessed the ring-shaped UFO, both husband and wife saw the ring of lights hovering above the road. It was sitting there, but she could not tell what it was.

They drove closer to it; Cahill could see that it had a circular shape and "what looked like windows and lights around the bottom."[3] As they approached closer and closer to it, they noticed that the object was not making any noise.

At this point, her husband exclaimed, "You're right! That's something. That's very, very strange."

Cahill saw figures inside the craft, and she told her husband, "I swear there are people in there." Then the UFO shot off to their left at a very fast rate of speed. "I mean it just disappeared. Within a split second it had gone."[4]

They continued driving, and after a short distance, less than a mile, they were confronted by a blinding light that forced Cahill to shield her eyes with one hand. She kept looking out the window, yet was unable to see anything due to the light's intensity.

At that point, she asked her husband, "What are you going to do?"

He responded, "I am going to keep driving."

It was at that point that something very strange—yet not unknown in the annals of UFO history—occurred to the couple. They lost a segment of time and the experiences that occurred during that missing time frame. As Cahill noted:

> From there, that is the last we remembered until . . . I knew I was going to see a UFO, you know, I just knew, because of what we had seen, I'd seen it twice in one night and he had seen it once . . . and the adrenalin is pumping, the heart is thumping, I'm so excited.[5]

But then her anticipation evaporated, and she and her husband found that they were just sitting in the car.

> And I'm saying to my husband, "What happened?" And he says to me, "I don't know. We must have gone around a corner or something." By the time we got home, he was definite of everything, but at that time he didn't know what happened either. I said to him, "I

swear I've had a blackout," because adrenalin just doesn't disappear in a split second like that. I mean your heart is going mad! And all of a sudden . . .⁶

As they resumed the drive home, Cahill noticed the pungent odor of vomit, which started a long babbling rant. Before they reach their destination, she observed a tall, odd, dark figure standing on the side of the road. She did not know why, but it caught and held her attention.

Cahill told the investigator Bill Chalker, who wrote an article for the *International UFO Reporter,* that she had argued with her husband about what happened for part of the drive back home. They agreed that they had seen a UFO but could not agree on her feeling of having experienced a blackout and being amnesiac, or a missing segment of time, or seeing people aboard the UFO. But both agreed they could smell vomit, and both experienced stomach pains that they could not account for.

Cahill experienced the pain as a severe muscle fatigue that radiated from her lower abdomen to her upper shoulders. After they returned home, she experienced menstrual bleeding and soon became ill. Oddly, she had just finished her period only the week before.

Not long after these events, Cahill went into the hospital with a womb infection. After examining her, the doctors concluded that she must have been pregnant; either that or she had had some kind of gynecological operation. But she rejected those conclusions because neither had occurred to her recently. The doctors noted a peculiar triangular mark on her abdomen along with a scar.

She had actually discovered the triangular mark, located below her navel, the night of the incident after returning home.

Cahill described the sequence: "I also started bleeding that night. Three and a half weeks later I ended up in the hospital. . . . [The hospital] actually did a laparoscopy, another laparoscopy. This was not when I first went in. I went back in later, another six weeks after that, because I had a lot of pains in my stomach and just wanted to have it checked to see what it was. And I still had the triangular mark there."⁷

By the time she had gone to the hospital, she had completely forgotten the UFO encounter. In fact, her memory of the incident was blank, which was revealed by a comment her husband made when a friend expressed his disbelief in UFOs. Her husband cut in, saying, "If you had seen what Kelly and I saw, you might change your mind."

She jumped in asking, "What are you talking about?"

In fact, ironically, while her husband (the ex-disbeliever) recalled at least seeing the UFO, the experience had somehow been erased from her mind. She struggled with this mystery for days because she knew her husband would not make something like that up.

She said, "He was telling me, 'Remember, on the way home from [your girlfriend's], remember, it wasn't making any noise?' And I was just sitting there. I couldn't remember it."[8]

After a few days of struggling to recall the event, without success, it finally came back in a rush. "All of a sudden I remembered it! It hit me! And . . . then I remembered going into the light, and then I couldn't remember anything else. A couple of weeks after that, this started to really bug me, because I remembered that light, and I remember arguing with him all the way home, but it was all I did remember."

Cahill told the investigator, Bill Chalker, that apart from her husband with her in their car, she was aware of another vehicle farther down the hill from their own position. That car contained at least two people, a man and a woman. She paid little heed to them at the time because she and her husband had their attention riveted on a massive UFO that had landed in the field opposite them.

What follows is from the investigator's report:

Because Kelly lived in Victoria and I live in New South Wales, I passed details of Kelly's experience on to John Auchetti of Phenomena Research Australia (PRA) and urged Kelly to contact him. PRA got on the case immediately.[9]

By November 17, PRA had located the man and woman Cahill had seen that night. It turned out that the couple also had a friend (a woman) with them. These witnesses took Auchetti to the encounter site, a spot consistent with Cahill's description. The group's drawings of the UFO and the entities also closely coincide with Cahill's.

Here we have a striking situation.

Chalker, the investigator, found that two groups of people unknown to each other had witnessed the same UFO, and they were located by and cooperated with competent investigators. They also experienced missing time. Independent witnesses also provided information that enabled the investigators to cross-check and correlate details, which revealed a remarkable amount of similar information.

The probe widened and was further strengthened by the finding of a range of apparently related physical traces, including ground impressions and a magnetic anomaly, as well as similar psychological effects on some of the witnesses.

Together, the Cahills were able to regain their memories of the events, which they reconstructed as follows:

> It was a dark, cloudy night. Evidently, Kelly could see the second car only because it was backlit by the headlights of a third car.
>
> From the trio's testimony, investigators determined the exact location of this third car. They established that a male was looking at the UFO's position through a break in the vegetation cover. The trio's evidence coupled with Kelly's allowed for triangulation of the encounter site with the UFO. The location was consistent with the anomalies discovered.[10]

What follows is a verbatim quote from the investigator's report:

> If the August 8 encounter had revolved only around Kelly, it could be argued that the experience may have been some sort of psychological episode. But the presence of other witnesses—a married couple and their friend, plus a possible other observer in a third car—forcefully argues for a real encounter.
>
> Indeed, the PRA contends that the focus of the incident was not Kelly but the two other women.
>
> As in Kelly's situation, the females in the other group seemed to play a dominant role. Bill, the male witness in the trio, appears, like Kelly's husband, to have had only limited involvement. The two women consciously recalled onboard episodes. They remembered the UFO and the tall black beings. Their description did not feature the red eyes Kelly saw.

For the trio the experience apparently started when they approached the site. All three could hear a strange noise and suddenly felt ill. Bill thought he was going to faint. He lost control of the car and ran off the road, striking a pole. After checking for damage, they drove off.

A few minutes later, a speeding car with its high beams on, shot past them. Then another passed. They came to a bridge with a sharp turn following it almost immediately.

Farther along this section, the trio stopped. As all this was going on, Bill's vision was impaired. Obviously, he had some type of vision as he was driving, but he was unable to remember seeing the UFO. The two women with him recall the UFO clearly, and their descriptions closely match Kelly's.

In some unexplained manner, Bill was isolated from the central experience. He has conscious recall of smells and sounds and remembers that a lot of activity was going on. He does not recall seeing anything.

He subsequently underwent hypnosis, which expanded his apparent recollections to seeming onboard components, but once again these were through the senses of smell and hearing only.

The two women did not think of theirs as an "*abduction*" experience. They felt as if they had exercised free will all through it. Yet, the principal element of their onboard experience was a form of examination—not, however, visually remembered. Other parts of their onboard experience exist in visual images and conscious memory. Hypnosis in their cases appears to have only reinforced what they recall already.

The entities did not speak and provided very little information. Neither woman saw the other or any of the others while in the alien environment, presumably aboard the UFO. Curiously, each was still aware of what was happening to her companion, ostensibly through psychic means.

The trio apparently did not have the complex background experiences described by Kelly. Their experience seemed limited only to the August 8 encounter.

There is also some physical evidence. PRA found a possible related ground trace and low-level magnetic anomaly at the encounter site.[11]

CONCLUSION

The Cahills had a close encounter that was corroborated by other witnesses. Unfortunately, abduction cases are always full of ambiguity and a dreamlike quality. Though they begin with a sense of reportage and realism, when the contact-and-abduction sequence begins, it seems that elements of mind control intervene and affect the abductees.

Memory loss is commonly reported by abductees, as are physical examinations. Nonetheless, Kelly Cahill's physical symptoms and trips to the hospital were very real.

SECTION V

• • • • • • • •

GOVERNMENTAL
DISCLOSURES

18

The COMETA Report

A very important document related to the disclosure of extraterrestrial activity on Earth as evidenced by UFO encounters, contacts, and sightings was released in France in 1999. It revealed to the world that not all governments take the position of the U.S. government where the reality of UFOs is concerned.

In fact, it prompted a wave of public disclosures by other governments, who opened their previously secret files for all to read.

The image* shows a classic disc-shaped UFO, as found throughout the history of sightings dating back to Ezekiel.

On Friday, July 16, 1999, the world was stunned when a report titled "UFOs and Defense: What Must We Be Prepared For?" was published by the French Institut des Hautes Études de Défense Nationale (Institute of Advanced Studies for National Defense; IHEDN). This ninety-page document, which is commonly called "The COMETA Report," was written at the behest of COMETA, a private UFO study organization known as Comité pour des Études Approfondies (Committee for In-Depth Studies). COMETA included among its members high-ranking military personnel, public officials, and scientists in the aerospace industry. Therefore, the report was taken seriously.

The in-depth study covered many aspects of the UFO subject, particularly as they related to issues of national defense. It was conducted over the course of several years by an independent group of former

*(not shown) The image is from the Peruvian military archives.

IHEDN auditors and by military and scientific experts, from various pertinent fields.

Before its public release, the conclusions of the study were sent to then–French president Jacques Chirac and to Prime Minister Lionel Jospin.

What follows is my summary:

The report was prefaced by French Air Force general Bernard Norlain, former director of IHEDN, and it began with a preamble by André Lebeau, former chairman of the Centre National d'Études Spatiales (National Center for Space Studies; CNES), the French equivalent of NASA.

In his introductory remarks regarding the appearance of UFOs in the skies over Earth, Lebeau asked, "Could some of these phenomena be the work of extraterrestrial beings?" He also wrote, "This report is useful in that it contributes toward stripping the phenomenon of UFOs of its irrational layer."[1]

The preface makes it clear that the scientific method has been strictly adhered to by COMETA, though there is a speculative thread as regards the extraterrestrial hypothesis.

It is of great importance that the French officials included space scientists in their studies. If NASA officials had ever been involved in UFO investigations in the United States, it was kept top secret because NASA is never mentioned by U.S. military officials as ever being consulted.

Just how important this document was, and still is, can be understood by the credentials of the committee's membership. An exhaustive list of members, which is very impressive, is given at the beginning of the report. It includes:

- Air Force General Bruno Lemoine (former auditor of IHEDN)
- Admiral Marc Merlo (FA of IHEDN)
- Michel Algrin, Ph.D. in political sciences and attorney at law (former auditor of IHEDN)
- General Pierre Bescond, engineer for armaments (former auditor of IHEDN)
- Denis Blancher, chief national police superintendent at the Ministry of the Interior

- Christian Marchal, chief engineer of the national Corps des Mines and research director at Office National d'Etudes et de Recherches Aérospatiales (National Office of Aeronautical Research; ONERA)
- General Alain Orszag, Ph.D. in physics and armaments engineer

(That these officials would in no way wish to compromise their reputations and careers is obvious. Most of the committee members then held, or had held, important positions in defense, industry, education, and research, or as government administrators.)

In a short preface, Norlain explained how the committee was created.

In brief, Air Force General Denis Letty came to see him in March 1995, when he was director of IHEDN, to discuss his idea that a committee to investigate UFOs should be formed. Norlain assured him of his interest and referred him to the Auditors Association of IHEDN, which in turn gave him its support, and COMETA was formed.

Then Letty, as president of COMETA, wrote that after careful consideration of many well-documented UFO observations, the committee was compelled to consider all hypotheses as to the origin of UFOs, especially the extraterrestrial hypotheses.

Following the general's comments, the committee presented the contents of the study. The first part consisted of the presentation of some remarkable cases from both France and other countries.

In the next section of the report, they described the then-current research efforts in France and abroad and studies made by scientists around the world, which they noted might provide partial explanations of the UFO phenomenon, in accordance with known laws of physics.

The main global explanations were then reviewed; they ranged from the theory that UFOs were secret military aircraft to the possibility of their being extraterrestrial manifestations.

In the third part, the committee examined issues regarding national defense based on information from both civilian and military pilots. They noted that many concerns, including strategic, political, and religious consequences, had to be considered should the extraterrestrial hypothesis be confirmed.

Next, I present the actual cases that COMETA evaluated and included in their report.

PART I: FACTS AND TESTIMONIES

The group studied the most well-documented, credible cases available. Many of the cases chosen were already well known by most UFO researchers but not to the general public. I include my comments in italics.

Testimonies of French Pilots

1.1 M. GIRAUD, PILOT OF MIRAGE IV (MARCH 7, 1977)

The incident occurred on March 7, 1977, at 9:00 pm local time during the Dijon flyover when the Mirage IV was returning, with the autopilot system engaged, to Luxeuil following a night mission. The aircraft was flying at an altitude of 9600 meters and approaching the speed of "Mach 0.9."

The flight conditions were very good. Suddenly the pilot, Herve Giraud and his navigator, observed a very bright glow at "3 o'clock" (time code) from their aircraft, at the same altitude, coming on a collision course and approaching very rapidly.

Pilot Giraud queried the Contrexeville military radar station that controlled their flight, to ask whether they had radar contact on the aircraft coming toward them. In fact, the pilot and navigator thought that it was an air defense interceptor, seeking to intercept their aircraft to identify it.

The radar controller did not have a corresponding radar contact on his scope, gave a negative response, and asked the pilots to check their oxygen. This request is a standard emergency procedure. It shows that the controller is so taken aback by the crew's question that he suspects an oxygen problem capable of causing a "hallucination."

The UFO maintained its course toward the Mirage IV. The pilot initiated a bank to the right toward it; a bank that he was forced to keep tightening (3 to 4 g) in order to try to maintain visual contact with the object and to keep it from positioning itself to the rear. Despite this maneuver, the UFO moved behind the Mirage IV at an estimated distance of 1500 m.

At this point the pilot reversed his bank to regain visual contact with the UFO. He then saw the glow move away to "11 o'clock." He resumed course to Luxeuil. But 45 seconds after he resumed course, he began feeling like he was being "watched" according to his own words,

Giraud told his navigator, "You wait and see it's going to come back."

And in fact, an identical glow, appeared at "3 o'clock." The pilot then initiated a very tight bank (6.5 g) to disengage his aircraft from what he now considered to be a real threat. The glow followed the Mirage IV's maneuver in order to position itself to the rear again at an estimated distance of 2000 m.

The pilot reversed, as before and again saw the glow disappear as it had previously. The controller still did not have a radar contact on the UFO. The pilot and navigator continued their flight, returning to the Luxeuil base without further incident.

Those are the facts. Two points should be emphasized:

- Only a combat aircraft could have had performance comparable to that of the UFO (speed, maneuverability). In this case, the controller would have had a radar contact on this aircraft, especially at that altitude, a contact that he would have seen all the better since there was no other traffic in the vicinity of the Mirage IV.
- Given the apparent maneuvers of the UFO(s), regardless of whether or not they were the same craft, their speed could only be supersonic, which, in the case of combat aircraft, would be manifested on the ground by a very loud sonic boom due to the phenomenon of the focusing of the shock wave generated by the bank. This would have been noticed in the surrounding area, especially since it was nighttime. But no sound was heard in the region.[2]

[This is a high-quality case because of the testimony of a trained pilot and his navigator and the inclusion of an on-ground controller. Anyone who believes a flight crew would risk their licenses and careers by fabricating such an event is out of touch with reality. I totally concur with COMETA that this case constitutes a completely credible event.]

1.2 Testimony of a Fighter Pilot (March 3, 1976)

On March 3, 1976, Colonel Claude Bosc, then a student pilot at the Combat Flight School at Tours, was making a solo night flight in a T-33 training aircraft. The mission consisted of navigating at an attitude of 6000 meters following a Rennes-Nantes-Poitiers itinerary; then landing at Tours. Several trailing aircraft were following the same itinerary at 5-minute intervals.

It was a clear night and the towns could be seen at the flight altitude in question. Visibility was greater than 100 km. While he was flying in a stable pattern at an altitude of 6000 m—and speed of 460 km/h—Bosc observed a green light, very far off in the distance (at the detection limit of lights on the ground), that he initially assumed was the launching of a green signal flare.

In 1 to 2 seconds, the "flare" exceeded the altitude of his aircraft by 1500 m and seemed to level off before descending in his direction. It approached at a dizzying speed on a collision course with his aircraft and filled the entire front windshield of the cockpit.

Thinking that impact was inevitable, the pilot let go of the joystick and crossed his arms in front of his face in a self-protective, reflex gesture.

The aircraft was completely enveloped in a brilliant, phosphorescent green light; the pilot saw a sphere that avoided his aircraft, at the very last moment, passing over his right wing but slightly grazing it, all occurring within a fraction of a second.

The pilot related the following memory of this incident:

- the UFO was not very large (1 to 2 m in diameter),
- it had a trailing tail, like that of a comet, which was also a fluorescent green color,
- the center of the sphere (UFO) consisted of a very bright white light (magnesium-fire type),
- the sighting lasted a total of less than 5 seconds.

Colonel Bosc related that he was very shocked by this phenomenon, informed the radar controller, ensuring the control of the mission on the ground; the controller had not detected anything on his radar scope. Upon return, two other pilots—who had followed the same itinerary as Bosc—stated that they had seen the phenomenon, but from a distance.[3]

[*Again the testimony of a military pilot, corroborated by other pilots, is virtually unimpeachable. Of note is the fact that the UFO did not appear on ground radar equipment in either of the above cases. This suggests that the UFOs have stealth technology.*]

1.3 Air France Flight AF 3532 (January 28, 1994)

At 1314 on the night of Jan 28, 1994 Jean-Charles Duboc (P), captain of Air France flight AF 3532 and his Co-pilot Valerie Chauffour (CP) were making the Nice-London connection.

They were cruising at an altitude of 11,900 meters in the vicinity of Coulommiers in Seine-et-Marne [Department]; the weather conditions were perfect; the chief steward, who was present in the cockpit at the time, suddenly pointed out a phenomenon that he thought to be a weather balloon.

His sighting was immediately confirmed by the copilot. The pilot, who in turn saw it, initially thought that it was actually an aircraft banking at a 45° angle. However, all quickly agreed that what they were seeing did not resemble anything that they knew of.

The excellent visibility and the presence of altocumulus clouds permitted the pilot to estimate that the phenomenon was at an altitude of 10,500 meters and at a distance of approximately 50 km. Taking into account its apparent diameter, they deduced that the craft was large.

They were struck by the changes in the shape of the craft, which first appeared in the form of a brown bell, before transforming into a chestnut brown, lens shape, then disappearing almost instantaneously on the left side of the aircraft, as if it had suddenly become invisible. The pilot reported to the Reims Air Navigation Control Center, which had no information on any flight traffic in the vicinity.

However, following standard procedures, Reims informed the Taverny Centre d'Opération de la Défense Aérienne (Air Defense Operations Center; CODA) of the sighting made by the crew and asked the pilot to follow the "Airmiss" procedure upon landing.

CODA did in fact record a radar track initiated by the Cinq-Mars-la-Pile control center at the same time that corresponded in location and time to the [UFO] phenomenon observed. This radar track, which was recorded for 50 seconds, crossed the trajectory of flight AF 3532 and did not correspond to any flight plan filed.[4]

[*It should be noted that the phenomenon disappeared from the view of the crew and the radarscopes at the same instant.*]

The investigations that were subsequently conducted by CODA ruled out the weather balloon hypothesis and established the crossing distance of the two trajectories to be determined, consequently bringing the approximate length of the craft to 250 m in length [a monstrous-size UFO].

It should be noted that the Northern Regional Air Navigation Center (CRNA), which handles 3000 movements per day, has investigated only three cases over the last seven years [prior to 1999, when the report was issued], one of which was that of flight AF 3532.[5]

[*This case involves the testimony of a commercial flight crew backed up by ground radar tracking, making it highly credible.*]

Aeronautical Cases throughout the World

The next section of the report involves cases that occurred in other parts of the world outside of French jurisdiction that included radar confirmation and were investigated by the nations involved.

2.1 LAKENHEATH (UNITED KINGDOM) (AUGUST 13–14, 1956)

The joint USAF—U.S. Air Force—and RAF [Royal Air Force] military bases of Lakenheath and Bentwaters are located 30 km northeast of Cambridge with respect to the first; and near the coast to the east of this city with respect to the second.

Unknown aerial objects appeared on their radar screens during the night of August 13 to 14, 1956, and were later judged "unidentified" by the report published in 1969 by the Condon Commission; tasked with evaluating the research of the U.S. Air Force on UFOs. . . .

In September 1971, the magazine *Astronautics and Aeronautics* published a study of the case by Thayer, the radar expert on the Condon Commission, which was based in part on a study presented in 1969 by Professor MacDonald, an atmospheric physicist.

The incidents began at the Bentwaters base, between 2100 and

2200 hours, when unusual sightings were made by the approach control radar center.

After those events the following took place:

- At 2255 hours, the radar detected an unidentified object moving east to west passing over the base, into the wind at an apparent speed of 2000 to 4000 miles per hour (mph). No sonic boom was reported. The personnel of the Bentwaters control tower said they saw a bright light flying over the ground from east to west "at an incredible speed" at an altitude of approximately 1200 m. At the same time, the pilot of a military transport plane flying over Bentwaters at an altitude of 1200 meters stated that a bright light passed under his plane rocketing east to west "at an incredible speed." The two visual sightings confirmed the radar detection.
- The Bentwaters radar operator reported these concurring radar and visual sightings to the shift supervisor at the Lakenheath [air] traffic radar control center. He was an American noncommissioned officer who produced a detailed report of these sightings and those that follow. The report, which was sent to the Condon Commission in 1968 by the then retired NCO, is coherent and does not contradict the documents in the USAF [Project] Blue Book file except in a few minor points: among these documents, the regulation telex sent by Lakenheath to the Blue Book team on the day of the incident and the report forwarded two weeks later to that same team by American Captain Holt, an intelligence officer at Bentwaters.
- The shift supervisor at the Lakenheath base alerted his radar operators. One of them detected a stationary object approximately 40 km southwest of the base, almost in the axis of the trajectory of the supersonic object seen at 2255 hours. The shift supervisor called the Lakenheath approach radar [center], which confirmed the sighting.

    The radar technicians at the air traffic control center suddenly saw the object immediately go from immobility to a speed of 600 to 950 km/h. The shift supervisor notified the base commander.

The object changed direction several times, describing line segments ranging from 13 to 30 km, separated by abrupt stops for 3 to 6 minutes; the speed always went from a value of zero to a value of some 950 km/h without any transition.

Visual sightings were made from the ground and confirmed the high speed and astounding accelerations. The regulation telex sent by Lakenheath concluded: "The fact that rapid accelerations and abrupt stops of the object were detected by radar and by sight from the ground give the report definite credibility. One can only believe that these sightings may have some meteorological or astronomical origin."

- After 30 to 45 minutes, the RAF sent a night fighter, a Venom two-seater, in pursuit of the object. The Lakenheath air traffic radar control center guided it in the direction of the object 10 km east of the center. The pilot acquired the target visually and on radar, and then lost it. The center then directed the plane 16 km to the east of Lakenheath; the pilot again acquired the target and said, "My machine guns are locked onto him." A short time afterward, he once again lost his target; but the target was followed by the radar operators at the center.

   They informed the pilot that the object had made a rapid movement to position itself behind him and was following him at a short distance. The pilot confirmed [this]. As radar technicians watched, for about ten minutes the pilot tried every maneuver to get back behind the object (steep climbs, dives, sustained turns), but he did not succeed: the UFO followed him at a constant distance according to the ground radars.

   Finally, with his fuel running low, he returned to base, asking that someone tell him whether the object continued to follow him. The UFO did, in fact, follow him for a short distance, and then came to a standstill. The radar technicians then saw the object make several short moves, then leave in a northerly direction at about 950 km/h and disappear from radar range at 0330 hours.

- A second Venom dispatched to replace the first was quickly forced to return to base due to mechanical problems prior without establishing any contact with the (UFO) object.

Thayer concluded his article in the journal *Astronautics and Aeronautics* in this manner: "If one considers the strong credibility of the information and the coherence and continuity of the reports, as well as their high degree of 'strangeness,' this UFO case is certainly one of the more troubling cases known to date, the case is compelling."[6]

What follows is an examination of one important case.

2.2 THE RB-47 AIRCRAFT IN THE UNITED STATES (JULY 17, 1957)

This case, which appears as "unidentified" in the Condon report, has been cited and studied extensively for 40 years. Physicist James MacDonald published the results of his investigation in 1971 in the journal *Astronautics and Aeronautics*.

We will summarize here the important sequences of events of the case, which show a luminous unidentified flying object detected at night not only by sight and on radar, but also by pulsed microwave emissions coming from its direction:

- The RB-47 was a bomber; the bomb bays of which had been converted to hold three officers each equipped with means enabling emissions from ground radars to be detected and their azimuth direction, but not their distance or the nature of the signals, to be specified. In the south central region of the United States, where the aircraft was making a training flight that day, numerous radar stations were emitting signals the frequencies of which were close to 3000 MHz and the pulses of which lasted 1 microsecond and occurred every 600 microseconds. The radars scanned the horizon four times per minute.
- Three other officers (pilot, copilot, and navigator) were in the cockpit and, as a result, could themselves see out of the aircraft. The six officers were questioned by MacDonald in 1969.

They related that:

- The first incident took place above Mississippi, probably at around 0930Z (0330 local time) when the aircraft, going back to the north from the Gulf of Mexico, was approaching the coast a little to the east of the Mississippi delta, flying at Mach 0.75. Captain MacClure detected on his screen a blip corresponding to a pulsed microwave source located behind and to the right of the RB-47 (at "5 o'clock") that rapidly passed the aircraft and turned around it, departing again on its left in the other direction (between "6 o'clock" and "9 o'clock").

The source was therefore airborne and supersonic. MacClure noted the characteristics of the signal: they were those of the aforementioned ground radars, with the exception of the length of the pulses, which were 2 microseconds. He did not report this incident immediately, thinking that it was perhaps a malfunction of the electronics. As Klass writes, at the time there were no supersonic aircraft either in the United States or in the USSR large enough to transport a radar signal that possessed the characteristics that were observed.

- The following incident occurred at 1010Z in Louisiana, when Commander Chase, pilot, and Captain MacCoyd, copilot, saw an intense bluish-white light aim at the aircraft from "11 o'clock" then jump from their left to their right and disappear while it was at "2 o'clock." Klass showed that this object was perhaps a meteorite the trajectory of which caused an optical illusion, but, at the time, Chase and MacCoyd wondered whether it wasn't a UFO. Hearing them, MacClure remembered his prior detection and looked for a signal of the same type.

- He found this signal at 1030Z, which was identical to the previous one and, perhaps by coincidence, came from "2 o'clock." This signal was confirmed by Captain Provenzano, whose detector was also able to operate at around 3000 MHz. It could not have been the signal from fixed radar, because its "2 o'clock" direction remained unchanged when the aircraft followed its route to the west for several minutes. The aircraft entered Texas and then came within range of the "Utah" radar [center] located near Dallas. The crew reported to Utah, which detected both the aircraft and an object maintaining a constant distance of 18 km from it.

- At 1039Z, still in Texas, Commander Chase perceived a large red light, which he estimated was moving 1500 m below the aircraft at approximately "2 o'clock." The aircraft was flying at an altitude of 10,500 m, and the weather was perfectly clear. Although the commander was not able to determine either the shape or the size of the object, he had the distinct impression that the light was emanating from the top of the object.

- At 1040Z, he received authorization to pursue this object and notified Utah. He slowed down, and then accelerated; Utah informed him that the object was mirroring his movements, all the while maintaining a constant distance of 18 km.

- At 1042Z, Chase accelerated and saw the red object turn to the right in the direction of Dallas; this was confirmed by MacClure.

- At around 1050Z, a little to the west of Dallas, the object stopped and simultaneously disappeared from the view of the radars (Utah and the onboard radar that had just detected the object when the RB-47 had approached it) and from MacClure's screen (the disappearance of an object from a radar screen is less surprising nowadays; it calls to mind the active stealth technologies currently in development and even in operation). The aircraft then banked to the left. MacClure picked up a signal that was perhaps the one from Utah. Visual and radar contact were regained.

- At 1052Z, Chase saw the object drop to around 4500 m. He had the RB-47 make a dive from 10,500 to 6000 m. The object then disappeared from his view, from the Utah radar, and from MacClure's screen simultaneously.

- At 1057Z, still near Dallas, the object reappeared on MacClure's screen, and Utah indicated that it had prepared a "CIRVIS" (Communications Instructions for Reporting Vital Intelligence Sightings) report, a secret urgent radio report sent to the Air Defense Command, which is mandatory in the event of a sighting by the Air Force of an unidentified aerial object.

- At 1058Z the pilot regained visual contact at "2 o'clock." A few minutes later, seeing his fuel reserves drop, he decided to return and headed roughly north toward Oklahoma City. The object then positioned itself behind the aircraft at a distance of 18 km, as reported by Utah, which tried to send fighter jets in pursuit of the unknown [object]. The object, flying lower than the RB-47 and behind it could not be seen from the cockpit, but it was detected on MacClure's screen until Oklahoma City, well outside the range of the Utah radar. Then it suddenly disappeared from the screen at 1140Z.[7]

The above case was obviously very intensively studied and well documented.

PART II: THE EXTENT OF OUR KNOWLEDGE

This section of the report begins with a survey of how the government conducted UFO research in France, from the first instructions given to the gendarmerie in 1974 for the recording of reports to the creation of Groupe d'Étude des Phénomènes Aérospatiaux Non-identifiés (Unidentified Aerospace Phenomenon Research Group; GEPAN) in 1977; this organization collected more than three thousand reports from the gendarmerie, cases studies, and statistical analyses.

It then surveyed agreements made by GEPAN and, later, Service d'Expertise des Phénomènes Rares Aérospatiaux (Rare Aerospace Phenomena Expertise Department; SEPRA) with the air force and the army, civilian aviation groups, and other organizations, including civilian and military laboratories, which analyzed samples and photographs taken from various UFO cases.

Chapter 8 of the report, "UFOs: Hypotheses, Modeling Attempts," discusses some models and hypotheses that were under study at the time in several countries.

Noted is the fact that partial simulations of potential UFO propulsion systems had already been made. They were based on observations of various aspects of the phenomena, such as speed, movements, rapid acceleration, the engine failure of nearby vehicles, and paralysis of witnesses.

One model is MHD propulsion, which had already tested successfully in water. The report suggested that such propulsion might be achieved in the atmosphere with superconducting circuits in a few decades. Other studies are briefly mentioned regarding both atmospheric and space propulsion, such as particle beams, antigravity, or reliance on planetary and stellar impulsion.

The report goes on to suggest and note the following:

> The failure of vehicle engines, often reported by witnesses, may be explained by *microwave radiation*. High power hyper frequency generators are under study in France and other countries; one application is microwave weapons. Particle beams, such as proton beams, which ionize the air and therefore become visible, might explain the observation of truncated luminous beams. Microwaves might explain body paralysis as well.[8]

In the same chapter, various hypotheses are studied. The study concludes that hoaxes are rare and easily detected. Some nonscientific theories are discarded, such as conspiracy and manipulation by very secret, powerful groups.

Also rejected are paranormal phenomena and collective hallucinations. The hypothesis of secret weapons is also regarded as very improbable, as is intoxication or hysteria during the cold war era, along with natural phenomena.

In the final analysis, we are then left with various extraterrestrial hypotheses. One version has been developed in France by astronomers Jean-Claude Ribes and Guy Monnet, based on the "space islands" concept of American physicist Gerald K. O'Neill, and it is compatible with present-day physics. The astronomers theorized that

> Interstellar space travels towards other stars are possible thanks to gigantic spaceship, at subluminic speed (the original idea is from the physicist O'Neill). These spaceships are gigantic units, carrying a full ecosystem and hundreds of thousands pf people for a no-return odyssey to reach the closest star after a 40,000 years long trip. Those giant spaceships get their energy from hydrogen collected from the traveled space and from which energy is extracted by fusion . . .[9]

Next, the efforts by the independent UFO research organizations in the United States, Great Britain, and Russia are surveyed in the report.

In the United States, the media and the polls showed a marked interest and concern of the public, but the official position, especially of the air force, was still one of denial; *more precisely, that there is no threat to national security.*

That limited definition does not rule out the existence of UFOs; it just states that they pose no threat.

(Actually, declassified documents more recently released under the United States' Freedom of Information Act paint a very different picture, one of surveillance of nuclear installations by UFOs and the continued study of UFOs by American military and intelligence agencies.)

The report goes on to stress the importance of private, independent UFO research associations in the United States. It mentions the briefing document "Best Available Evidence," which was sent in 1995 to one thousand leaders in government, science, and the press worldwide, and the Sturrock Panel, a four-day workshop held in 1997 to review UFO evidence, both sponsored by American philanthropist Lawrence Rockefeller.

The report then notes the emergence of alleged insiders into the public spotlight, such as U.S. Army Colonel Philip Corso,* a former army intelligence officer, and concludes that his testimony, despite its many critics, might be partially revealing as to the actual situation in the United States.

The report continues with a brief description of the situation in Great Britain, with a special mention of journalist Nick Pope, who ran the British government's UFO study project from 1991 to 1994, and wonders about the possible existence of secret studies being pursued jointly by British and American services. It also mentions research efforts in Russia, in passing, and the release of some information by the KGB in 1991.

It is important to note that only the U.S. and British governments continue to maintain secrecy where UFOs are concerned. Could it be that perhaps the British, being America's closest allies, were let in on the Roswell truth?

---

*Corso was an army intelligence officer who claimed to have been assigned to the study of the UFO phenomenon. He wrote a controversial book, *The Day After Roswell,* published in 1998 by Pocketbooks. In it he detailed his involvement in the Roswell Case, confirming that it was authentic. Corso was a member of Eisenhower's Security Council.

PART III: UFOS AND DEFENSE

In the third part, the report notes that no overt, hostile actions have been reported in the history of UFO observations or encounters. However, it goes on to say that at least some acts of UFO intimidation have been recorded in France (e.g., the Mirage IV case).

Since the extraterrestrial origin of UFOs cannot be ruled out, the report asserts, it is therefore necessary to study the consequences of that hypothesis at the strategic level, and also at the political, religious, and media/public information levels.

The first chapter of Part III is devoted to prospective strategies, and it begins with fundamental questions: What if UFOs are extraterrestrial? What intentions and what strategies can we deduce from their behavior?

These direct questions open up the most controversial part of the report.

Possible motivations of extraterrestrial visitors are then explored, such as the protection of planet Earth against the dangers of nuclear war, which is suggested, for instance, by the repeated UFO flyovers of nuclear missile sites (as noted in chapter 11, regarding Roswell).

The committee takes the time to ponder over the possible repercussions on the behavior, official or not, of different nations and focuses on the possibility of *secret, privileged contacts that might be "attributed to the United States."*

The attitude of the United States is seen as "most strange" since the post–World War II sighting wave of 1947 and the Roswell event. Since that time, the report states, a policy of increasing secrecy seems to have been applied. This, it is asserted, might explain how America acquired such military and technological superiority in the decades following 1950.

This is a fascinating conjecture made by high officials of a foreign government. Many independent researchers have also hypothesized that the U.S. government reverse-engineered UFO technology and that this is why America has so rapidly leaped from one breakthrough to another over the course of the decades following Roswell.

Next, the report poses the question, "What measures must we take now?" The answer offered is that, at the very least, whatever the nature of UFOs, they require "critical vigilance."

The authors were especially concerned about the risk of "destabilizing manipulations." They suggested that a kind of "cosmic vigilance" be implemented by the elites, nationally and internationally, in order to prevent any shocking surprises, erroneous interpretations, or hostile manipulations.

COMETA then urged France to strengthen SEPRA and recommended the creation of a committee at the highest level of government to be entrusted with the development of hypotheses, strategies, and preparations and to make cooperative agreements with countries in Europe and elsewhere.

A suggested further step, the report notes, would be that European states and the European Union undertake diplomatic action with the United States within the framework of political and strategic alliances.

A key question is then framed: *What situations must we be prepared for?* Mentioned are such scenarios as an extraterrestrial move for official contact, discovery of a UFO and alien base on Earth, invasion (deemed improbable) and localized or massive attack, and manipulation or deliberate disinformation aiming at destabilizing other states.

The COMETA Report devotes special attention to "aeronautical implications," with detailed recommendations aimed at various personnel, such as aircraft crew members, air traffic controllers, weathermen, and engineers. It also makes recommendations at the scientific and technical levels, aimed at developing research with potential benefits for defense and industry. The report further explores the political and religious implications of UFOs, using as a model the perspective of our own exploration of space.

How would we do it? How would we handle contacts with less advanced civilizations?

In fact, that question has already been answered by Western civilizations' repeated contacts with remote, nontechnological cultures on Earth. The results are always the same; the less developed culture suffers damage, even ruin, as a result of the contact.

COMETA's concluding statements claim that the physical reality of UFOs under control of intelligent beings is "quasi-certain." It says that *only one hypothesis takes into account the available data: the hypothesis of extraterrestrial visitors.* This hypothesis is, of course, unproved, but it has far-reaching consequences. The goals of these alleged visitors remain unknown, but they must be the subject of speculations and prospective scenarios.

In its final recommendations, the COMETA Report stresses the need to:

1. Inform all decision makers and persons in positions of responsibility
2. Reinforce means of investigation and study at SEPRA
3. Consider whether UFO detection has been taken into account by agencies engaged in the surveillance of space
4. Create a strategic committee at the highest state level
5. Undertake diplomatic action with the United States for cooperation on this most important question
6. Study measures that might be necessary in case of emergencies

A final note: the report contains seven appendices, which are worth reading even by highly informed UFOlogists:

- Radar Detection in France
- Observations by Astronomers
- Life in the Universe
- Colonization of Space
- The Roswell Case and Possible Disinformation
- Antiquity of the UFO Phenomenon and Elements for a Chronology
- Reflection on Various Psychological, Sociological, and Political Aspects of the UFO Phenomenon

CONCLUSION

The COMETA Report is a game changer in the fields of government disclosure and the rational scientific study of UFOs. The French have systematically studied the phenomenon in detail, and that has paved the way for an eventual scientific understanding of our extraterrestrial heritage.

19

The Russian Roswell Case

In a speech at the 1992 MUFON [Mutual UFO Network] Symposium, Major-General Pavel Popovich, a pioneer cosmonaut who had been designated a "Hero of the Soviet Union" and was the president of the All-Union Ufology Association of the Commonwealth of Independent States, said:

> Today it can be stated with a high degree of confidence that observed manifestations of UFOs are no longer confined to the modern picture of the world. . . . The historical evidence of the phenomenon . . . allows us to hypothesize that ever since mankind has been co-existing with this extraordinary substance, it has manifested a high level of intelligence and technology. The UFO sightings have become the constant component of human activity and require a serious global study. . . . The scientific study of the UFO phenomenon should take place in the midst of other sciences dealing with man and the world.[1]

January 29, 1986, Dalnegorsk, Soviet Union: About 8 p.m., many citizens of this small mining city near the southeastern coast of Russia began observing a reddish spherical object flying parallel to the ground; it made no sounds as it continued its flight. It was later determined that the speed of the object was slow, approximately 15 meters per second (34 miles per hour) and that it had been flying about seven hundred to eight hundred meters (2,500 feet) above the ground.

The process of the descent was described differently by different eyewitnesses. Some said the object fell down with a flash and was not visible after that; others claimed it oscillated in altitude above the hill, radiating light of varying intensity as it went up and down. The light given off by the object was described by some as resembling the flames of a forest fire, and the light lasted for approximately one hour.

Two days later, Valeri Dvuzhilini, a member of the Academy of Sciences, was the first to arrive on the scene. He collected samples of an unidentified *metallic mesh* that was scattered around the site and samples of rocks and vegetation that had been scorched in the crash.

The impact site was two meters wide and two meters long (six feet by six feet). The ground looked like it had been burned at very high temperatures. The rocks at the impact site were covered with a black film, and the remnants of a burned tree were found within the landing zone. The remnants were not typical of a forest fire.

On some of the rocks were drops of a silvery metal, which were later analyzed and determined to be lead. The type of lead found in local lead deposits. In addition, black, glassy, drop-shaped beads were found scattered about the site. In all, approximately seventy grams of lead, five grams of metallic mesh fragments, and forty grams of beads were discovered.

Geiger counter readings determined that the radiation level in the landing zone was normal. Dvuzhilini's group took pictures of the site using two different cameras; however, the film later developed as blank.

Chemical analyses of the beads showed they were mostly composed of lead, silicon, and iron. Some of the drops contained significant amounts of zinc, bismuth, and rare earth mineral elements. An analysis of the soil, rocks, and burned wood taken from the landing ground was also performed. It was noted that the chemical composition was similar to the composition of similar samples taken from the site of the Tunguska event, a large explosion that flattened 770 square miles of forest in central Russia in 1908. That event is generally attributed to an exploding meteor.

The mesh fragments were also analyzed. It was found that the fragments were composed of a material that did not dissolve in strong acids or organic solvents, even when exposed to high temperatures for prolonged periods of time. One of the mesh fragments was discovered to be composed of scandium, gold, lanthanum, sodium, and samarium.

An analysis of another mesh fragment showed gold, silver, and nickel. After that fragment was heated in a vacuum, these elements did not show up; however, molybdenum and rhenium were detected.

The concentration of gold detected in one of the mesh fragments was equivalent to 1,100 grams per metric ton. This is much higher than gold deposits in the region. Ore becomes economic to extract when the concentration of gold reaches four grams per metric ton. There are no gold deposits in Dalnegorsk that contain gold at concentrations high enough to extract.

Altogether, three Soviet academic centers and eleven research institutes analyzed the materials from the alleged UFO crash site. Additional conclusions of these analyses include that the distance between atoms is different from ordinary iron and that radar signals cannot be reflected from the material.

Elements in the material may disappear and new ones appear after heating. One piece disappeared completely in front of four witnesses. The core of the material is composed of a substance with antigravitational properties.

This is a better case than the Roswell incident because it was properly investigated, with the materials collected and then immediately turned over to a number of reputable labs for analysis. At the time, during the cold war, the Soviets assumed it was probably the result of American technology. However, nothing quite like it has ever turned up in the United States.

CONCLUSION

This "Russian Roswell" case was not dismissed by the government. It appears that the debris material in this case was anomalous in several ways. The various elements are well known on Earth, but we should not necessarily expect extraterrestrial objects to be otherwise. However, we should expect that different fabrication techniques and processes would produce unknown features, as shown in the samples from this incident.

· · · · · · · · ·

NASA, ASTRONAUTS, AND THE SPACE PROGRAM

20

Enigmas of the Space Program

"To boldly go. . . ." It sounded so compelling back in the 1960s. In its early days, the space program lit a fire in the public imagination like few things ever have. It came on the heels of several decades of UFO reports, which the media did pay attention to in those days.

People were filled with questions about the possibility of extra-terrestrial visitations and also, from a more practical perspective, about the nature of the moon and planets.

It all came together, and everyone was behind Captain Kirk and the adventures of his starship, the *U.S.S. Enterprise*. But William Shatner was just an actor playing a role. He issued his commands from a Hollywood studio, not interstellar space. Nonetheless, there was another side to the actual space program that focused the public's attention: the cold war and the competition between the Soviet and American space programs.

The Soviets took the early lead with their *Sputniks* and cosmonauts orbiting Earth. Then U.S. astronauts made the big score by landing on the moon first. The world watched these events with mounting excite-ment and anticipation.

It really seemed like we would soon see astronauts going on long-term voyages, landing on the moon and establishing a base, then ven-turing to Mars . . . and then who knew beyond that? Perhaps after exploring the planets in the solar system, they would be mounting expe-ditions into interstellar space.

Stop. That was nearly fifty years ago. Not only did we not get to

Mars, but the highly publicized lunar mission also was scrapped for as yet unexplained reasons. The focus was shifted to much more pedestrian programs, such as the space shuttles and sending unmanned probes to investigate the planets and moons in our solar system.

What happened to the bold, stirring vision that once captured our attention and imaginations? That question is not as easy to answer as you would think.

Stripped of the science fiction elements, space—which begins where Earth's atmosphere and magnetosphere end—is a brutal, inhospitable place. To say that it is an extremely rigorous environment would be an understatement; space is lethal. Out there between the stars, it is absolutely frigid. Even within the bounds of our solar system, it is either too hot or too cold to support life as we know it on Earth. And space is a vacuum with no atmosphere to breathe.

In addition, the planets have roiling toxic atmospheres. The public was not clearly thinking these realities through when the Soviets and then the Americans launched the space race. Did astronomers, astrophysicists, engineers, and various other scientists know all this? Absolutely!

The questions that the lay public should have been asking were simple. Where are our astronauts going to get the constant supply of oxygen they need? After that, where is the water they also need in constant supply going to come from? Given the *Star Trek* scenario, that was all taken care of; in reality, NASA still cannot overcome these issues.

Sure, they could build a space vehicle that could orbit the earth for a few days and even get to the moon and back, but a lunar base, then a long-term voyage to Mars? These were fantasies that were spun in the early heyday years of the space program.

NASA did not, and still does not, have the technological capability needed to build a lunar base or send astronauts to Mars on a long-term mission.

President Obama's recent statements notwithstanding, administrations dating back to the Nixon-Agnew era have been chanting that mantra.

However, the galactic vision steadily got squeezed down to the redundant space shuttles and unmanned-probe missions that the public has grown less and less interested in. I, too, have seen my interest wane. I was very much alive back in the '60s and was as caught up in the drama and promises as anyone else. Like everyone else, I also was a bit naive and too willing to accept official proclamations that should have been questioned.

The following is a direct quote from NASA's website about the agency's mission:

> To reach for new heights and reveal the unknown so that what we do and learn will benefit all humankind. To do that, thousands of people have been working around the world—and off of it—for 50 years, trying to answer some basic questions. What's out there in space? How do we get there? What will we find? What can we learn there, or learn just by trying to get there, that will make life better here on Earth?[1]

After fifty years, enough time has elapsed to examine the record and see whether or not that mission has been fulfilled and those questions answered. What follows is a brief overview of the space program.

To begin, NASA was "launched" in 1958, partially in response to the Soviet Union's launch of the first artificial satellite the previous year. Looking back, even NASA officials admit that in those days the agency was as much about politics as it was about science.

Then President Kennedy focused NASA and the nation on sending astronauts to the moon by the end of the 1960s. Through Project Mercury and the Gemini Program, NASA developed the technology and skills it needed for the journey. On July 20, 1969, as part of the Apollo 11 mission, Neil Armstrong and Buzz Aldrin became the first two men to walk on the moon.

That encapsulates the "heady" champagne days of the space era. Landing astronauts on the moon was a huge achievement of American science and technology, a triumph over the Soviets during the cold war. But on the science side of it, what did NASA learn about the moon that has actually been of any practical benefit to taxpayers?

Other than bringing back a few geological samples to Earth, nothing much really was achieved; NASA did not add much to our knowledge, not directly from examining the moon anyway. Astronomers knew that the moon was constantly hammered by cosmic object impacts and that its surface was cratered and pockmarked, so what was the point of the mission in strict scientific terms?

At that point, NASA was envisioning the construction of a manned lunar base. That was supposed to be the real endgame of the lunar missions following the landing. In fact, a project toward that goal had been in the works for a decade prior to the lunar landing.

Project Horizon was a 1959 study regarding the U.S. Army's plan to establish a fort on the moon by 1967, according to Heinz Koelle, a German rocket engineer with the Army Ballistic Missile Agency's Project Horizon study.

The first landing was to be carried out by two "soldier-astronauts" in 1965, and more construction workers would soon follow. Through numerous launches (sixty-one Saturn I and eighty-eight Saturn II rockets), 245 tons of cargo would be transported to the outpost by 1966. Space was to be quickly militarized.

Next, the Lunex Project was a U.S. Air Force program that planned a manned lunar landing in 1961, prior to the Apollo Program. It envisaged a twenty-one-airman underground air force base on the moon by 1968, at a total cost of $7.5 billion.

In 1962, John DeNike and Stanley Zahn published their idea of a subsurface moon base located at the Sea of Tranquility. The proposed base was to have housed a crew of twenty-one in modules placed four meters below the surface The scientists believed the underground base would shield the operation as well as Earth's atmosphere does: our magnetosphere shields the sun's deadliest rays from hitting the earth; an underground base would be required to do this on the moon since it has no magnetosphere . . .

DeNike and Zahn envisioned nuclear reactors for energy production because they are more efficient than solar panels. In addition, atomic power would have been used to overcome the problems of the long lunar nights, and for the life-support system, an algae-based gas exchanger was proposed.

But were all of these plans real or simply smoke and mirrors? Where were these space soldiers going to get their oxygen and water? How were they going to deal with the lunar dust? A lunar base meant that soldiers would be stationed on the moon for a prolonged period.

Scientists aren't magicians or miracle workers, but everyone was so pumped about the lunar landing that anything seemed possible . . . at least for a while.

There is no question that the plan was to follow the moon landing with some kind of manned lunar base. However, just when it seemed that all the groundwork had been accomplished and the next step was at hand, NASA pulled the plug on the lunar mission. Not only did NASA turn its focus away suddenly and inexplicably, but so did the Soviet Union. Why?

Before attempting to answer that question it may first be necessary to backtrack and take a quick look of events that led up to the Apollo 12 mission, which was the second manned lunar landing. Manned exploration of the lunar surface began in 1968 when the Apollo 8 spacecraft orbited the moon with three astronauts on board. This was mankind's first direct view of the dark side of the moon.

The following year, Apollo 11 landed two astronauts on the moon, proving the ability of humans to travel to the moon, perform scientific research work there, and bring back sample materials. It is at this point that anomalous exchanges between ground control on Earth and the astronauts emerge, as do enigmatic events.

Aldrin and Armstrong were onboard the Apollo 11 mission. They allegedly observed some UFOs in a crater, and Aldrin filmed them as Armstrong got out of the spacecraft.

APOLLO 11 TRANSCRIPT (AUTHOR'S COMMENTS IN ITALICS)
With the post landing checks completed, Armstrong climbed out of the LM and descended to the lunar surface. . . . Armstrong's attention was first directed at the nature of the surface material. He reported that the top layer was a fine, powdery material. He noted that he sunk in only a quarter of an inch or less, and that the foot-pads of the LM, which are convex discs 32 inches in diameter, had penetrated only a few inches.[2]

[*This description makes it clear that the surface is powdery, but the powder or dust is not deep; beneath that it is hard because his boots do not sink in far, nor does the lunar module sink in deeply.*]

After a quick visual check of the LM, Armstrong went ahead with his scheduled task of collecting the contingency sample—several pounds of lunar surface material which he stowed in a spacesuit pocket. In the course of his collecting, he noted that as he dug down five or six inches below the surface, he encountered hard, cohesive material.[3]

[The nature of the surface and subsurface is confirmed.]

Once the LM inspection and the sample collection were completed, Aldrin got out of the LM and climbed down the ladder, with Armstrong providing voice guidance. Armstrong was taking pictures of the event at the same time. The two then "unveiled" the plaque mounted on the strut behind the ladder by removing a protective covering. They read the inscription for the benefit of their world audience.

> *Here Men From Planet Earth*
> *First Set Foot Upon The Moon*
> *July 1969 A.D.*
> *We Came In Peace For All Mankind*[4]

[Who was NASA expecting would eventually read this plaque?]

The collecting of samples in bulk went forward without incident. Armstrong and Aldrin between them bagged upwards of 50 pounds (earth weight) of the loose surface material and selected rocks. These were stowed in small cloth bags and sealed and then packed in two large containers—also sealed—for eventual storage aboard the LM.[5]

[The next experiments seem a bit arcane and one can but wonder why they would have been so high on the agenda of the first manned lunar landing: a highly sensitive tremor measuring instrument and an equally sophisticated laser device to gauge distances and orbital pathways were deployed.]

The seismometer, designed to record and report events affecting the physical structure of the moon, began returning data immediately. It was sensitive enough to record the impact of the astronauts' feet on the moon's surface as they walked.

The laser reflector which was supposed to provide very precise information on the moon's distance from earth and its orbital path did not immediately function. The reason for this is not clear. A few days later it commenced operating.[6]

[*I question why a seismometer experiment was on the top of the priority list. Do we, on Earth, really need to know that much about moonquakes? (After all, taxpayer money funded this effort.) I can understand the logic of collecting the soil and rock samples, but measuring lunar tremors does not fit in the context of the first lunar landscape exploration.*

In addition to these basic experiments, the astronauts were doing a lot of filming. This raises a serious issue. The transmission log contains a two-minute gap where NASA claims a camera overheated. If that is true, then why is that event omitted from the NASA summary of Apollo 11? What the summary does include is the following:]

During the moon walk, the TV transmission had a ghostly quality. The astronauts' white space suits, the grey tones of the moon's surface, the buoyancy of their movements, and the strange configuration of "Eagle" combined to give the impression that what viewers were seeing was truly from another world.

Besides the TV camera, the astronauts used a trio of other cameras for surface photography. They got both stilt [*sic*] and sequence coverage with a Hasselblad still camera, a Maurer data acquisition camera and the Apollo Lunar Surface Close-up camera.[7]

They had cameras and backup cameras of all kinds, and the filming went just fine. Two minutes was a very long period of silence for the first lunar landing, which was broadcast live to a billion people around the world. With multiple cameras recording the event, how could the image and sound be totally interrupted for two minutes? The astronauts had cameras covering many different angles.

When questioned about the silence, NASA insisted that the problem was the result of one of the television cameras being overheated, thus interfering with the transmission. That is a less-than-satisfactory answer.

This unexpected problem surprised even the most qualified of viewers, who were unable to explain how—in such a costly project during a live worldwide broadcast—one of the most essential elements could break down.

During the two-minute interruption, thousands of amateur radio (ham radio) operators dialed their stations onto the same frequency that the astronauts and the NASA capsule communicator on Earth were transmitting on.

During transmission of the Apollo 11 moon landing of astronauts Aldrin and Armstrong in 1969, two minutes of silence occurred in which the image and sound were interrupted. NASA insisted this problem resulted from one of the television cameras, which had "overheated," thus interfering with the reception.

Some time after the historic moon landing, project director of the base in Houston, Christopher Kraft, made some surprising comments when he left NASA. Some of those comments are included at the end of this piece. The following conversation has been corroborated by hundreds of amateur radio operators who had connected their stations to the same frequency through which the Apollo 11 astronauts transmitted.

During the interruption—which was not as it seemed—it appears that NASA, Armstrong, and Aldrin, along with Cape Kennedy, censored both image and sound.

Below is the gist of the exchange, during the two-minute radio silence, that reportedly took place between the astronauts and NASA's Mission Control Center in Houston:

ARMSTRONG AND ALDRIN: Those are giant things. No, no, no—this is not an optical illusion. No one is going to believe this!

HOUSTON (CHRISTOPHER CRAFT): What . . . what . . . what? What the hell is happening? What's wrong with you?

ARMSTRONG AND ALDRIN: They're here under the surface.

HOUSTON: What's there? (Muffled noise). Emission interrupted; interference control calling "Apollo 11."

ARMSTRONG AND ALDRIN: We saw some visitors. They were here for a while, observing the instruments.

HOUSTON: Repeat your last information!

ARMSTRONG AND ALDRIN: I say that there were other spaceships. They're lined up in the other side of the crater!

HOUSTON: Repeat, repeat!

ARMSTRONG AND ALDRIN: Let us sound this orbit . . . in 625 to 5. . . . Automatic relay connected. . . . My hands are shaking so badly I can't do anything. Film it? God, if these damned cameras have picked up anything—what then?

HOUSTON: Have you picked up anything?

ARMSTRONG AND ALDRIN: I didn't have any film at hand. Three shots of the saucers or whatever they were that were ruining the film.

HOUSTON: Control, control here. Are you on your way? What is the uproar with the UFOs over?

ARMSTRONG AND ALDRIN: They've landed here. There they are and they're watching us.

HOUSTON: The mirrors, the mirrors—have you set them up?

ARMSTRONG AND ALDRIN: Yes, they're in the right place. But whoever made those spaceships surely can come tomorrow and remove them. Over and out.

If one camera malfunction caused the blackout due to overheating, then how was it cooled down enough to resume normal transmission so quickly? Why weren't the other cameras used as a backup?

Certainly, NASA engineers would have anticipated such a failure and had a redundancy sequence in place. After all, we are talking about the whole world watching this event on live television with the reputation of America's space program on the line.

Moreover, anyone who has read the entire transmission log knows that the cameras, the quality of the images, the angles, and the lighting were not just incidental, secondary parts of the mission. They were, in fact, equal to or more important than the two experiments that were conducted on the lunar surface.

NASA and the astronauts were discussing the operational status of the cameras and the resolution of the images they were taking from the time that the Apollo spacecraft that was above the earth to until and after it landed. Furthermore, the camera functions were the issues gone over more than any other technical component during the mission. To claim that the transmission went down due to a camera failure is highly questionable.

This excuse would be revived in the next lunar mission, Apollo 12, when NASA claimed that Astronaut Alan Bean accidentally pointed the camera he was operating at the sun! Seriously, the man goes through the most intense selection and training program on Earth, only to destroy the camera assigned to visually document the mission?

Keep in mind that the subject of UFO sightings by astronauts was already a hot one since early manned space missions had produced inexplicable events and reports of sightings.

For instance, a sighting occurred during the December 1965 Gemini 7 mission. Astronauts Frank Boorman and James Lovell reported sighting a "bogey" at ten o'clock high. Exchanges with Mission Control confirmed this was not the rocket booster, and subsequently, a variety of small particles—never properly explained—were observed at a distance of three or four miles.

An earlier event, from June of that year and perhaps the best-documented astronaut sighting, occurred aboard Gemini 4. Astronaut James McDivitt reported observing "a cylindrical object with an antenna-like extension." According to McDivitt's account of the incident, the distance of the object, which was silvery in appearance, was impossible to gauge, but it initially appeared at least miles away.

The object was in "free drifting flight" over the Pacific Ocean. Suddenly, the craft appeared to change direction so that it was on a collision course with the astronauts. They instantly started preparations for avoiding a collision, but the craft flew by them without incident.

Then, in 1966, two bright red, glowing objects captured the attention of Gemini 10 astronauts John Young and Michael Collins as they circled Earth.

Suddenly, both astronauts observed the objects in the same orbital path their craft was in. The astronauts immediately informed Mission Control personnel, who in turn requested further information. In their words, "If you can get a bearing maybe we can track them down!" Just at that particular moment, Young radioed back, "They just disappeared!"

At the time of the Apollo 11 and 12 moon-landing missions, the public knew of these encounters and reports, but while they were still buying the official NASA explanations, it was with mounting questions.

(Each of the above-mentioned incidents was thoroughly investigated by the famous [or should I say "infamous"?] Condon Committee. The conclusion was that the incidents were "unexplained" and were in the "highest category of credibility.")

Keep in mind that these sightings were part of a sequence that went back to Roswell; the buzzing of Washington, D.C.; the Socorro incident; and more. The UFO phenomenon was not kept under wraps by the media as it has been since the 1980s. Of course, the astronaut sightings were unimpeachable, so they added a huge amount of credibility to the UFO phenomenon.

Now, given how the military and the government handled Roswell and Washington, would NASA be inclined to air or to black out yet more evidence that UFOs were real? It does not take a Sherlock Holmes mentality to answer that question.

The NASA explanation for the Apollo 11 broadcast interruption does not wash. If they had sent only one camera to film the entire event, perhaps, although who would want to give them more tax dollars after that, especially given that on the next mission, they did send only one camera, which Bean allegedly destroyed by pointing it at the sun?

After the Apollo Program, NASA focused on creating reusable ships to provide regular access to space: the space shuttles. First launched in 1981, the space shuttles flew more than 130 flights before the fleet was retired in 2011.

In 2000, the United States and Russia established a permanent human presence in space aboard the International Space Station, a multinational project representing the work of sixteen nations. In reality, the space shuttle was really a space truck that had a very pedestrian mission. The actual exploration of other planets has been conducted by probes since the last manned lunar mission.

The question now is, why did NASA and the Soviet space program both abandon their lunar missions, but now both claim they want to return to the moon? We shall delve into that in chapter 23, but before doing so, it should be enlightening to read the views of some astronauts regarding extraterrestrials, presented in the following chapters.

CONCLUSION

After a string of early successes that ended with the first lunar landing, NASA backed off the lunar-base mission. Some astronauts have reported UFO sightings during space flights. Fifty years thereafter, the agency is still talking about building a space base on the moon.

21

Astronaut
Gordon Cooper

The following quote from astronaut Gordon Cooper is taken from the article "Message to the United Nations Addressing a Panel Discussion on UFOs and ETs in 1985," published in *UFO Universe Magazine*. Following Gordon's quote is the full text of an article by Timothy Green Beckley titled "Gordon Cooper and UFOs: An Astronaut Speaks Out," which is taken from Beckley's book *MJ-12 and the Riddle of Hangar 18.*

Cooper was one of America's original seven Project Mercury astronauts. He orbited Earth for a then-record thirty-four-hour, twenty-two-orbit flight in the spacecraft *Faith 7* in May of 1963. He was outspoken about the need for an open inquiry into UFOs, based on his personal experience of sighting UFOs both in space and on Earth and the testimony of other Mercury, Gemini, and Apollo astronauts.

In 1985, Cooper addressed a United Nations panel on this topic, which was chaired by former U.N. Secretary-General Kurt Waldheim. Cooper told the U.N. panel:

I believe that these extraterrestrial vehicles and their crews are visiting this planet from other planets, which are a little more technically advanced than we are on Earth. I feel that we need to have a top level, coordinated program to scientifically collect and analyze data from all over the Earth concerning any type of encounter and to determine how best to interfere with these visitors in a friendly fashion.

We may first have to show them that we have learned how to resolve our problems by peaceful means rather than warfare, before we are accepted, as fully qualified, universal team members. Their acceptance will have tremendous possibilities of advancing our world in all areas. Certainly then it would seem that the U.N. has a vested interest in handling the subject quickly and properly.

I should point out that I am not an experienced UFO professional researcher—I have not as yet had the privilege of flying a UFO or of meeting the crew of one. However, I do feel that I am somewhat qualified to discuss them, since I have been into the fringes of the vast areas of which they travel. Also, I did have occasion in 1951 to have two days of observation of many flights of them, of different sizes flying in fighter formation, generally from west to east over Europe. They were at a higher altitude than we could reach with our jet fighters. . . .

Fig. 21.1. Exploration on the Moon. Photo courtesy of NASA.

If the U.N. agrees to pursue this project and lend their credibility to it, perhaps many more well-qualified people will agree to step forth and provide help and information.[1]

"GORDON COOPER AND UFOs: AN ASTRONAUT SPEAKS OUT"

Article by Timothy Green Beckley
[My comments in italics]

One of the few individuals whose prominence is beyond question has, however, over the past few months, dared to open his mouth and challenge the status quo.

Gordon Cooper was one of America's original astronauts. He helped pioneer this country's space exploration efforts when, aboard a tiny space capsule known as *Mercury [Faith] 7,* Cooper orbited the Earth for 34 hours, proving that man could live outside our atmosphere for prolonged periods. His patriotism, bravery and respectability go without saying . . .

Cooper has recently made several public pronouncements concerning his strong belief in UFOs. While a guest on the Merv Griffin Show, Cooper shocked the viewing audiences by speaking for over five minutes on a topic that was only within the past few years often considered too bizarre for polite conversation.

[Too bizarre because the U.S. government made a mockery out of anyone who seriously proposed that UFOs were real but had a hard time doing that with Cooper.]

Nonetheless, there were some things that Cooper wouldn't even discuss on the air in front of the curious multitudes.

Luckily, Lee Spiegel *[sic]* is a personal friend of Gordon Cooper. They have conferred on several occasions, and while in the company of the man who is bound and determined to crack the "Cosmic Watergate," which he is convinced exists within the higher echelon of government, the former space traveler is more than happy to talk about his UFO experiences—and they are many.

In the early 1950s, Cooper was assigned to a jet fighter group in Germany. While stationed there, he remembers very vividly the week an entire formation of circular objects passed over the Air Base on almost a daily routine.

"We never could get close enough to pin them down, but they were round in shape and very metallic looking," Cooper points out. UFOs were to continue to haunt him when the Air Force Colonel was transferred several years later to Edwards Air Force Base Flight Test Center in the California desert.

What happened one afternoon while he was on duty at this military base is evidence enough that the government definitely does keep a lot of secrets when it comes to UFOs!

The incident took place in the late 1950s—either 1957 or 1958—as Cooper can best recall; and to this day, the photographic evidence of an actual UFO touching down upon the Earth is being kept under wraps.

During this period, Cooper was a Project Manager at Edwards Air Force Base, just three or four years before entering America's space program. After lunch this particular day, Cooper had assigned a team of photographers to an area of the vast dry lake beds near Edwards.

In a taped interview with UFOlogist Lee Spiegel, the former Astronaut disclosed that while the crew was out there, they spotted a strange-looking craft above the lake bed, and they began taking films of it.

Cooper says the object was very definitely "hovering" above the ground. And then it slowly came down and sat on the lake bed for a few minutes. All during this time the motion picture cameras were filming away.

"There were varied estimates by the cameramen on what the actual size of the object was," Cooper confesses, "but they all agreed that it was at least the size of a vehicle that would carry normal-sized people in it."

Col. Cooper was not fortunate enough to be outside at the time of this incredible encounter, but he did see the films as soon as they were rushed through the development process.

"It was a typical circular-shaped UFO," he recollects. "Not too many people saw it, because it took off at quite a sharp angle and just climbed straight on out of sight!"

Cooper admits he didn't take any kind of poll to determine who had seen the craft, "because there were always strange things flying around in the air over Edwards." This is a statement Lee Spiegel was able to verify through his own research efforts, having obtained closely guarded tapes of conversations between military pilots circling the base and their commanding officers in the flight tower, tracking the presence of unknown objects.

"People just didn't ask a lot of questions about things they saw and couldn't understand," notes Cooper, who adds that it was a lot simpler to look the other way, shrug one's shoulders, and chalk up what had been seen to "just another experimental aircraft that must have been developed at another area of the air base."

[*This is the reason so many UFO sightings and encounters go unreported. Why go through the hassle, public scrutiny, potential ridicule, and all?*]

But what about the photographic proof—the motion picture footage—that was taken? "I think it was definitely a UFO," Cooper states, as he makes no bones about it. "However, where it [the object] came from and who was in it is hard to determine, because it didn't stay around long enough to discuss the matter—there wasn't even time to send out a welcoming committee!"

After he reviewed the film at least a dozen times, the footage was quickly forwarded to Washington. Cooper no doubt expected to get a reply in a few weeks' time as to what his men had seen and photographed, but there was no word, and the movie "vanished"—never to surface again. . . .

On coast-to-coast television, Cooper recently made a blockbuster statement that had the telephone lines tied up the next day, as viewers telephoned the stations that carried the syndicated Merv Griffin Show, anxious to find out if their ears had been playing tricks on them the night before.

Toward the end of the talk-show host's interview with the former Astronaut, Merv broke into a secretive tone of voice, right on the air, and aimed a hundred-thousand-dollar question at his guest: "There is a story going around, Gordon, that a spaceship did land in middle America and there were occupants, and members of our government were able to keep one of the occupants alive for a period of time. They've seen the metal of the aircraft, and they know what the people look like—is that a credible story?"

For all intents and purposes, Cooper should have laughed, for assuredly such a speculative story belongs in the category of science fiction or space fantasy. Cooper kept a straight face when he replied: "I think it's fairly credible. I would like to see the time when all qualified people could really work together to properly investigate these stories and either refute or prove them."

[Of course, Griffin was referring to Roswell.]

The bombshell had been dropped. Cooper went on to say that from the various reports of UFO contacts and abductions he had been privy to, he was convinced that the occupants of this crashed UFO were "probably not that different from what we are," that they are almost totally humanoid (i.e., have two arms, two legs, a torso, and readily identifiable facial features) in appearance.

Taken aback by what Cooper had said over the national airwaves, Lee Spiegel telephoned Cooper's office the following morning and managed to get past his private secretary, though others in the media were getting the cold shoulder.

"Cooper admitted to me that he could have revealed more on the air, but he decided not to play his entire hand because he felt certain that some 'official eyebrows' were going to get raised."[2]

22

Astronaut Mitchell
TV Interview

The following is the full transcript of Dennis Murphy interviewing astronaut Edgar Mitchell on the *Dateline NBC* television show, which aired on April 19, 1996. The interview covers many topics. At one point, Murphy notes that Mitchell does not accept the government's official explanation of the events that occurred at Roswell in 1947. Mitchell makes some interesting claims about that incident that should be taken with the utmost seriousness.

MOONSTRUCK ANNOUNCER: From our studios in Los Angeles, here again is Maria Shriver.

MARIA SHRIVER: Their names are legendary. Shepard, Glenn, Armstrong, Aldrin: Men who led America into space and to the moon. And after seeing the universe in ways mankind had only dreamt of, they came back changed from the experience. But their journey transformed some of them in ways you might not expect. Tonight the story of a man who walked on the moon and returned with some ideas that could be called out of this world. Here's Dennis Murphy.

ADAM MITCHELL: (Watching moon with father) How big is the moon?

DENNIS MURPHY REPORTING: (Voice-over) A father and son, a silver moon floating over a Florida beach.

(Edgar and Adam Mitchell sitting on beach watching moon)

EDGAR MITCHELL: (Watching moon with son) It's about a fourth the size of the earth . . .

MURPHY: But when Adam Mitchell learns about craters . . . his astronomy teacher isn't just his dad. Edgar Mitchell is one of only a dozen men to ever walk about the lunar landscape.

(Edgar and Adam on beach; lunar equipment and man on moon)

MURPHY: And that's the pad you went to the moon from?

EDGAR MITCHELL: This is the one we're standing on. That structure's different, but the pad we're standing on is it.

MURPHY: (Voice-over) Does it seem like a long time ago?

(Film footage of *Apollo 14* rocket on launch pad)

EDGAR MITCHELL: Yes and no. There are moments when it seems like yesterday and other moments when it's forever.

MURPHY: (Voice-over) Mitchell's moment came in 1971 when Apollo 14 thundered into the history books, but since then he's been on an even more profound journey to a world where he says the paranormal is normal and extraterrestrials are fact, not fiction.

(*Apollo 14* launching; moon and cloudy sky)

EDGAR MITCHELL: I'm convinced there's life throughout the universe. It's just a question of how developed. Are they a few thousand years ahead of us? It doesn't take much.

MURPHY: (Voice-over) Edgar Mitchell has always marched to his own definitively different drum. He's the son of a New Mexico cattle rancher, but he gave up punching cows for punching supersonic holes in the sky as a Navy test pilot. He went on to become an MIT physics scholar and ultimately one of NASA's best and brightest.

(Murphy and Mitchell walking near launch pad; old photo of Edgar on pony; plane taking off from aircraft carrier; photo of younger Edgar Mitchell; photo of Mitchell in spacesuit)

MURPHY: Was it intimidating to show up at NASA on the first day of school, and here's the original seven, and here's Deke Slayton . . .

EDGAR MITCHELL: Mm-hmm.

MURPHY: . . . the awesome astronaut program and you're the new kid in school?

EDGAR MITCHELL: Well, sure. But I would say for most of us having been through the selection process, we were a little brash. You know, the Mercury astronauts called themselves the original seven. Our group called ourselves the original nineteen.

PRESIDENT JOHN F. KENNEDY: (speaking in press conference) I believe that this nation should commit itself to achieving the goal before this decade is out of landing a man on the moon and returning him . . .

EDGAR MITCHELL: To me, the purpose of going to the moon was to discover more about ourselves, to discover more about humanity, to be the bear that goes over the mountain to see what he can see.

MURPHY: (Voice-over) And in 1970, Ed Mitchell thought he would get to that mountaintop. He was called up with Stew Roosa and Commander Alan Shepard for a mission to the moon on *Apollo 13*. (Mitchell and Shepard in spacesuits)

MURPHY: How come you didn't go on that one'!

EDGAR MITCHELL: Headquarters said, "Allan, you need some more training time. Let's not rush this." So we negotiated with—with Jim Lovell's crew.

(Excerpt from *Apollo 13* shown)
MURPHY: (Voice-over) As the movie *Apollo 13* showed so vividly, the mission became much more than a trip to the moon.

(Excerpt from *Apollo 13*)
MURPHY: (Voice-over) Of course, as it turned out, you missed a very bad ride.

(Excerpt from *Apollo 13*)
EDGAR MITCHELL: That's the way it turned out, and as Jim Lovell said in the movie, "These blessings come in great disguises."

MURPHY: (Voice-over) Mitchell was part of that triumph of human ingenuity, the rescue team that brought the crippled capsule home and saved the *Apollo 13* crew from what looked like certain death—a hero in Houston, but not in Hollywood. He was written out of the movie.

(Excerpt from *Apollo 13*)

ED HARRIS: (From *Apollo 13*) I believe this is going to be our finest hour.

MURPHY: (Voice-over) Mitchell's finest hour would come a year later when he got a ticket to ride. After the *Apollo 13* cliffhanger, this was the mission that had to work. Pressure . . .

(Excerpt from *Apollo 13* footage from preparations for Apollo 14 mission)

UNIDENTIFIED ANNOUNCER: (Voice-over) On January 31st, 1971, the crew of Apollo 14 would leave earth on their mission to the moon.

(*Apollo 14* on launch pad: moon)

MURPHY: (Voice-over) And they made it to the moon in style.

(Liftoff of *Apollo 14*)

EDGAR MITCHELL: (From footage of moon landing) We're on the surface.

ALAN SHEPARD: (Shepard and Mitchell walking on moon) We've made a good landing, and it's been a long way, but we're here.

EDGAR MITCHELL: (Holding American flag on moon) How's this? Look OK?

ALAN SHEPARD: (Standing on moon) Oh yeah. That's the good side.

MURPHY: (Voice-over) Shepard and Mitchell spent 33 and a half hours on the dry lunar sea of Tomorrow. It was an almost glitch-free mission, exactly what the doctor had ordered for the space program. Shepard fired a memorable six-iron shot and they were gone, headed home with 95 pounds of moon rock. And according to space documentarian and co-writer of *Apollo 13,* Al Reinert, they came back with a secret.

(Footage of Mitchell and Shepard on moon—liftoff from the moon; Al Reinert)

AL REINERT (*APOLLO 13* SCREENWRITER): He had a couple of people, or at least one or two people back on Earth that he was trying to contact telepathically.

MURPHY: (Voice-over) Mitchell was conducting some extracurricular experiments on his own time. While the others were asleep in the capsule, Mitchell tried to transmit his thoughts from deep in outer space to friends back on Earth. He had a table of random numbers matched up with these symbols, at a set time, he would choose a sequence and concentrate. Tens of thousands of miles away, his friends tried to read his thoughts and jot down the same numbers and symbols. Later Mitchell thought the results were dramatic, but not as dramatic as the fallout. The press found out about it, and the headlines caught everyone by surprise, particularly *Apollo 14*'s commander.

(Astronauts in *Apollo 14*—numbers and symbols; Earth as seen from space; newspaper headlines)

MURPHY: Alan Shepard's going over the newspapers.

EDGAR MITCHELL: Mm-hmm.

MURPHY: . . . and he says, "Here are some guys saying, that you're playing with ESP on the way to the moon."

EDGAR MITCHELL: Yep.

MURPHY: "What a bunch of bologna."

EDGAR MITCHELL: Yeah, he was—he was kind of tickled about that, and thought it was—here the press is being creative. And again I had to say, "Well, boss, I did it."

MURPHY: (Voice-over) Edgar Mitchell, branded forever as the ESP astronaut, came back a changed man. He found his entire belief system thrown up in the air, like a game of pick-up-sticks.

(Earth as seen from space; space capsule with parachute landing in water; astronauts exiting ship)

EDGAR MITCHELL: Looking at the moon, looking at the sun, looking at beyond the earth to these billions and billions of brilliant stars and galaxies was simply the feeling of connectedness, the feeling that the molecules of my body in this spacecraft were manufactured in those stars. We're connected.

MURPHY: (Voice-over) This man who had mastered a world of rules, regulations, and strict science had experienced nothing less than a spiritual transformation, an epiphany that happened to several of the number-two guys, the rookies. *Apollo 12*'s Alan Bean became a painter of haunting lunar seas. *Apollo 15*'s Jim Irwin became an evangelical Christian missionary and set off to find Noah's Ark, *Apollo16*'s Charlie Duke a minister.

(Moon; surface of moon and spacecraft; Bean, Irwin; Duke)

MURPHY: It's interesting. There's something about that second seat on the lander.

AL REINERT: The commanders were the guys who were in charge. They were very responsible.

UNIDENTIFIED ASTRONAUT (ON MOON): Oh boy, it's beautiful up here.

AL REINERT: The rookies had the chance to kind of just, you know, "Wow, we're on the moon." I think there's a spiritual element to the whole journey if you're open to it. Again, you're talking about very different people. Some of them, you could have sent them to Dallas for two weeks for all the impact it made on their soul.

MURPHY: (Voice-over) Not Edgar Mitchell. The moon trip drove him to try to reconcile his two conflicting natures: the test pilot scientist and the spiritual pilgrim. He was off on his own voyage now to inner space, and there he met a shaman, a Tibetan healer, about the time his mother was ill. (Mitchell in spacesuit; Mitchell in pinning ceremony; spacecraft on moon; Earth as seen from space; photo of Mitchell's mother and other women)

EDGAR MITCHELL: Well, she was suffering and was legally blind, so I got the healer and my mother together just to see what would happen.

MURPHY: Wait—wait a second. Here you are, a guy from MIT, there's a lot of Edwards Air Force Base in you, a lot of translunar injection, and here you are talking to a guy from Tibet saying he's going to heal her.

EDGAR MITCHELL: Well, I have to admit that—that it was incongruous, but my perverse curiosity said, "Let's find out if this guy's real."

MURPHY: (Voice-over) And what Mitchell found out amazed him.

(Mitchell and Murphy in interview)

EDGAR MITCHELL: Well, I got them together, and he did his thing. which is primarily passing his hands over her head. And at 6:00 the next morning, mother came rushing into my room, her Bible in one hand, her glasses in the other and said, "Son. I can see. I can see."

MURPHY: What did you make of that?

EDGAR MITCHELL: I was dumbfounded. So, I took the next logical step. I invited the man to come live with me for a while so I could figure out what was going on.

MURPHY: The astronaut who'd been to the moon is bunking with a Tibetan healer?

EDGAR MITCHELL: Yep, and he's quite a guy.

MURPHY: (Voice-over) Almost two years after his moonwalk, Mitchell left the astronaut core and started delving into the paranormal, and on that path less traveled, he shocked his old NASA buddies once again when he aligned himself with the controversial psychic Uri Geller, most famous for bending spoons, supposedly with his mind.

(Mitchell on moon; Mitchell at work with NASA; person rotating hands above a glass object; photo of *Apollo 14* crew; Mitchell and Geller)

OFF-SCREEN VOICE: (Footage of Geller bending spoons) The spoon turns to plastic in his hands.

MURPHY: (Voice-over) Mitchell personally championed Geller's research in the United States.

(Spoons; Geller)

MURPHY: But there are people, Doctor, who say, "Fraud, charlatan, this guy's . . ."

EDGAR MITCHELL: Sorry.

MURPHY: I've been sold a bill of goods.

EDGAR MITCHELL: They're the ones that have to say, have to look a little deeper.

MURPHY: (Voice-over) And now Mitchell is taking another step beyond, past healers and ESP. Get ready, this man who's been to the moon is saying publicly for the first time that he believes we have been visited by inhabitants of other planets, extraterrestrials, here. He says he's talked to people who've had close encounters of the third kind. (Stars in galaxy; planet; clouds; Mitchell walking; stars; Earth)

EDGAR MITCHELL: I have no firsthand experience, but I have had the opportunity to meet with people from three countries who in the course of their official duties claim to have had personal firsthand encounter experiences.

MURPHY: With extraterrestrials.

EDGAR MITCHELL:—With extraterrestrials.

MURPHY: Aliens from some other place?

EDGAR MITCHELL: That's what they claim.

MURPHY: (Voice-over) Take for instance what may be the most famous sighting of UFO-ology, the wreckage of something that fell out of the sky and was found in the the desert of Roswell, New Mexico, in 1947. Mitchell is in the camp of those who believe it was a spacecraft. He scoffs at the government's explanation of a crashed high-atmosphere balloon.

(Newspaper headlines; desert; headlines; photo of man with wreckage)

EDGAR MITCHELL: The people that were there say that's utter nonsense. Come on. Let's have the truth.

MURPHY: Do you think it's more likely than not that extraterrestrials have been to this planet?

EDGAR MITCHELL: From what I now understand and have experienced and seen the evidence for, I think the evidence is very strong, and large portions of it are classified.

MURPHY: Classified by whom?

EDGAR MITCHELL: By governments.

MURPHY: You're saying it—it—it not only likely happened, but there's been a cover-up?

EDGAR MITCHELL: Oh I—I think if it has happened the way it seems to be, there's definitely been a cover-up.

MURPHY: (Voice-over) Mitchell wouldn't name names, but he says some of his information comes from former highly classified U.S. government employees, people who say our government picked up sonic engineering secrets from UFOs. The Department of Defense declined to comment on Mitchell's allegations, but gave us the U.S. Air Force's standard handout on unidentified flying objects, stating: "There has been no evidence indicating that sightings categorized as 'unidentified' are extraterrestrial." Case closed.

(Murphy and Mitchell walking; Pentagon; Air Force handout on unidentified flying objects)
MURPHY: (Voice-over) So, is Edgar Mitchell lost in space? Not to audiences like this one at Cambridge University in England.

(Murphy and Mitchell; Cambridge audience)
UNIDENTIFIED MAN: (At assembly at Cambridge) This is a man who's traveled farther than almost any of us.

MURPHY: (Voice-over) Scientists and new-agers find something provocative in this quiet man from the moon.

(Mitchell at Cambridge)
EDGAR MITCHELL: (Speaking to Cambridge audience) There is no unnatural or supernatural experience. There is just experience.

MURPHY: (Voice-over) Mystic, astronaut, and now author, Edgar Mitchell has written a book, *The Way of the Explorer,* telling all about the incredible journey that is his life.

(Mitchell, woman, and child walking on beach; front cover of Mitchell's book)

MURPHY: (Voice-over) It's been almost three decades since man first hopped about the moon and we're finding out that our astronaut heroes really were far more complex human beings than the image of *The Right Stuff,* A-OK pilots of NASA's public relations machine.

(Astronauts on moon; Astronauts on the cover of *Time* magazine; photo of astronauts by spacecraft; astronauts on moon)

AL REINERT: At the time they were going to the moon they were so worried about all those little details, but as the years go by they forget all of those technical things, and what sticks in their minds are the powerful human moments that would have been in any tourist's mind, you know? (Voice-over) I mean, in a way, they were guys on a giant camping trip.

(Astronauts on moon)

MURPHY: (Voice-over) And back at the pad where he began his journey twenty-five years ago, the astronaut nicknamed "the brain" appreciates a rainbow while marveling at the engineering that sent him into space.

(Murphy and Mitchell walking at launch pad; rainbow)

EDGAR MITCHELL: (Voice-over) It's like an alive machine sitting there getting ready to go. It's impressive, it's emotional.

(Launchpad equipment)

MURPHY: (Voice-over) What a long, strange trip it's been for Edgar Mitchell.

(*Apollo 14* taking off)

MURPHY: You have been the subject—let's face it—over the years of a kind of wink, wink, nudge, nudge, oh there's Edgar Mitchell.

EDGAR MITCHELL: Mm-hmm.

MURPHY: ESP, all of that stuff, that's . . .

EDGAR MITCHELL: Yep.

MURPHY: . . . that's Edgar's thing.

EDGAR MITCHELL: Yep. Yep.

MURPHY: Nice guy, but there he's—he's off—he's off in the asteroid belt.

EDGAR MITCHELL: Yep.

MURPHY: Does it bother you when colleagues and friends regard the way you have thought in the last twenty years in that way?

EDGAR MITCHELL: It is always difficult when you're a pioneer.

SHRIVER: Mitchell once dreamed of being part of a manned mission to Mars, and indeed sometime before the year 2020, NASA does hope to send men back to the moon and on to Mars.

Author's note: The 2020 lunar mission was scrapped in 2010.

23

In the Shadow
of the Moon

As we have seen in previous chapters, NASA's UFO position was simply adhering to the strategy adopted by the military, vis-à-vis the Roswell (1947) and Washington (1952) incidents, as well as the conclusions of various investigations (U.S. Air Force sponsored) that declared there were no UFOs or, more precisely, that there was no threat to U.S. national security interests.

Consider the options if they had not publicly denied what the astronauts had proclaimed, that they had observed UFOs; the astronauts would have directly contradicted the whole strategy and wrecked the credibility of the U.S. government.

NASA is, after all is said and done, a government agency with a very strong military component, orientation, and structure, especially back in the 1960s. The astronauts were the best-trained *soldiers* in the service, period.

They knew what they were observing, and their reports put NASA in the uncomfortable position of having to explain them away without undermining the reputations of their astronaut corps.

This all seems obvious and transparent, in retrospect, but at the time all these contradictory reports coming from astronauts, then being refuted by NASA, simply put the public in a state of confusion.

NASA has basically kept the public confused ever since.

First, they report signs of life on Mars. Next, they issue a slight disclaimer; perhaps those signs were prematurely identified, the public is told, and those indications are then questioned. Thereafter, a new mission is proposed using more sophisticated devices, which then determine that there really might be evidence of water on Mars, but then those results are questioned and a new mission is . . . we all know the cycle.

So why were the planned further missions that would conclude with the building of a lunar base terminated? As the record indicates, though there were some notable exceptions, the manned Apollo missions fulfilled their objectives. So the public was primed for the next phase, and the vision of men living and working on the moon had been implanted.

Oddly, in the middle of the cold war and right on the heels of the intense competition between the United States and the Soviet Union in the space race to get to the moon first, the two countries apparently made up and decided on a joint venture. This fact has not been given the close scrutiny it deserves.

Let us consider this very strange alliance between two avowed enemies who were on the brink of a nuclear exchange in 1962, just ten years earlier.

Literally, out of nowhere, on May 24, 1972, hawkish U. S. president Richard M. Nixon and equally hawkish Soviet Premier Alexi Kosygin announced they had signed an agreement for a joint manned space mission. This came out of the blue amidst the cold war's arms race. They said they would put international manned spacecraft capable of docking with each other in orbit.

What? This was more unlikely than the air force suddenly admitting that Major Jesse Marcel had told the truth and that the Roswell debris was an alien artifact.

The mass media reported it as if it were the most natural thing in the world. Strange that this came immediately following *the conclusion of the manned lunar missions* that both countries had conducted. Curiously enough, both countries, which had their citizens believing that their astronauts and cosmonauts would soon be building a base on the moon, scrapped those plans without good explanations.

Not only did these cold war warriors suddenly embrace each other, quite unexpectedly, but they also went on to authorize the Apollo-Soyuz Test Project, involving the rendezvous and docking in Earth orbit of a surplus Apollo command/service module with a Soyuz spacecraft.

The mission took place in July 1975. This was the last U.S. manned space flight until the first orbital flight of a space shuttle in April 1981.

To say that these were enigmatic twists that did not fit the geopolitical reality would be an incredible understatement. What in hell was actually behind all of that? The cold war was still in progress, deeply so, if we are to believe the media reports generated by both countries during that time.

In fact, the citizens of both nations were expecting the world to end in a nuclear war. How did it come to pass that both countries suddenly had concluded, behind the scenes, that it was advisable to cooperate where space ventures were concerned?

President Jimmy Carter would be elected in 1976. He was warmly embraced in UFO proponent circles because he claimed to have personally witnessed a UFO in flight. Carter assured the public that he would get to the truth of it and fully disclose whatever he found once in office. Four years went by, but that disclosure was never made.

What did Carter learn that made him renege on his campaign promise?

Then President Ronald Reagan got elected and started portraying the Soviet Union as being the "Evil Empire," at the *very same time* the United States was involved in joint space missions with that big devil (strange to say the least). Why the duplicity on the part of both countries? The saber rattling was for public consumption, clearly.

It is obvious now that, behind the scenes, both countries had learned something from their lunar missions; whatever that was prompted the immediate cessation of lunar missions by both countries.

Instead of the proposed lunar bases that the United States and Soviet space programs were going to install, a wildly unexpected joint venture came flying, like a UFO, out of the blue. Note the date: May 1972. That year would end the manned lunar missions of both the United States and the Soviet Union. *In their places, a new era of joint cooperation for the scientific study of space ensued.*

These were fascinating and inexplicable geopolitical developments that were completely out of synch with the alleged cold war that the media were actively reporting on a daily basis.

(Side note: during the Apollo Program, NASA informed the U.S. astronauts that the Soviet spacecraft had missed [been diverted from?] from their lunar trajectory. How convenient.)

Did the mass media truly fail to notice how weird it was to be reporting on the cold war in one article and on the joint space ventures in an article alongside that one? The guys with the white hats suddenly joined hands with the guys in the black hats *to go boldly where no man has gone before* . . . and no one noticed that the whole thing did not jibe with the political reality, not at all?

Those born shortly before, during, or after these events cannot appreciate just how unlikely—at least as they were portrayed by the respective governments and media outlets—they actually were. If you were an adult then, you are probably a bit shocked and upset by looking back and considering how thoroughly we were manipulated.

Maybe the citizens of the Soviet Union were not really fooled. Soon thereafter, the Soviet Union would melt away like hot butter under a merciless New Mexico summer's day.

The Apollo mission astronauts ran into things such as artificial structures, and their UFO sightings are a certainty, established by the transmissions between Houston and the astronauts. However, the general public accepted the NASA explanation. that the two-minute silence was caused by a camera malfunction.

(I suggest that you would not agree if you read the transmission and realized that the camera operations were as important as, if not more important than, the several experiments that were conducted on the lunar surface.)

During Apollo 11, Houston brought up the quality of the images, the resolution, the lighting, and other optical features as if they were in the process of filming a major Hollywood movie—even more consideration than a film crew gives to its work. To claim that one of its cameras failed, causing the live blackout that was witnessed live by a billion people, was dishonest at best.

Then using the same lame excuse during Apollo 12 went over the top and into never-never land. Could anyone really accept the premise that a highly trained astronaut could be incompetent enough and dumb enough to point the main camera at *the sun?* Absurd. Gone was that visual documentation (how convenient, indeed).

While the Soviet space program took the early lead and had great success, their manned lunar program entirely crashed and burned. This meant the Apollo Program proved that the United States had the superior technology and that America, did indeed, win the space race.

The Soviet leadership had made public pronouncements about landing a man on the moon and establishing a lunar presence as early as 1961; serious plans were not made until several years later. Sergey Korolyov, the senior Soviet rocket engineer, was apparently more interested in launching a heavy orbital station and in manned flights to Mars and Venus. With this in mind, Korolyov began the development of the superheavy N1 rocket, with a seventy-five-ton payload.

However, in August 1964, Vladimir Nikolayevich Chelomey, a Soviet missile and aircraft engineer and designer, was told to develop a moon-flyby program with a projected first flight by the end of 1966. He was further instructed to develop the moon-landing program with a first flight by the end of 1967. However, a number of unforeseen complications delayed the implementation of the program.

The Soviets did succeed in orbiting their Luna 9 spacecraft around the moon in 1966. At that point, it was thought that cosmonaut Alexey Leonov would be the first man who would walk on the moon. Research and development of various N1 rockets and spacecraft continued.

Four N1 test launches were attempted in 1969, 1971, and 1972, and all were failures, despite engineering improvements after each crash. The second launch attempt, on July 3, 1969, just thirteen days prior to the launch of Apollo 11, was a catastrophic failure that destroyed both the rocket and the launch complex, and this delayed the N1 program for two years more.

The Soviet Luna 20 mission landed an unmanned craft on the moon on February 21, 1972. Historians who try to explain away the sudden termination of both the United States' and Soviet Union's manned lunar missions brush it aside with the following interpretation: the Soviets were so discouraged by the United States triumphantly landing men on the moon first that they just gave up.

Wrong, as the evidence shows.

The Soviets were just as rational as their American counterparts, and they knew full well that the only way to prove the concept of a base on Mars was building one on the moon first. That, in fact, is still the only logical way to proceed, and NASA has revived the plan in recent years.

Curiously, ardent anti-Commie Richard Nixon slipped across the Pacific Ocean to pay a visit to China's chairman Mao Tse-tung on

February 28, 1972, a completely unexpected event that was without precedent. Then the manned Apollo 16 mission, bound for a lunar landing, was launched on April 16.

(Next, on July 25, U.S. Health Department officials made a shocking admission [which may seem totally off the subject at this juncture]; they admitted that African-Americans were used as guinea pigs in a report they handed over titled, "Tuskegee Study of Untreated Syphilis in the Negro Male." The release of this report clearly showed that the *U. S. government can and has kept secrets* and that it conducted experiments on its own citizens without their permission.)

Anyone who thinks that Roswell or lunar findings could not be suppressed is simply wrong and ignorant of these cases.

More of that kind of evidence would follow in the 1970s and 1980s. Yet the UFO and Roswell debunkers raved on and on (and still do) about the impossibility of the government keeping secrets from the prying media and inquisitive public . . . blah, blah, blah.

The unmanned Soviet Luna 20 mission and the manned Apollo 16 mission both showed that the Soviet Union and United States were actively engaged in examining the moon right up until 1972. (There was nothing in the mass media suggesting that the lunar program was about to be terminated prior to its cessation. However, its end was nearing.)

On December 7, 1972, the Apollo 17 spacecraft (with astronauts Eugene Cernan, Ronald Evans, and Harrison Schmitt) was launched; this was the last manned lunar mission to date. As noted above, the joint United States/Soviet space program was announced in May 1972, six months earlier. Detente was still a long way off, as was the cold war thaw. In fact, that would not really happen until twenty years after the Soyuz-Apollo deal was announced.

Next, both countries not only shifted their focus from the lunar base objective, they also shifted to space shuttle–type operations.

Not surprisingly, the program formally commenced in 1972; the space shuttle was originally sold to the public as a "space truck," which would, among other things, be used to build a United States space station in low Earth orbit in the early 1990s, and then be replaced by a new vehicle.

Talk about a lowering of expectations. In one fell swoop, the "*boldly go where* . . ." proposition was turned into a meat-and-potatoes, low-orbit, truck-delivery operation.

NASA seemingly went through a transformation overnight. No more manned missions; they were replaced by robot probes, which still remain the strategy. The *Star Trek* vision came down to Earth, where it had always really been. The lunar base fantasy was not discussed much after that.

(Lest you think I am joking, the first shuttle orbiter was originally planned to be named the *Constitution,* but a massive write-in campaign from fans of the *Star Trek* television series convinced the White House to change the name to the *Enterprise.* The TV series had a lot to do with the space program.)

The space shuttles did not ignite the public imagination the way that the lunar program had. Then, two terrible tragedies—the in-flight destructions of the *Challenger* in 1986 and the *Columbia* in 2003— soon marred NASA's reputation. I contend, ironically, that NASA backed itself into a corner by disavowing the UFO phenomenon. Public interest in space exploration would have remained high if NASA had been completely open and honest from the onset.

The shuttle program was decommissioned in 2011. Now what? According to NASA, it is déjà vu all over again. We shall go back to the moon, build a base, and then travel to Mars and start setting up a manned base, perhaps in 2020. Why? You (the U. S. government) have already told us in no uncertain terms that there are no extraterrestrials around, so if there are no other more advanced civilizations out there, why should we bother?

NASA astronomers and engineers pooh-pooh the idea of extra-terrestrial visitation because of the vast distances that would have to be spanned, so why should we be confident they can solve that problem?

Killing the extraterrestrial idea has, in essence, killed public enthu-siasm about the space program. The NASA budget has plummeted since the 1960s.

What could manned missions learn that computerized space probes have not already discovered? There are huge, perhaps insurmountable obstacles to long-term space flights or interplanetary bases.

First, they require perfection since both oxygen and water have to be continuously supplied and any life-support systems breach would be lethal. One accident and the mission is doomed. Have we been able to create a perfect, foolproof technology yet?

It seems time to call NASA's bluff and to expose their public relations strategy. We are not going to have lunar or Mars bases any time in the near or intermediate future. The NASA budget has been cut in recent years, and putting together a manned spacecraft capable of sustaining a crew while they set up a base is nowhere near accomplished.

The ideas being offered by various scientists and engineers, who are eager for new contracts and grants, are silly at best. Some contend that we should get ready to leave Earth in case we ruin the planet and need to leave. Just how many spaceships would be readied to ferry how many of Earth's seven billion inhabitants? Others claim that we should go on pursuing the exploration of the solar system for the sake of science.

Why, what have we learned so far that is of earthshaking importance? The moon is different from Earth; it is gray and full of meteor craters. It is also frigid; the solar nights are long, and lunar dust would make living on it and breathing a very costly proposition. So why should we bother going there—just to make work for overqualified, underemployed NASA engineers and administrators?

The global economy is not in any shape to support manned missions or lunar bases at any time in the near future. We are not going to be gaining any military advantage by further space exploration. NASA does not have the technology to land, set up, and establish a lunar or Martian mining base.

In fact, our public research dollars could be better spent on deeper investigations of Earth's oceans rather than on continued investigations of the solar system. The recycling of the notion of establishing a lunar base at this time borders on senility. If NASA is not careful, this idea could backfire if not carried out by 2020. Not all of us out here have short memories. (As of this book's release, that mission has been scrapped, though NASA has not come clean about the reasons.)

CONCLUSION

In fact, the record shows that NASA was planning to return to the moon after the successful Apollo missions. However, that plan was derailed by as yet unidentified factors. Now the notion is being recycled, but in doing so the agency is putting its reputation and neck on the line. If there is no follow-through, the space agency will continue to shrink and decline.

· · · · · · · · ·

DNA, ABO Genetics, the Genome Project, Clones, Chimeras, Hybrids, and the Genetic Insertion Event

24

The Genetics of the ABO Blood Groups

Type O negative blood (red cells) can be transfused to patients of all blood types. It is always in great demand and often in short supply.

Type AB positive plasma can be transfused to patients of all other blood types. AB plasma is also usually in short supply.

Type O negative blood is needed in emergencies before the patient's blood type is known and with newborns who need blood.

About forty-five percent of people in the U.S. have Type O (positive or negative) blood. This percentage is higher among Hispanics—57 percent, and among African Americans—51 percent.

AMERICAN RED CROSS,
"BLOOD FACTS AND STATISTICS"

ABO GENETICS

We are all subject to the laws of nature, and chief among these are the laws of genetics, which are definitely superior to the laws made by humans. Each of us is controlled, to a large extent, by the unique genetic blueprint that is stamped into our cells. That biological plan has many instructions that must be obeyed; the penalty for not doing so can be sickness or death.

The most basic laws of genetics involve those contained in our blood groups.

There are four main ABO blood type groupings: A, B, AB, and O. These blood groups are determined by the antigen on the blood cell surface and the antibodies present in the blood plasma. If you are human, then you have one of these four blood types.

Our blood groups, especially the ABO and Rh blood types, fall into the above categories. In modern times, we have come to know our own particular ABO blood group (A, B, O, or AB); many of us also know whether we are Rh positive or Rh negative.

We have learned these things because this knowledge can be essential for healthy childbearing, a vibrant and disease-free life, and even survival.

While we are going to briefly examine the genetics of the ABO and Rh system for the sake of general knowledge, I have a greater purpose, of course, and that is to investigate it as it pertains to human origins.

Though the ABO blood group story can get complicated, in fact, the fundamentals are well within the layperson's grasp. You do not need to be a geneticist to comprehend the basics. In my view, without an understanding of this information, we simply do not know some of the most important biological data there are to know about ourselves, other humans, and our history.

Although most DNA is packaged in chromosomes within the cell nucleus, mitochondria, which are rod-shaped structures within cells that convert oxygen and nutrients into power for the cells, also have a small amount of their own DNA. This genetic material is known as mitochondrial DNA (mtDNA). (For more details on mtDNA, see chapter 25, page 287.)

Long before the human genome was unraveled and mtDNA became the rage, the ABO blood group system was discovered by Austrian scientist Karl Landsteiner in 1900. This marked a very important step in human development and survival because it allowed medical science to save lives through blood transfusions and, later, when medical technology improved, organ transplants.

Prior ignorance of the distinct differences between individuals in different blood groups resulted in severe illness, miscarriages, and infant mortality. Before this discovery, people simply assumed that all human beings shared the same blood.

However, the discovery of the ABO system showed that was an erroneous view; after the blood groups were studied it became clear that there were small but very significant genetic differences in human blood types.

For example, the type O, Rh negative mother who, in the past, tried to carry and give birth to a baby with type O, Rh positive blood often suffered a miscarriage, still birth, or infant mortality. This was a serious complication in Europe, where type O negative blood appears with a significant frequency in the overall population distribution.

For the moment, as a way of example, we will assume your blood is type A. That means that your antigens will recognize type A blood as "self" but will identify type B blood as alien. Not only will your immune system make that identification, it also will try to prevent the invader blood from mixing with your blood.

This is why your blood type becomes a critical issue if you need a transfusion. The hospital has to determine that you are a type A person first, then make sure you get blood from either another person with type A blood or from a person with type O blood.

Now it starts getting a little more complicated.

Type A blood reacts to type B by clotting (and vise versa with B to A), which can cause serious medical problems, even death. It will react to type AB blood in the same way. However, a type A person can receive a transfusion from a type O person. That is so because the latter blood type lacks the A and B antigens, and that means it is the *universal donor* blood type.

A type O person can give blood to people with all the other blood types. But types A and B people can only receive blood from their own or a type O donor, whereas type AB people can receive blood from an A, B, or O person; which makes them the universal recipients.

Now we have to add another factor that adds to the complexity of the situation a bit more. While there are four main blood groups, there is also another blood group antigen, located on red blood cell surfaces. It is known as the Rhesus factor (Rh factor), and this antigen is either present or absent (Rh positive or Rh negative, respectively).

While you are a basic type A person, you are also either Rh positive or Rh negative. In fact, the hospital needs to know the Rh status just as much as it does the ABO data. Why? If you have type A negative blood, you can only receive blood from another type A negative person or an O negative person.

A person who is Rh negative will produce antibodies against Rh positive blood cells if exposed to them. Exposure can be due to a blood transfusion with Rh positive blood or a pregnancy in which the Rh negative mother has an Rh positive infant in her womb.

The same is not true with Rh positive blood. If you have type A positive blood, you can receive blood from a person with type A negative or O negative blood. The Rh positive blood type does not attack the Rh negative blood, as the latter does the former. So an Rh positive mother can carry an Rh negative fetus without any problems.

This body of knowledge may seem of academic interest only until you get to the emergency room and have to receive a blood transfusion or need an organ transplant. Then it becomes critical (even life-saving) genetic knowledge that you will be grateful for.

Every human being is either Rh positive or Rh negative; this is really the main genetic division where human ABO blood group distribution is concerned. Why do people have different blood groups?

Shouldn't we all have the same blood group and Rh type if we originated in Africa from a single ancestral mother (mtDNA Eve) in whom the Rh factor occurred? If not, where did this difference originate?

Anti-A antibodies are hypothesized to originate from an immune response toward an *influenza* type virus; anti-B antibodies are hypothesized to originate from antibodies produced against gram-negative *bacteria,* such as *E. coli.*

It appears that the A and B blood groups developed to reduce the transmission of viruses and bacteria within a human population. This possibility suggests that individuals in a human population supply and make a diversity of unique antibodies to fend off invading antigens (i.e., viruses and bacteria) so as to keep the population as a whole more resistant to infection.

On the other hand, it may be that the force driving evolution of blood group diversity is that cells with rare variants of membrane antigens are more easily distinguished by the immune system from pathogens carrying antigens from other hosts. Thus, individuals possessing rarer types (A, B, AB) are better equipped to detect pathogens.

The high within-population diversity observed in human populations would then be a consequence of natural selection on individuals. Note that while humans have four basic blood groups, chimpanzees are virtually type A homogenous, and gorillas are type B only.

From this, it is apparent that people who are types O negative and AB positive are, in effect, opposites, as the former can be the universal donor and the latter can receive blood from any other blood group. The fact that the vast majority of people are Rh positive and a minority is Rh negative further reinforces the probability that humanity evolved in diverse regions and not just one: Africa.

We can envision that at some point in human evolution there were splits between at least two and probably more human groups. In all probability, one group in Africa was exposed to the Rh factor and reacted to it; in a different locale another group, the type O negative population, was not exposed to it, so the Rh negative group does not have that genetic trigger.

This has far-reaching implications as regards human history and the evolution of different human populations.

The Rh negative population lacks the gene composition that Rh positive people possess, which means their blood is more neutral and the other groups do not react to it with antibodies. However, the reverse is not likewise true.

Before delving into that issue, we need to return to the basic ABO distinctions with the Rh factor added to them. Now we see that a type A negative person can give blood to a type A positive or another A negative person, but a type A positive person cannot donate blood to an A negative person.

Next, type B negative individuals can give blood to type B positive or B negative individuals, but a B positive person cannot give blood to a B negative person; likewise an O negative person can give blood to an O positive or another O negative person but an O positive person cannot give blood to an O negative individual.

For instance, to reinforce a scenario presented above, we can envision that the type A blood group was exposed to a certain *virus,* which caused the bodies of people in that group to react by creating specific antibodies to fight off the invader.

Likewise, the type B blood group did the same in another environment to a different *bacterial* invader. This resulted in two distinct blood groups that have basic antibody incompatibilities.

In fact, those incompatibilities are so great that people with different blood types can neither give nor receive blood to or from one another, even if the donor and recipient are from the same family.

Of course, this does not mean that type A and type B blood is so different that such people cannot marry and reproduce and have healthy offspring; they can. However, on the ABO level they cannot give or receive blood to or from each other.

The ABO blood groups represent profound genetic differences in the human population that must be taken into consideration. In fact, these differences mean that even members of the same family cannot cross these genetic ABO blood barriers.

Now, since types A and B represent mutations, then type O must represent the ancestral blood group that existed prior to these mutations. The O allele (a variant form of a gene) occurs most frequently in modern humans. It carries a human-specific *inactivating deletion* that produces a nonfunctional enzyme at the point along the gene sequence in a DNA molecule where functional enzymes are produced by people with types A and B alleles.

In a sense, type O positive blood is inactive (or silent), whereas types A positive and B positive blood are reactive.

Therefore, a person with O positive blood can be a donor to someone with either A or B positive blood, but those with types A positive and B positive cannot give blood to a person who is O positive.

In effect, type O positive blood has a simpler molecular structure than either A positive or B positive blood. Then when we bring type O negative into the picture, we see that it represents an even simpler molecular model in that it also lacks the Rh factor.

So we can now appreciate why the type O negative person is the only *universal blood donor;* it is due to the fact that this is the most stripped-down blood type, in genetic terms, offering no mutations for the antibodies or the Rh factor to react to.

In April 2007, an international team of researchers announced in the journal *Nature Biotechnology* an inexpensive and efficient way to convert types A negative, B negative, and AB negative blood into type O negative.

This was achieved by using glycosidase enzymes from specific bacteria to strip the *blood group antigens* from red blood cells. However, they noted that removal of *A and B antigens* still did not address the problem of the Rh blood group antigen.

Now let us focus on the population genetics of the basic Rh factor. An Rh negative mother carrying an Rh positive fetus causes major problems. The type O negative blood of the mother will react to the Rh positive fetus by treating it as a "nonself" (very much as if it were an alien invader).

This can result in hemolytic disease, which can be fatal for the fetus or newborn. It was not an uncommon experience for women in Europe, where type O negative blood was and still is more common than anywhere else on Earth.

This is, in part, why our collective memory recalls the concern that every birth evoked prior to the twentieth century, the reaction of an Rh negative mother to an Rh positive fetus. From this, it becomes apparent that the Rh factor is the genetic barrier that points to a significant division in the human population. Why?

While the type A and B blood groups are divergent, the Rh positive members of both groups can receive blood from similar Rh positive people as well as their Rh negative counterparts. But the Rh negative people cannot receive blood from the Rh positive people. This makes the Rh positive gene dominant. Of course, this is also true of type O positive genes.

We saw above that the type O negative mother could not successfully carry and give birth to a type O positive baby; however, a type O positive mother can carry and successfully give birth to a healthy baby of either Rh group.

This gives a great advantage to the transmission of Rh positive genes, while conferring distinct evolutionary disadvantages to the type O negative blood group.

In addition, the A and B antigens and antibodies have advantages over both type O positive and negative blood groups. Types A, B, and AB positive are more resistant to certain environmental pathogens because they are mutations that occurred in response to certain pathogens. Therefore, they are codominants, making the latter blood group recessive. This too presents some enigmas where human history and evolution are concerned, which we will examine shortly.

In sum, to this point we have seen that the high rate of differentiation in the human ABO blood group gene seems to be related to susceptibility to different pathogens (viruses, bacteria, etc.). It has been estimated that all genetic variation underlying the human ABO alleles appeared along the human lineage, *after the divergence* from the chimpanzee lineage.

This means that the human ABO blood group mutations came about after the alleged branching off of protohumans from the chimpanzee lineage. If this scenario is accurate, then we are not nearly as similar to chimpanzees or other great apes as evolutionary geneticists would have us believe.

Why do I make that assertion?

Chimpanzees are almost all type A, never B, and virtually never O. We humans are mostly type O, slightly lesser A, with an even smaller frequency of B, and a fourth blood group, type AB, which neither chimps nor gorillas display at all. Gorillas are strictly type B.

As we learned above, type O is the result of a recessive gene that is rather quickly displaced by the genes for types A and B, since they are codominant. We can see that in the chimpanzee population, where type O is a mere remnant since type A displaced type O in succeeding generations over time.

If we descended directly from a common ancestor along with chimpanzees, down the great ape genetic pathway, then why is type O our major group to this day?

This has confounded genetic biologists for some time.

Our ABO blood groups differ from those of chimpanzees; though their blood grouping also uses the ABO nomenclature, none of our blood groups could be exchanged for the blood of chimps.

In addition, we also cannot interbreed due to our mismatched chromosomes. A chromosome is the basic stuff of cells, an organized structure of DNA and proteins housed in cells. It comes as a single piece of coiled DNA containing many genes, regulatory elements, and other nucleotide sequences. Chromosomes also contain DNA-bound proteins, which serve to package the DNA and control its functions.

While evolutionary geneticists try to emphasize how close we are to chimpanzees by pointing to our similar number of chromosomes, forty-six for humans to forty-eight for chimps, in fact, this allegedly small difference prevents us from interbreeding.

We are obviously not as close to our so-called primate cousins as horses are to donkeys or lions to tigers, which can interbreed.

It is obvious that one or two chromosomes and several major ABO divergences represent a huge amount of information and not the insignificant amount inferred by evolutionists.

If we were so similar, then our blood group distribution pattern should be in relative synch since we, supposedly, came from a common ancestor. But we cannot share blood nor can we interbreed and produce offspring. Are we being lied to by our scientists about being virtual "humanzees"?

Now, for the time, please forget the history you have been taught that claimed that (1) we all came out of Africa, and (2) Native American populations originated in Asia. Why? Because those ideas do not square with the known ABO and Rh factor genetics facts given above.

If type O blood is from a recessive gene and humans branched off from a common ancestor shared with chimps, then why do the latter display virtual homogenous type A blood, while we humans are largely type O? And no other primates display Rh negative blood, by the way.

Trying to claim, which some evolutionary biologists do, that type O blood actually confers some survival advantages does not explain how it has cheated its recessive status and overcome the A-B codominance factor. (They can argue this if they want to also argue that modern humans arose no more than five thousand years ago.)

The out-of-Africa or Bering Strait theories present problems that defy not only the rules of common, deductive logic, but also the rules of genetics and population statistics.

Since the O gene is recessive, the only way to have type O blood is to have an O father and an O mother (OO); both parents have to have it. The A and B genes are dominant, so AA and AO blood types both give the offspring type A blood; similarly, BB and BO both yield type B blood.

So ancestors with the combination AO and BO would yield the

following expected values for the prevalence of types A, B, AB, and O blood:

A: 5/16

B: 5/16

AB: 1/8

O: 1/4

These genetic values make it clear that types A, B, and AB will be transmitted about 75 percent of the time. So how did an Asian population that had a high percentage of types A and B (OA, OB) supposedly migrate to the Americas to produce a Native American population that was virtually absent those two blood groups? Did only one OO couple float across the Pacific on a raft to populate all the Americas?

In fact, no matter what the genetic situation, type O blood should be rarer than A or B. In fact, we see no such thing: type O blood is the most common human blood type worldwide.

Different populations vary, but almost half the world's people have type O blood, roughly a little more than a third have type A, an eighth or so have type B, and about four percent have type AB.

This means that their type O positive homogeneity shows that the precontact Central and South American populations had been in isolation from other human populations. This explains why they lacked the antibodies necessary to fend off the contagious diseases that Europeans brought from Europe.

Disease, and not warfare, is what killed off native populations for the most part.

Moreover, we have a five-hundred-year, unplanned, natural laboratory experiment that further calls the two theories on the carpet. When Europeans began colonizing Central and South America in the sixteenth century, the indigenous population was virtually 100 percent blood group O positive.

This has been shown to still be the case in native populations that resisted intermarriage or remained isolated until recently.

However, native peoples, like the Aztecs and others in central and northern Mexico, did mix with Europeans to produce a largely Mestizo (mixed) population. Today, that mixed population displays about the same ABO/Rh factor distribution pattern as the people of Europe do (type O: 45 percent, A: 38 percent, and B: 10 percent). That proves just how quickly types A and B displace type O.

Some very torturous and improbable logic has to be used to get an African population carrying O and A alleles to Asia, then an Asian population carrying A and B alleles across the Pacific without finding any A or B codominant alleles in the migrating population.

(It does not matter what the newer mtDNA evidence that is used to support these theories claims to show; the blood group data sit on a priority position in the gene pool.)

The indigenous population of Central and South America had fixed type O positive dominance prior to contact with European populations. It only required five hundred years of intermarriage to dilute type O from 100 percent dominance to less than 50 percent, which is exactly what the A and B codominant mathematics would predict.

Clearly, type O would not have been homogenous if this native population had had any type of contact with either Africa or Asia. The theories that today dance around the science of ABO genetics by using mtDNA studies and ignore the more reliable ABO/Rh factor genetics fall apart under the filter of the latter.

Several more sharply conflicted issues remain.

How has type O remained dominant in the global human population if it was in the ancestral blood group? If the ABO distribution dates back even several tens of thousands of years, then types A and B should have displaced O to the remnant level, or very near that fractional frequency, that we already see in chimpanzees.

Next, an equally enigmatic issue revolves around the Rh factor: where did type O negative come into the picture? This question has long plagued biologists and anthropologists.

As we have seen, Rh positive is the dominant gene by far. In fact, the global distribution of type O negative today actually masks the historic genetic background of this blood group.

The O negative blood type did not exist in the indigenous populations of sub-Saharan Africa, Asia, or the Americas; *it did not exist at all.*

The O negative blood type is truly an outlier blood group that is difficult to account for. While the general literature claims that about 15 percent of the human population is Rh negative, that is an average that actually hides the reality. Most of the world's populations have less than 1 percent who are Rh negative, while Europe and the countries that were colonized by Europeans five hundred years ago show frequencies from 6 percent to as high as 35 percent.

(Moreover, the 15 percent figure that is still used today actually came out of research conducted seventy years ago. If you carefully examine the Rh factor numbers kept in blood bank graphs, you will find they are closer to a 10 percent average frequency today.)[1]

In fact, blood type Rh negative is very concentrated among Europeans (especially Basques) and a few North African peoples (Berbers, Canary Islanders); O negative, therefore, is the least likely to have prevailed.

How can this radical departure from the rest of the human population be explained? It cannot be accounted for using the conventional out-of-Africa hypothesis.

This could only have occurred if the O negative population spent a long period in isolation, as the pure type O positive population did in the Americas—separated from the O positive, A positive, B positive, and AB positive populations.

The narrow locus of type O negative suggests that this was the case. Since the Basque population predates the Indo-European population in Europe and the Basques still retain a 30 percent type O negative frequency, then it must have been far higher in the remote past.

Clearly, the Basques are culturally, linguistically, and genetically different from the other European cultures, a fact established long ago. They predate the rest of the population of Europe by thousands of years. Yet despite contact and intermarriage, they still retain a high level of type O negative blood, whereas, the Inca and Bororo indigenous populations of South America have 100 percent type O positive and zero percent type O negative blood types, even today.

Next, the Berbers are also a distinct population in North Africa. Though they have become more and more assimilated into the Arab culture over the past seven hundred years, like the Basques, the Berbers retain a strong sense of autonomy and distance from other cultural groups.

What is of great interest is that some Berbers still show seemingly Caucasian-type traits such as blond or red hair, fair skin, and even blue or green eyes.

(In ancient times, the people of North Africa were referred to as the Atlantoi or the Atlantes by the Greeks, who also cast them as outliers.)

The Berbers also display a high Rh negative frequency today, about the same as the Basques, a 25 to 35 percent distribution. Just as fascinating are the inhabitants of the Canary Islands, which lie off the northwest coast of Africa, close to southern Europe and Morocco.

Spanish sailors landed on the Canary Islands in the fourteenth century and found an indigenous population of people who resembled other Europeans. (They called themselves Guanches.) However, they spoke a dialect related to Amazigh, which the Berbers speak. This native group had built a step pyramid, and they practiced mummification of their dead.

The sailors were mystified by this unknown race of people, who resembled them in appearance yet were not Europeans. Blood group ABO studies of the mummies and of the modern population showed that they also had a high level of type O negative blood, up to 35 percent.

A world map depicting the ABO/Rh blood group data shows that the locus of the Rh negative group is in the region of southwestern Europe and northwestern Africa, including the Canary Islands. This is a small geographic spot on the globe, a tiny dot really.

From this region, the Rh negative blood group radiates outward in all directions.

This is obviously a great historical enigma given the present hypothesis, the out-of-Africa and out-of-Asia theories. Even today, native African people who have never married outside of their tribes do not display any Rh negative blood.

Not surprisingly, the populations of Western Europe display the next highest frequencies of type O negative blood. The distribution steadily drops off in Asia and approaches near zero in eastern Asia. It also drops off steeply in sub-Saharan Africa. Then, as we have noted previously, it never existed in the Americas until the postcolonization era.

It would appear that the Basque, Berber, and Canary Island populations, who all share the highest frequencies of type O negative blood in the world by far and are known to be cultural outliers, once existed in near total isolation, as did those people who had type O positive blood in the Americas.

Remove these populations and the rest of Europe and the countries where European colonization occurred from the global ABO Rh factor distribution averages, and the type O negative group drops radically to less than 1 percent.

This blood group represents a gene pattern that is so recessive to the A positive and B positive codominant types that it simply should not exist at all in modern times, and probably would not save for colonization, and will not in another five hundred to one thousand years.

Every individual stands a 1 in 4 chance of inheriting the O positive blood type, a 7.5 in 10 chance of inheriting an A, B, or AB group, and a less than 6 in 100 chance of inheriting the Rh negative gene, depending on where one lives in the world. You stand an almost zero chance of inheriting the Rh negative gene if you are a member of an indigenous tribe in Central or South America or sub-Saharan Africa.

We have to add the Rh negative blood group to the isolated O positive homogenous blood group of the Americas, as another population that was once isolated from the populations that were predominantly O, A, and B positive.

The latter populations, in ancient times, were in sub-Saharan Africa, Asia, the Middle East, and Europe.

So where did type O negative originate if not Europe as we know it today?

It was most likely the ancestral blood group of a population that existed in geographical isolation. Type O negative blood is so recessive to the other blood groups and to Rh positive blood that it could not have survived long in a mixed population.

The mere existence of this blood group strongly supports Plato's history of Atlantis, as that would explain both why these groups are all on the Atlantic and where the isolation occurred.

Rather than a single population carrying type O positive and type A positive blood out of Africa to Asia, where the type B mutation was added, and then having that ABO mixed population migrating to the Americas, we will examine another possibility.

Let us assume that there were several genesis events that caused the type O positive blood group to appear. One took place in the Americas, another in sub-Saharan Africa, and a third involved an O negative implant.

The out-of-Africa migration eastward ended in a mixed Asian population that produced and added the type B mutation to the mix. That
meant that both Africa and Asia had the ABO distribution long ago.
But that mixed population did not carry their ABO gene pool to the
Americas.

Remember, it took only five hundred years of intermixing to clone
the European ABO distribution pattern into the mixed modern population of Mexico. That meant a 50 percent reduction in type O positive
and the complete insertion of A and B as well as Rh negative blood
types in that time frame.

(I do not care what the mtDNA evidence is supposed to show; I cat-
egorically dispute those interpretations since they are at complete odds
with the more critical and reliable ABO data. We shall examine more
reasons in the next chapter.)

Now we have two outlier groups, one type O positive (Americas)
and one type O negative (unknown), to account for. Neither could have
been in contact with any mixed ABO group for an extended period.
Then we must assume that they were both isolated populations. What
do those two groups have in common, if anything?

The Maya and Aztecs claimed that they originally arrived in
Central America from a land to the east. The Aztecs called that land
Aztlan, coincidentally enough. The Canary Islanders told the early
European explorers that they were refugees from some greater islands
that once existed to their west.

Other European cultural groups, mostly along the western coastal
regions of Europe, also claim to be from other lands that vanished
long ago.

The Aztec city of Tenochtitlan, now Mexico City, was said to have
been built on the civic plan of that culture's ancient, lost empire. How
was it laid out? An artificial lake was first constructed. Then bridges
were built to connect the roadways that led in and out of the city. Each
house had direct access to a complex canal system.

In fact, it sounds remarkably similar to Plato's description of the
supposedly mythical land of Atlantis.

Would it not, in fact, be entirely logical for the oldest surviving cultural groups in southwestern Europe and northwestern Africa to have
fled an isolated group of islands to settle in the lands closest to them?

Would the same not also be true for the Maya and Aztecs on the western side of the Atlantic? Of course it would!

It has been easy for the proponents of the *out-of-Africa* and *Bering land crossing* theories to dismiss the whole lost continent theory, skirt around the ABO blood group enigmas, and latch onto mtDNA data, which, coincidentally enough, support their theories. However, as we saw above, the ABO/Rh data are factual, are proven every day, and cannot be ignored.

In fact, the Berbers and Canary Islanders are indigenous populations of North Africa. Whoops! Even the recent mtDNA studies show that these populations are very ancient and indigenous, much to the chagrin of orthodox historians.

One would at least expect black Africans to have made it to the northern part of their own continent regardless of the Sahara; there are ways around it, given tens of thousands of years to migrate and settle the world. But the appearance of O negative blood in North Africa and the lack of it in sub-Saharan Africa derail the out-of-Africa theory.

In fact, it appears that some people came out of Africa while others did not. The ABO data suggest multiple sources of origin for various human groups.

There are only two ways that type O could predominate as it does today: (1) if the human population was split up and lived in isolation for an extended period, or (2) if the human population represents a *recent insertion* event by an external agency.

We could account for the fact that chimps and gorillas have replaced the ancestral type O blood group with the codominant A and B blood groups and humans have not, if the latter represents a genetic intervention event. But aren't we closely related to the great apes in terms of sharing such a large proportion of our genes and chromosomes? Yes, so what?

We shall address that neo-Darwinian propaganda shortly.

Consider the oral traditions of ancient human cultures that claimed that we are the product of an intervention by "gods" from the heavens. Can geneticists rule this out by resorting to any branch of science, including microbiology, physics, or astronomy? No, they cannot.

In fact, does the Bible not say that "gods," an advanced race, created human beings? It most certainly does, and it does so in the first chapter of Genesis. It does not say that a singular God created humans; it says, "Let us create them in Our image and likeness."

The very concept of God means a singularity, not an "Our," not a plurality. The Old Testament always switches to the plural when referring to the beings that intervened in human development in Genesis.

Perhaps geneticists are more caught up in their own cultural baggage than they realize. Nowhere does the Bible evoke the concept of a miracle when it comes to human generation.

It is quite specific, and it should be interpreted in terms of our understanding of genetics today, not the lack of understanding that generations have approached the Bible with in the past.

In fact, Genesis 1 refers to the first act of genetic intervention, when an ancestral race was created to inhabit Earth and "eat the herbs and fruits" that the earth freely provided. Is this not a clear reference to the earliest, primitive, premodern human types (Neanderthals), which were not even hunters but, like other great apes, largely gatherers?

Please reread Genesis without the interpretations overlaid on it by many generations of traditional misinterpretation. Note that the humans are created, male and female, not Adam first and then Eve, which happens in the next chapter, Genesis 2.

At the end of chapter three, Adam and Eve (the new prototypes) become the forerunners of modern, crop-and-agriculture-based civilization. That is the true distinction that is made between the earliest humans, who gathered and subsisted on plants, fruits, and nuts, and the next genetically engineered humans, who were told they must plow the earth and plant seeds and harvest crops.

I am not making this up; that is what the Old Testament actually says in no uncertain terms. There were at least two genetically engineered human types. Each embraced a different way of earning a living.

The first race was a hybrid of the advanced race and a great ape species, probably the ancestral type O group that predated the chimpanzee lineage. This hybrid died out, which is not at all inconsistent with the scenario envisioned by anthropologists. The modern human hybrid was inserted into several branches at different points around the globe.

The Bible (only one of many ancient texts that include this kind of information) goes on to tell how the offspring of this advanced race, *the sons of the gods,* interbred with human females, producing a distinctly alien subrace (Genesis 6:1–9). It also tells how this advanced race intervened to prevent humans from evolving a homogenous civilization (Tower of Babel) too early (Genesis 11:1–9).

When read through technologically informed eyes, the Old Testament becomes a history of early human and nonhuman genetics. No document is more careful about tracing bloodlines than the Talmud or the Old Testament. That even crosses over into the New Testament, where it is made very clear that Christ is a direct descendant of the King David lineage.

In fact, when the obsolete, pretechnological interpretations are discarded, what is Genesis but a history of how one group of people was selected to completely expunge the genetics of several other groups after the Flood?

The ancient Hebrews were told, in no uncertain terms, to spare not a single inhabitant, not even women and children; all were to be exterminated.

The Dogons of Northern Africa relate a different extraterrestrial intervention, from a people called the Nommo, as do other cultures, including the Sumerians, who allegedly created the first civilization on Earth.

Is it possible that an advanced race genetically created several different human hybrids that were crosses between their own genetics and those of the great apes? Yes. There is nothing in the science of genetics that precludes this possibility.

In fact, the astronomical data strongly suggest that such a civilization should exist out there in the infinite reaches of space, as was shown in the early chapters of this volume.

The genetic anomalies noted above can be addressed and resolved by inserting the activities of an outside, quasi-human population intervening to direct human (and planetary-wide) genetic development.

CONCLUSION

The ABO/Rh blood groups present a situation that is directly at odds with several conventional theories about human origins and historical migrations. The existence of a pure type O positive population in the

Americas contradicts the Asian migration theory, and the existence of a type O negative population in southern Europe and North Africa contradicts the out-of-Africa theory.

The genetics underlying the ABO blood groups is superior, in importance, to the mtDNA data, which are now being used to shore up those theories, while the enigmatic ABO data have been shoved aside.

25
Genome Project Revelations

Several orthodox explanations of the universality of the genetic code can be suggested, but none is generally accepted to be completely convincing. It is a little surprising that organisms with somewhat different codes do not coexist.

FRANCIS CRICK AND L. E. ORGEL

As noted in the previous chapter, mitochondria within cells have their own mitochondrial DNA (mtDNA).

There are approximately twenty-three thousand genes in the human genome, well within the same range as in mice, roundworms, mammals, and primates. Scientists tell us that understanding how these genes express themselves will provide clues to how diseases are caused.

Here are some rather anomalous facts about the genome.

1. The genetic code is fairly uniform; though biologists thought that the human genome would be four to five times larger than that of other species to account for human complexity, the number of genes in a genome does not correlate to the complexity of the species.

2. The human genome has significantly more segmental duplications (nearly identical, repeated sections of DNA) than do other mammalian genomes. These sections may underlie the creation of new primate-specific genes.

3. In 2003, when the first version of the report of the genome sequence was published, less than 7 percent of protein families appeared to be vertebrate specific.

The Human Genome Project was started in 1989 with the goal of decoding the human genome by sequencing and identifying all of the approximately 3.3 billion base pairs—that is, the chemical units in the human genetic instruction set—finding the genetic roots of disease, and then developing treatments. With the report of the sequence in hand, the next step was to identify the genetic variants that increase the risk for common diseases like cancer and diabetes.

Project scientists used white blood cells from the blood of two male and two female donors (randomly selected from twenty of each), with each donor yielding a separate DNA library. One of these libraries (RP11) was used considerably more than others, due to quality considerations.

One minor technical issue is that male samples contain just over half as much DNA from the sex chromosomes (one X chromosome and one Y chromosome) compared with female samples (which contain two X chromosomes). The other twenty-two chromosome pairs (the autosomes) are the same for both sexes.

All of this recent work began when Francis Crick and James Dewey Watson codiscovered the shape of the DNA molecule in 1950. That was an amazing breakthrough at that time. However, less than forty years thereafter, it was announced that a far more incredible undertaking was going to take place, the mapping of the human genome (which begat the Human Genome Project).

By 2003, the first rough draft of the genome sequence was finished. It was an almost unbelievable accomplishment coming so soon after the rather basic, by way of comparison, discovery that Crick and Watson had made.

During the intervening years—from the time of the project announcement to the rough draft being made public—people on both sides of the evolution versus creation debate waited anxiously to see what story our human genes would tell when scientists finally deciphered their secret language.

Before the Human Genome Project, some microbiologists had estimated that the known *three billion or so DNA letters* combined to form a hundred thousand or more genes. However, Christopher Wills, professor emeritus at the University of California, San Diego, says:

> But the amazing thing is that there are much fewer genes in the human genome than expected [only about twenty thousand to twenty-five thousand], which means that each gene has to be very sophisticated in what it does.[1]

Because the number of DNA letters per gene is limited, the new, lower gene count made clear that about 98.5 percent of our DNA seemingly had little or nothing to do with genes; it was *junk DNA*, as some scientists called it.

When the results were published, neo-Darwinians were shocked. Ironically, the head of the Human Genome Project, Francis Collins, was not a Darwinist but a devout Christian.

The discovery that the approximately twenty-three thousand genes in human beings were in the same range as those in mice and roundworms came as a humbling surprise. That was a not-so-flattering fact, and it was not at all anticipated because of our "superior" brains.

Evolutionary microbiologists were surprised to learn that the human genome was not the long, much more complicated code they had predicted; not only that, they soon learned that it was not even substantially different from the codes of various plant species.

So the notion that "size matters" was quickly tossed out by geneticists. Apparently, the number of genes was not the good predictor of the complexity of a species that they had envisioned it would be.

The focus then shifted to the great similarities that existed between the human and chimpanzee genomes. That became the battle cry of evolutionists then and still is to this day. Of course, creationists took their humbling when it was revealed that the chimp and human genomes only differed by a mere 2 to 3 percent.

However, I submit that the concept of similarity is misplaced and taken way too far by Darwinian microbiologists and other scientists who share their philosophy. Why?

If we look at the animal classification referred to as mammalian, we will find creatures that have many things in common, such as eyes, ears, mouths, teeth, noses, lungs, hearts, and so forth. This entire very large kingdom shares certain characteristics that make them mammals. We humans have those same features, so we can say that we are a similar species but mean it in a very general way.

In fact, most mammals share at least 85 percent of their genomes with humans.

Using the figure 98 percent makes it sound like we are so close to being the same as chimpanzees that it is a virtual certainty that we emerged from the same ancestor. But wait a minute. Perhaps most of the 90 percent is also shared by other mammals and especially other great apes as well (93–95 percent).

In fact, that is true. We could also say that we are genetically very similar to gorillas, about 95 percent, and even horses and dolphins, more than 90 percent for both species.

That calls the entire meaning of the statistical comparison methodology into question.

By using this method, geneticists have made several assumptions that might not be valid. First, they assume that they have examined and understood all of the important details of different genomes and made one-to-one, side-by-side comparisons of each gene in the entire genome sequence. They have not done so.

The second assumption is that the 2 to 3 percent difference is of lesser importance than the 97 percent similarity. Is it?

In fact, it is apparent—due to the relative uniformity of the genetic code—that up to a point the code is like a template, a foundational framework that does not mean much, in terms of speciation, until the final speciation genes responsible for divergence are added.

Since the human and chimpanzee genomes are very similar up to a point, then the genes that make up the uniformity are not nearly as pivotal and potent as the genes that give expression to the two distinct species (chimps and humans).

As Wills noted above, "Each gene has to be very sophisticated in what it does."

Keep in mind that when the genomes were first deciphered, geneticists considered a sizable portion of the code to be nonfunctional *junk*. Wrong.

Time has shown the geneticists that their original perception was erroneous, and they have since learned that their assessment of some genes as being junk was, in fact, just a reflection of their own ignorance. The so-called junk genes play a functional, regulatory role in the genetic code.

When a geneticist tries to argue the case for neo-Darwin theories by using the apparent similarity of the human and chimp genomes, I respond with the following: please explain then why you are studying chimpanzee DNA while they are eating bananas in the forest like they have for millions of years.

If we are so close to being the same, then why do humans act more like social insects by clustering together in vast cities, like hives, while chimps live in extended family clans of fewer than a dozen individuals?

Humans have a definite herd instinct that goes beyond just being social animals, which chimps are, too. However, chimps do not try to mass together to form insect-like hives, which humans have done all over the planet. Not only that, chimps are environmentally and habitat stable; we humans are the most *unstable creatures* on the planet, always seeking to venture over the next horizon.

The genome dissimilarity actually points to the issues that we should be focused on: Why are humans so radically different in their social behaviors, technological innovativeness, language, customs, migration, and violent impulses? What is it about the 2 to 3 percent of the genetic code that differs so much from that of animals that it makes humans want to go to Mars, meddle with plant and animal genes, and in engage in mass murder (i.e., warfare)?

Let us examine the human race through a different lens: *males and females.*

This examination definitely prevents this presentation from slipping into a mere academic debate and keeps the discussion real. A man shares about 97 percent of his genes with a woman. That's right. Even on an intraspecies level, we are not the same, though we are very similar, of course.

All embryos start out female.

Different creatures have different ways of determining sex. However, in the mammal kingdom, sex is determined by genetics. A handful of Y chromosome genes cause maleness by turning on a few biochemical switches during the early gestation period. *This is universal in all mammals.*

It means that, if you are male, the basic genes that made you male extend back to the earliest mammal species, if not earlier. In regard to those genes, *you are closer to a male rabbit or horse than you are to a female human.* You see, this whole similarity thing is very much a matter of which information you select to focus your attention on.

Does that mean that human males are closer to rabbits and horses than to human females? Of course, that is not the case. It means that in one *narrow* context the genes that determine the male sex traits are more similar to those in males of other mammal species than to females of the same species. But only in that very limited context.

As noted above, all fetuses start as female, and a handful of Y chromosome genes causes the fetus to turn into a male. What is more important: the fact that females and males are both human or the fact that the former has the capability to reproduce either sex? Are the similarities important, or are the dissimilarities that define how a male differs from a female, and the reverse, of equal or even greater significance?

It is all a matter of perspective.

Chimps and horses do not speak English, nor do they feel the need to learn to read Stephen King novels. Does that mean they share a close genetic bond? Some humans also do not speak English, nor do they read horror fiction. Should we put them in the chimp or horse category, too?

Levity aside, this whole genetic arena has an important underlying reality to it, of course. But if we are not careful, that reality can be distorted and tweaked to mean just about anything anyone wants it to.

THE CHROMOSOME BARRIER

Now that we have established some caveats and ground rules, let us proceed to objectively find out what it is that makes us human and chimpanzees themselves. First, one of the initial findings in the field of genetics was the fact that humans have *one fewer pair of chromosomes* than do the great apes.

As noted in the previous chapter, we humans have twenty-three pairs of chromosomes, and chimpanzees and gorillas have twenty-four pairs, forty-six and forty-eight chromosomes in total, respectively.

Chromosomes are of paramount importance because they are the vectors of heredity. The ABO and Rh blood groups are defined in them.

In humans, they can be divided into two types: *autosomes and sex chromosomes*. Certain genetic traits are linked to a person's sex and are passed on through the sex chromosomes. The autosomes contain the rest of the genetic hereditary information. All chromosomes act in the same way during cell division.

As noted above, human cells have twenty-three pairs of chromosomes (twenty-two pairs of autosomes and one pair of sex chromosomes), giving a total of forty-six per cell. In the human evolutionary lineage, it is thought that two ancestral ape chromosomes fused, producing human chromosome 2.

This is considered to be the main divergence between the human and chimp genomes.

In the preceding chapter, we learned that the human and chimpanzee ABO distribution pattern is very different. Chimpanzees completely lack two blood types that we humans possess (B, AB) and have minimal occurrences of type O, which forms our major blood group, and no Rh negative group.

(Clarification: the human and chimp [A, minimal O] blood groups are not identical; the chimp type A is a *species-specific* blood group. Human type-A individuals could not receive type A chimpanzee blood or donate their type A blood to a chimp in need of a transfusion.)

A two-chromosome difference does not sound like much (mathematically), but this seemingly small difference means that our genetic codes are not compatible enough to produce offspring. That is a wide genetic divergence between two species that supposedly branched off from the same ancestor. (It is even wider with the gorilla.)

The major structural difference is that human chromosome 2 was apparently derived from two smaller chromosomes that are found in the great apes. A simple fusion of two separate chromosomes is said to be the main difference between human and chimp chromosomes.

Once again, a seeming small mathematical difference, when translated into the variations between genomes, turns out to make a huge difference. So far, we have seen that humans and chimps have dissimilar blood groups and dissimilar chromosome patterns.

Once again, neo-Darwinists want to emphasize *the closeness of the two species* using numeric relationships that imply a near match. However, genetics *does not* seem to work that way.

A small number of gene differences can cause sharp distinctions between species.

In the genetic code, an apparently minor variation can translate into very different species-specific genetic expressions, such as the simple biochemical switches that trigger a female fetus to change into a male. At the point that the human and chimp genomes depart, this may translate into a small number, but that is irrelevant. The departure produces major differences, such as a new blood type or fewer chromosomes that act as species partitions and so forth.

As we noted in the previous chapter, the ABO/Rh factor blood groups are inherited from both parents. Chromosomes are also inherited; one copy from each parent forms one of the pairs so that the offspring inherits one-half of the mother's chromosomes and one-half of the father's as well.

Now this genetic transmission system produces some interesting and unanticipated results. Since each succeeding generation is the product of the combination of twenty-three chromosomes from the mother and twenty-three from the father, it only takes seven generations to disconnect from the original ancestor or founder.

What does that mean? For example, if I try to trace a person's heritage back two hundred years to the late seventeenth century, there is a problem. He probably does not have any of the chromosomes that his remote ancestor back eight generations possessed. Why?

This is due to the fact that each intervening generation only received 1/2, 1/4, 1/8, 1/16, 1/32, 1/64, and then 1/128 of that eighth-generational ancestor's original chromosome makeup.

Since the last figure is less than one, my chromosomal makeup is entirely different, which means that it does not take that long to depart entirely from the alleged ancestral chromosome. This is very counter-intuitive to the way we consciously think about our ancestral lineage. We tend to think of genetic inheritance going back in a straight line to the original block (we were chipped off), right to our remotest ancestors, with a conservation of traits and a high degree of genetic uniformity.

Yet genetics does not work that way. We are not really chips off the direct-line ancestral block.

The ABO/Rh factor blood group transmission genetics underscores this fact. We all believe that we are virtually identical genetic copies of our parents. Given this assumption, it is natural to think that we could freely exchange blood or donate or receive organs from our parents (at the very least), if not our siblings, if necessary. Not true.

I am a type A negative, and my mother is a type O positive, meaning that I can neither give nor receive blood to or from my own mother. We may be close emotionally and genetically in many ways, but not in terms of blood groups; in that specific area, we are rather distant relatives.

Both family ties as well as shared ethnic and racial traits give us a false impression of the underlying genetic reality. You may be able to save the life of a neighbor down the street with a transfusion, but not a family member. Blood groups unite and divide us genetically, not eye, hair, or skin color and so forth, which are very superficial traits.

In fact, our senses of family, racial, and ethnic uniformity are delusions. Even though everyone in your family may have black hair and brown eyes, if you are a type A negative, you might find that only an individual outside of your family or ethnic group can save your life in a crunch.

Though this book is not written to support the Creationist version of human origins or of Judaism or Christianity, the Bible made a crucial point by flatly stating that *all life is in the blood*—not in the color of your eyes, skin, or hair, but in your bloodstream.

The chromosomes have a story to tell, and it is simply this: if you possess forty-eight of them, you go that way and join the chimpanzees and gorillas in the forests of central Africa; if you possess forty-six, then you are a card-carrying *Homo sapiens* and go wherever you want to.

THE MYTH OF mtDNA EVE

We just saw that all of our assumptions about familial and racial closeness in terms of a shared blood type and chromosomal pattern are more often wrong than right. We also learned that the alleged similarity between chimps and humans is really a matter of perspective, and in fact, we are two very separate and distinct species in terms of blood groups and chromosomes.

However, there is another component of the genome that evolutionists insist tells the real story of human history and evolution: mtDNA, to which we were introduced in the previous chapter.

Exactly what is mtDNA?

A human cell contains two types of DNA—nuclear and mitochondrial. The first constitutes the twenty-three pairs of chromosomes contained within the nuclei of our cells, which we examined above. As we learned, each parent contributes to the genetic makeup of these chromosomes.

On the other hand, mtDNA is found outside the nucleus, in the mitochondria, and is inherited *solely from the mother.*

Mitochondria are very small *cell structures* wrapped up within all of our cells. They are the power plants of the human body, providing about 90 percent of the energy that the body needs to function.

Each cell contains hundreds to thousands of mitochondria; this effectively means that there are hundreds to thousands of mtDNA copies in a human cell. This compares to just two copies of nuclear DNA (*chromosomes*) located in that same cell.

Whereas nuclear DNA is composed of a continuous linear strand of nucleotides to make up the gene sequence (a multitude of combinations of just four nucleotides: adenine, thymine, cytosine, and guanine [A, T, G, and C]), mtDNA is constructed in a circular or loop configuration. Each loop contains a sufficient number (usually 16,569) of nucleotide combinations to make up the thirty-seven genes involved in mitochondrial energy generation.

In addition to energy production, mitochondria also play a role in several other cellular activities. For example, mitochondria help regulate the self-destruction of cells and are also necessary for the production of substances such as cholesterol and heme (an iron-containing component of hemoglobin).

In effect, we do not get exactly half of our DNA from our father and half from our mother since a tiny piece of our DNA is inherited only down the *female* line in the mtDNA bundle.

While males, like females, receive and use their mother's mtDNA, they cannot pass it on to their children. Their sperm have their own mitochondria to power the long journey from the vagina to the ovum. However, upon entry into the ovum, the male mitochondria quickly dissipate and die. This leaves the female as the sole carrier of mtDNA.

Given this set of characteristics, according to microbiologists, each of us inherits our mtDNA from our own mother, who inherited her mtDNA intact from her mother, and so on back through the generations—right back to what they call "the Eve gene" from "mtDNA Eve."

This scenario, if taken to its ultimate conclusion, means that every person alive today has inherited their mtDNA from one single great-great-great- (long series) grandmother, who begat the ancestral mito-chondria nearly two hundred thousand years ago.

Our first question then, in light of the ABO/Rh factor blood group data, is, Which blood type did our mythical Eve possess? She had to have one.

She had to have carried and transmitted one blood group (ABO and Rh factor) as well as twenty-three chromosomes to her children, both sons and daughters. In addition, her husband would have also made a similar genetic contribution, though none to the mtDNA gene group.

As we learned above, it is impossible to retrace the chromosomes backward in time from a specific living individual to a specific ancestor because of the way they are transmitted and the genes are combined, lost, and recombined so quickly.

As for our Eve, we only know she had forty-six chromosomes and twenty-three went to each child, but the exact nature of each division remains unknown. In terms of chromosomes, none of us is a "chip off the old block" because the block disassembles and is replaced by a new one in eight generations.

If this is true in terms of the human lineage, and it certainly is, then how much more true is it in relation to the chimpanzee lineage, which does not even possess the same overall number of chromosomes?

We will return to the blood group question a little later. For now, let us simply acknowledge that trying to establish a direct line of ances-try backward to a point in time, or to a single individual ancestor, is like trying to trek through the Sahara Desert in a sandstorm.

First, you are blinded by the immediate swirls of sand stinging your eyes, and then, when the storm passes, you are confused by the shifting sands that have rearranged the environment.

In the previous chapter, we carefully walked through the vari-ous distinctions that exist between the ABO/Rh factor blood groups and what they imply about human origins and history. Through that basic genetic filter, it did not appear that there was either (1) a single place of origin or (2) a single human group that could have produced the diverse ABO/Rh blood group distribution pattern we see today around the globe.

Keep in mind that according to several of the key principles of evolution, *successful mutations are rare,* and natural selection processes favor simplicity over increasing complexity. Since that is true, it suggests that modern humans have appeared recently—very recently, in fact.

The chimpanzee population reflects those principles. They have not displayed any significant mutations in tens of millions of years; their homogenous blood group is the reflection of selective filtering, which produced a fixed blood group that is type A dominant.

Now we are faced with figuring out what basic genetic configuration our theoretical Eve possessed beyond the forty-six chromosomes that distinguished her from chimps. Was she type O positive? If so, when and where did the recessive O negative blood type enter the picture?

If it was an early mutation, given the fact that it is recessive, it should have been filtered out by the Rh positive type even before the type A and B mutations appeared to become codominants. Rh negative blood did not originate in Africa; we saw that in the last chapter.

But we have already seen that the current worldwide blood group distribution pattern not only has O positive on top of the chart, but O negative also has a significant minority in some regional populations.

To say that our mythical Eve (and Adam) presents a problematical model is therefore an understatement.

If she was type A, as some geneticists contend, then type O should have sunk into near oblivion long ago, just as was the case with chimpanzees and gorillas; that proposal begs the question of the origins of types O and B and Rh negative and their continued existence even more.

Of course, mtDNA Eve has produced billions of daughters, granddaughters, and so forth. If all of her descendants' chromosomes had been an exact copy of hers, then every daughter would be a virtual clone to this day. But we have seen that the chromosomal transmission method completely prevented that.

If she and her husband, the theoretical Adam, had both been type A positive, then the human blood group would be like the chimpanzee blood group, perhaps with minimal examples of type O, assuming Adam was type O or B, but no Rh negative blood would exist.

All the genetic evidence points to the fact that we are not clones, and we cannot even freely exchange blood group genes among ourselves. We are a diverse population now, and that suggests that we came from a diverse population in the past.

The theoretical mtDNA Eve is just an abstract model that is once again supposed to shore up the neo-Darwinian out-of-Africa hypothesis, but it does not really stand up under close scrutiny.

Ironically, one of the only scenarios that can be used to make it work is to radically shorten the time since modern *Homo sapiens* first appeared. If an ancestral Eve existed to transmit her mitochondria intact down through the generations, then she could have been a type O positive person and her husband a type O negative.

But then, to allow for the mutations within types A and B later, our hypothetical progenitors could not have started the race two hundred thousand years ago, but more like ten thousand years ago or even less. This also could not have happened in Africa because there is no Rh negative blood among native tribal Africans.

That prospect is not one that neo-Darwinians are going to embrace.

In the prior chapter, we saw that Earth has been an uncontrolled experimental genetics lab for the past five hundred years, where a pure type O positive population in the Americas was inundated by a mixed blood group European population, which quickly diluted the American people's historic O positive homogeneity.

The resultant ABO distribution pattern is now starting to reflect that of the mixed populations that existed and still exist in the colonized countries. Type O blood does not withstand an influx of types A and B, and the Rh negative blood type is quickly displaced by the Rh positive type.

If you are suspecting that something is amiss with the current switch from understanding the origins and distribution patterns of the ABO blood groups to the results quickly obtained using mtDNA genetics, *we are on the same page.*

Something has gone very wrong in the science of genetics when it comes to applying mtDNA to human evolution, history, and migration.

All of a sudden, mtDNA is being used as if it somehow supersedes the genetics of blood groups, which it clearly does not. Not too surprisingly, the results almost always confirm the out-of-Africa and Bering Strait theories.

The results seldom if ever are matched against the established ABO data, and there is this very aggressive rush to judgment, a push that implies that any skeptic just does not understand this new genetic paradigm. Right. . . . Where have we heard that elitist propaganda before?

I pose this challenge:

1. If you can show me, using the rules of population dynamics and the principles of ABO transmission, how the indigenous populations of Africa and Asia got to the Americas with nothing but type O positive blood in their gene pools, then my skepticism will drastically diminish.
2. If you can also prove that it is possible to start with type A positive blood and arrive at a large fraction of people with type O negative, in a descendant population over time, I will no longer be a skeptic.

But no real statistical simulation using the rules of ABO transmission can produce those results. Any population with a mixed ABO pattern, which both Africa and Asia have had for a prolonged time period, will produce a mixed ABO population during migration and settlement. It is not possible to have a homogenous type O positive population emerge.

Barring those events (and I do not expect any biologist or geneticist to pick up that gauntlet), I shall hold mtDNA studies, interpretations, and conclusions at greater than arm's length and suggest that all serious readers do the same.

PARSING THE GENETIC CODE

The DNA code is often compared to a human language. It has letters that combine in different sequences that mean different things. The main task of any language is to communicate something to someone.

Is the main task of DNA to copy itself to each new generation like the Old Testament was supposed to have been faithfully copied?

If Earth had provided each of our remote ancestors a manual that contained a detailed explanation of how to survive and thrive on the planet, then one of the jobs of our ancestors would have been to hand down an exact copy of that manuscript to us. *Of course, that is what oral traditions and sacred texts are supposed to represent.*

However, when a new individual is born, sometimes a small part of the DNA is not copied in every detail. One change can cause a very minor mutation, which is usually discarded rather quickly because mutations rarely prove beneficial.

But sometimes mutations do prove beneficial, as in the case of types A and B blood group antibodies. Then the genetic code goes through a slight revision, and the new mutations are added and copied by succeeding generations.

Now if we take the Old Testament as an example of a sacred book intended to convey critical information to succeeding generations, we must note several things up front.

Consider the language the version we are reading is written in. If it is the original Talmud, written in ancient Hebrew, and we have been schooled in that language, we have a pretty good chance of understanding the words as they were originally meant to be understood.

However, if it is in English and that was translated from Greek, we are removed several times from the foundation material, which was first translated from the ancient Hebrew; we may not understand what the original authors intended or understand only a portion of it.

The ancient Hebrews had many words for God that denoted various attributes, but they still referred to a singular deity. They also had a plural word for gods that does not translate well into English: *elohim.*

Each of the translations risks mutations, which are usually corruptions, of the original text. Does the text in Genesis 1 really say that the God of the universe created human beings, in his image, as it has been interpreted by generations of Christian Bible scholars?

No; parsed as carefully as a geneticist would the genetic code, it switches to the plural form and denotes that *gods,* not *God,* create man in *"Our image and likeness."* The switch to the plural has never been clarified by biblical scholars or believers.

Since it is understood that God is an invisible spirit or absolute presence, then he (or she or it) has no image or likeness; only a distinct physical entity has an image, form, or likeness. Deciphering the biblical code is not unlike trying to decode the human and chimpanzee genomes.

Human languages, like human civilizations, do not last very long, and even when they are alive and being spoken every day, as ancient Greek and Latin were not that long ago, they undergo constant permutations, additions, and deletions.

In a much, much broader context, this has also been the case with human evolution on the biological level.

It is bold but naive to think it is possible to retrace our ancestry back through countless generations to an alleged, mythical Eve (who were probably Eves anyway) and find all the alleged fossils of the various "missing links" that would then constitute the final pieces of the Darwinist puzzle.

There is actually no good basis for making that assumption. The reasoning is based on the notion that there were species extant upon Earth that represented intermediate stages of evolution between the common ancestor of the chimpanzee and us, modern humans.

However, there is no immutable law of genetics or biology that requires that to be the case.

Modern *Homo sapiens* is more likely the outcome of an external agency intervening in primate genetics to produce a hybrid race. That is what our ancient, sacred codes (like the Bible) tell us, as surely as our genetic code tells us that *we are not chimpanzees.*

Genetic intervention could and did happen, according to our most ancient oral traditions and sacred texts. There are no laws of physics, astronomy, or biology that can rule out extraterrestrial involvement in the evolution of life on Earth.

The Genesis Race (or Cosmic Ancestry) theory offers a third alternative that neither neo-Darwinians nor creationists are prepared to deal with, because it does not abrogate the laws of science or conflict with religious traditions.

Positing that an advanced race came from a distant solar system, seeded life on Earth, and then intervened in human affairs at infrequent intervals does not conflict with the Old Testament at all; it agrees with it. The theory also agrees with the early histories of the Sumerians and Hindus.

Neo-Darwinists dismiss creationism because, in the end, the arguments are faith based (involve miracles) and therefore are not scientific. Then they dismiss *intelligent design* by claiming it is religion pretending to be science.

How will they react to the theory that, while evolution exists, it did not start on planet Earth and the reason there are no missing links is because none ever existed on Earth?

Neo-Darwinists would rather argue with creationists because they know that intelligent design is a viable scientific thesis. As noted in chapter 1, directed panspermia (Cosmic Ancestry II) was conceived by two eminent scientists, Francis Crick and L. E. Orgel.

CONCLUSION

When deciphered, the human genome presented to scientists some enigmatic surprises that confounded their expectations. In fact, the DNA code is amazingly uniform for the most part, and it only branches off where speciation manifests.

Therefore, humans are very similar, in terms of DNA, to all primates and similar to all mammals as well. However, when evolutionists predicted that the human genome would be five times as large as it turned out to be, that was due to a false assumption. When it comes to the DNA sequence, quality, not quantity, is what matters.

Homo sapiens is likely a product of bioengineering on the part of an advanced, extraterrestrial civilization.

26

Clones, Chimeras, and Hybrids

Splicing human genes into animal DNA is a commonplace practice in biotechnology labs in advanced countries around the world today. Transgenic rodents, with human genes, have become a mainstay of medical research.

For instance, scientists have created a Down syndrome mouse by inserting three hundred human genes into its genome. By doing this, they can study this genetically caused disorder.

In addition, one of the most popular anticoagulant and anti-inflammatory medications on the market is created using goat's milk from ewes that have had human genes inserted into them. Moreover, a group of Chinese scientists recently inserted human stem cells into a goat fetus.

Other researchers around the world are quickly following in their footsteps. The picture goes from fascinating to extremely bizarre.

Cows have recently been genetically altered to produce milk that is virtually identical to human breast milk. The scientists responsible for this feat hope to have huge herds of these cows producing an alternative to human breast milk that will be on the market soon.

In earlier chapters, we noted that there are strong genetic partitions against different species mating and producing offspring. However, there are ways around this genetic wall. Two distinct species do not have to reproduce sexually; a cell from one can be inserted into an egg of another after the nucleus has been removed from the egg.

Even from our still-fledgling level of genetic knowledge, using second-generation methods of biogenetic engineering, our scientists can already create animal-human embryos.

They do this by plucking a cell from a person, then inserting it into a cow or rabbit egg after the nucleus has been removed. The final step is to zap it with a small jolt of electricity. The two cells are then fused to make an embryo that could be 99.9 percent human and 0.1 percent animal or whatever the researcher desires.

Esmail Zanjani, a researcher at the University of Nevada, Reno, has been able to grow mostly human livers in sheep. Zanjani achieved this by injecting human stem cells into growing sheep fetuses, either adult stem cells derived from bone marrow or embryonic stem cells from one of the federally approved stem cell colonies.

The research was originally aimed at finding out if it would be possible to transplant stem cells into developing sheep fetuses to correct defects in utero. But Zanjani observed the human cells integrating into and then proliferating within a wide range of sheep organs and tissues, including the pancreas, heart, skin, and liver.

This surprising development makes it possible to grow human cells inside animal cells, tissues, and organs that might later be suitable for transplants into people.

Here is how it works: if a patent needs a new liver, doctors would take some of the patient's bone marrow stem cells and inject them into a developing sheep fetus at the proper moment. After gestation, a lamb would be born with a liver made up chiefly of the patient's cells. The lamb would be slaughtered and the new liver transplanted into the patient.

Once installed, the patient's immune system would eliminate the lamb's liver cells, leaving behind a brand new organ that is perfectly matched since it was made from the patient's stem cells.

These types of transplants are possible because of early research in which single human genes were inserted into various plants, animals, and even bacteria to produce a number of therapeutic protein products, including *insulin* and *human growth hormone*.

It turns out that many genes can be mixed and matched across species. A gene crucial to building a fruit fly's eye will also trigger eye development in a frog.

As Robert Bailey stated, "Now that both the human and mouse genomes have been sequenced, researchers know that 99 percent of mouse genes have homologues in humans; even more amazingly, 96 percent are present in the same order on both genomes."

This shows that the human and chimp similarity is grossly overplayed. The truth is, as Crick and Orgel pointed out while presenting the directed panspermia theory, that the DNA code is amazingly uniform for the most part.

According to molecular biologist and writer Joan Slonczewski, "Until recently, genetic crossing of unrelated animals was considered untenable from the standpoint of biology."[1] However, new discoveries of genetic commonality across different species and new reproductive technologies have "led to chimerical combinations such as sheep and goat; and an early human embryo has been generated from the egg of a cow."[2]

CLONES

The cloning procedure is not all that complicated. Researchers clone animals simply by destroying the nucleus of an unfertilized egg from the host animal and replacing it with a nucleus from a cell of the body from another animal.

At this point, the egg of the host animal is considered fertilized and is planted into the womb of the host animal. By using this technique, the baby will develop into an animal that has identical genetic traits (a clone) as the animal that provided the cell nucleus to the cloning process.

In 1996, Scottish scientists successfully cloned the first mammal ever—a sheep, which they named Dolly. The cloned sheep developed premature arthritis and lung disease that led her creators to euthanize her after just six years—roughly half the life span of a normal sheep.

This shows that while human cloning is now possible, the process is not sophisticated enough to be considered reliable. Cloning is not that difficult in the lab, but producing a viable, healthy clone *is* difficult. Consider the following cases of cloning:

- South Korea's controversial stem cell scientist Hwang Woo-Suk succeeded in cloning endangered coyotes. Hwang cloned the coyotes by transferring the nuclei of somatic cells (all body cells other than reproductive ones) from a donor coyote to a female dog's eggs.

- A female dromedary camel was born on April 8, 2009, the world's first cloned camel. Nisar Ahmad Wani, who headed the research team in Dubai, United Arab Emirates, announced on April 14, 2009, that the cloned camel was born after an "uncomplicated" gestation of 378 days.
- In December 2001, scientists at Texas A&M University created the first cloned cat, named CC (for Copycat) Even though CC was an exact copy of his host, they had different personalities (i.e., CC was shy and timid; his host, on the other hand, was playful and curious.
- In 2004, the first commercially cloned cat, Little Nicky, was created by Genetic Savings and Clone.
- The world's first cloned calf (named Gene) was born on February 7, 1997, at American Breeders Service facilities in Deforest, Wisconsin. Later, it was transferred and kept at the Minnesota Zoo Education Center.
- A Holstein heifer named Daisy was cloned by Dr. Xiangzhong "Jerry" Yang using ear skin cells from a high-merit cow named Aspen at the University of Connecticut on June 10, 1999, followed by three additional clones, Amy, Betty, and Cathy, by July 7, 1999.[3]
- Second Chance, a Brahman bull, was cloned from Chance, a beloved celebrity bull. Second Chance was born on August 9, 1999, at Texas A&M University.
- Texas A&M University cloned a Black Angus bull named 86 Squared in 2000, after cells from his donor, Bull 86, had been frozen for fifteen years. Both bulls exhibited a natural resistance to brucellosis, tuberculosis, and other diseases that can be transferred in meat.
- A purebred Hereford calf clone named Chloe was born on March 28, 2001, at Kansas State University's purebred research unit. This was Kansas State's first cloned calf.
- Millie and Emma were two female Jersey cows cloned at the University of Tennessee in 2001. They were the first cows to be produced using standard cell-culturing techniques.

- Pampa was the first animal cloned in Argentina, in 2002 by Biosidus.
- Ten more Jersey cows were cloned at the University of Tennessee, all females, in 2002.
- Bonyana and Tamina were the first cloned calves in Iran; they were born at the Royan Institute in Isfahan, in the summer of 2009.
- In 2010, the first Spanish fighting bull was cloned by Spanish scientists.
- An Anatolian gray bull (Fee) was cloned in Turkey in 2009, as were cattle from the same breed (Eke, Eke, Pilfer, Kara).
- The world's first cloned female buffalo calf was conceived using the "hand-guided cloning technique" and was born on February 6, 2009, at the National Dairy Research Institute in Karnal, India. This calf lived only six days. A second female buffalo calf, named Garima, was born using the same technique at the same facility; this calf lived for two years.
- A cloned male buffalo calf, named Surest, was born on August 26, 2010, at the National Dairy Research Institute in Karnal, India.
- A cloned deer, named Dewey, was born on May 23, 2003, at Texas A&M University.
- A South Korean scientist, Hwang Woo-Suk, cloned the first dog, an Afghan hound named Snuppy, born on April 24, 2005. Later in 2005, Hwang was found to have fabricated evidence in stem cell research projects. This caused some to question the veracity of his other experiments, including Snuppy. In their investigation of Hwang's publication, however, a team from Seoul National University confirmed that Snuppy was a true clone of Tei, the DNA donor dog. South Korean scientists also have recently cloned "sniffer" dogs used in law enforcement.
- BioArts International held a dog-cloning contest in which people sent in submissions about which dog was the most suited to be cloned. The winner was Trakr, a K-9 police dog who was a 9/11 hero.
- In summer 2011, members of the same team at Seoul National University that had cloned Snuppy cloned a beagle named Tegon,

which glowed under ultraviolet light when it was given a doxycy-cline antibiotic. The researchers hoped that eventually this could help doctors detect the presence of diseases in humans.

Cloning research is going on around the globe. The point of this survey is to show how far genetic engineering has come in a very short time and to show that any advanced civilization that preceded human development could have easily manipulated the genome in any manner they wished.

In fact, our bioengineers are largely in that position today.

The process goes back to 1958, when John Gurdon, then at the University of Oxford, explained that he had successfully cloned a frog. He did this by using intact nuclei from somatic cells from a *Xenopus* tadpole. And Gurdon's success was an important extension of the previous work of Robert Briggs and Thomas King in 1952 on transplanting nuclei from embryonic blastula cells.

In recent years, a female rhesus monkey named Tetra, born in October 1999, was cloned by embryo splitting. This species is a genetic step removed from chimpanzees, and both rhesus monkeys and chimpanzees have about 97–98 percent genetic compatibility with humans. Science is moving ever closer to human cloning. The above list is by no means exhaustive, and it shows that cloning is not as mysterious and complicated a feat as is thought by the public.

Could you or I submit cells to be cloned today? Absolutely! But that is not allowed at present. However, as we have seen, there is nothing superspecial about the human genome. If a dead cow can be cloned and brought back to life, so to speak, so can a dead person. Think about that bizarre possibility.

If somatic cells had been recovered from Elvis or Michael Jackson at the appropriate time and cryogenically frozen, then later thawed and a surrogate mother found . . . well, this could be what the future has in store for cloning.

Science has taken a sci-fi premise and turned it into a reality. Cloning can be achieved by several methods. Nonetheless, it is still expensive, since it is difficult to produce a viable clone free of serious health problems. When those issues are resolved and it becomes easier and cheaper to produce healthy clones, who knows what is going to happen.

The Planet of the Apes series may have seemed like an interesting, if unlikely, premise some decades ago. But something far more fantastic is on the horizon right now. If our scientists are already creating mixed plant-animal hybrids using transgenetic techniques, then how far away are we from human-animal hybrids?

Already, scientists are cloning human embryos to see if they can develop normally, right along with cloned human embryos *made with animal eggs,* and then these results are being published in reputable journals. Moreover, the mass media make it sound like this is no big deal at all.

Biotechnology can, right now, create various combinations of animal hybrids, clones, and chimeras, which are organisms that contain a mixture of genetically different tissues. The biotechnology techniques are already capable of this, and scientists are actually doing just that. It is only the considerations of the various bioethics involved that are preventing the hybridization of humans and chimpanzees or the cloning of humans with superior abilities and skills; let's say geniuses and Olympic-level athletes.

Now it is important here to distinguish between a *chimerical* embryo and a *chimerical* adult. Placing animal DNA into a human embryo is entirely different from growing a human liver in a pig for transplantation into a human patient (xenotransplantation). It is different because adding animal DNA to a human embryo at *the embryo stage* fundamentally changes the entire organism, not just one organ.

Xenotransplantation of animal organs into humans is still in the developmental stage, but it will soon emerge from the shadows, so to speak. It will become a common medical practice in the near future. Patients waiting for organ transplants will be given organs or cells created in animals, such as pigs.

A *chimera* and a hybrid are similar, yet they differ in that the former consists of a combination between *two different species within an organism,* in which the genes of the two species do not combine as they do in a hybrid.

A *hybrid* is the product of the breeding of two *different species* (via normal copulation or in vitro fertilization) in which each cell in the hybrid's body has a mixture of genes from both of the parents. This process has been going on for a long time.

A mule is a hybrid since a male donkey can copulate with a female horse and the union will produce a hybrid species, though the mule off-spring is sterile. What follows is a partial list of hybrid animals.

Liger: This is a popular hybrid, a cross between a male lion and a female tiger.

Tigon: This is a cross between a male tiger and a female lion. This hybrid produces the world's largest felines.

Iron Age Pig: Domestic Tamworth pigs are crossbred with wild boars to create the famous "iron age pigs." The hybrids are tamer than wild boars, but less tractable than domestic swine.

Zebroids: A zorse is the result of crossbreeding a horse and a zebra. A zonkey is the result of crossbreeding a donkey with a zebra. The zony is the result of crossbreeding a pony with a zebra. All three are called zebroids—defined as a cross between a zebra and any other equid.

Cama: A cama is a hybrid between a camel and a llama. They are born via artificial insemination because of the huge difference in sizes of the animals, which disallows natural breeding. A cama usually has the short ears and long tail of a camel but the cloven hooves of a llama. Also, the hump is absent.

Wolphin: A wolphin is a rare hybrid formed from a cross between a bottlenose dolphin and a false killer whale. There are currently only two in captivity, at the Sea Life Park in Hawaii. A wolphin's size, color, and shape are intermediate between the parent species. The first captive wolphin was Kekaimalu, which showed mixed heritage even in its teeth: bottlenose dolphins have eighty-eight, false killer whales have forty-four, and Kekaimalu had sixty-six.

These kinds of similar-species hybrids do not seem to offend human sensibilities much. The blending of two similar species into a hybrid somehow is not disturbing, whereas the blending of dissimilar species seems freakish.

For example, scientists have inserted *silk spider* genes into the *goat* genome. The resulting *spoats* produce spider-silk protein in their milk. This spider-silk protein is collected, purified, and spun into incredibly strong fibers. These fibers are said to be more durable than Kevlar, more flexible than nylon, and much stronger than steel.

Cows that produce human milk and goats that produce spider silk in their milk already exist; now we must wonder what is coming next?

On September 5, 2007, the Human Fertilisation and Embryology Authority in the United Kingdom decided that "there is no fundamental reason to prevent cytoplasmic hybrid research" and agreed in principle to authorize the creation of human-animal embryos.

Subsequently, the authority granted two research groups in the United Kingdom permission to create human-animal hybrid embryos in January 2008. That same year, the UK's Human Fertilisation and Embryology Act was passed.

As of 2011, according to the *Daily Mail,* more than 150 human-animal hybrid embryos had been created in British laboratories.

Here we are not concerned about the ethics of biotechnology—and what should or should not be done—our focus is simply on *what can be accomplished right now* or is being developed at present. The U.S. Food and Drug Administration gives xenotransplantation the following definition:

Xenotransplantation is any procedure that involves the transplantation, implantation or infusion into a human recipient of either (a) live cells, tissues, or organs from a nonhuman animal source, or (b) human body fluids, cells, tissues, or organs that have had ex vivo contact with live nonhuman animal cells, tissues, or organs.[4]

The process behind xenotransplants involves several steps. Currently, researchers are investigating strategies to incorporate human anticoagulant or antithrombotic genes into genetically modified pigs to regulate the human inflammatory response.

To avoid the problems of animal organ rejection, it is proposed that the organ, probably from a pig or baboon, be initially bioengineered to alter it with human genes to trick a patient's immune system into accepting it as a part of its own body. This line of research is proceeding apace.

Previous trials revealed that transplantation of pig neuronal cells into nonhuman primates with a model of Parkinson's disease significantly improved several brain functions. During the study, some *monkeys received genetically engineered human neural precursor cells* and immunosuppressive therapy to prevent rejection.

For some animals, this was too much; they developed lymph-proliferative disease, which suggested that their immune systems had been weakened excessively. The authors of that research are still optimistic, saying, "If this issue can be resolved, an early clinical trial would seem justified in patients whose disease is refractory to therapies."[5]

Because of these problems, the longest time of survival for pig organs in nonhuman primates varies from a few days in lung transplants to approximately six to eight months in heart transplants.

Although researchers are still years away from conducting human trials of solid organ transplants of this nature, lifesaving transplants of a pig heart or liver could pose an alternative solution until a human organ becomes available.

Other genetic experiments have the mission of revealing knowledge about the functions of the human body, for instance, by creating mice with a humanlike immune system to study AIDS. Restrictions on cloning and stem cell research have made chimera research an attractive alternative. Below are some examples of the research that has been going on in this field:

1. A U.S. corporation has recently produced a very large, muscular "monster salmon" that can grow up to three times faster than normal salmon do.

2. Science can now produce cats that glow in the dark. A genetically modified cat named Mr. Green Genes was the very first fluorescent cat in the United States. The glow was used to track genes inserted into the cat's DNA. But Mr. Green Genes was not the first "glow in the dark cat" in the world. That honor went to a cat created by a team of scientists in South Korea.

3. In Japan, scientists have discovered that they can grow rat organs inside mice. The researchers hope to use the same technology to grow human organs inside pigs.

4. But Japan is not the only place where this kind of research is being done. In Missouri, entities *that are part pig and part human* are being grown with the goal of providing organs for human transplants.

5. Scientists at Rockefeller University have injected human genes into mice. These "humanized mice" are being used to study the spread of the hepatitis C virus.

6. In the United States, scientists have discovered that they can actually "grow" new human organs from scratch. A recent *Newsweek* article stated, "It might sound like science fiction, but growing new organs from scratch has already become reality. In addition to bladders, scientists have engineered new skin, bone, cartilage, corneas, windpipes, arteries, and urethras."[6]

Today, approximately 93 percent of all soybeans and approximately 80 percent of all corn in the United States *have been genetically modified*. Considering the fact that corn is in literally thousands of our food products, there is a very good chance that you consumed some genetically modified food today.

The general public and mass media are a decade or more behind the leading edge of genetic research that is taking place in labs around the world now. We are already living in a futuristic science-fiction world.

All of the foregoing goes to point up the probability that Earth is the product of terraforming and that genetic engineering created life on Earth; this is being proved possible every week by our own scientists.

One of the points I made in my first book, *The Genesis Race*, was that because we are the product of extraterrestrial bioengineering, we are recapitulating and will continue to recapitulate the evolution of our progenitors; that is the essence of Cosmic Ancestry.

CONCLUSION

Genetic engineering is proceeding at a much faster pace than even the most optimistic scientists imagined that it would. Clones and chimeras are being created every day, as are genetically modified organisms, such as plant-bacteria hybrids.

This shows that if we can make such rapid advances in this field, then genetically engineering humans would be child's play to an advanced extraterrestrial civilization. Science has already proven that the theory that humans are a genetically engineered species is viable.

27
Stalking the
Wild Humanzee

It is now common to place single human genes into plants and animals and even bacteria, to produce various therapeutic proteins, including insulin and human growth hormone. . . .

Now that both the human and mouse genomes have been sequenced, researchers know that 99 percent of mouse genes have homologues in humans; even more amazingly, 96 percent are present in the same order on the genome.

RONALD BAILEY, "WHAT IS TOO HUMAN?"

About a hundred years ago, a Russian scientist wanted to see if he could create a human-chimp hybrid; we shall call it a *humanzee*. As we shall see, that did not work out well for him at all—especially in the end.

However, though a humanzee is not really possible, a human-chimpanzee chimera is; in fact, geneticists could create such a creature, and it could be made to resemble those depicted in *Planet of the Apes*.

Illya Ivanovich Ivanov, an early-twentieth-century biologist, was a well-known biological researcher who specialized in creating and studying hybrid creatures. Ivanov perfected the techniques of using artificial insemination to create these hybrids and was well known at the beginning of the century for his work in breeding horses.

315

In 1910, he presented a paper to the World Congress of Zoologists suggesting the possibility of creating a human-chimp hybrid through artificial insemination. Fourteen years later, while working at the Pasteur Institute in Paris, he got his chance.

Ivanov obtained permission from the institute's directors to use its primate research station in Kindia, French Guinea, as the laboratory for his planned experiments; he obtained ten thousand dollars from the Russian Academy of Sciences to pay for them.

In March 1926, Ivanov arrived at the station, only to find it had no sexually mature chimpanzees to work with. So in November 1926, he traveled to the botanical gardens in Conakry, French Guinea, and set up shop there. Several adult chimpanzees from the interior of the country were brought to Conakry, and Ivanov artificially inseminated three female chimpanzees with human sperm.

None became pregnant as a result of that procedure.

He also wanted to impregnate human females with chimp sperm, but officials in French Guinea balked at that idea. When Ivanov returned to Russia in 1927, he designed an experiment to try to impregnate five human female volunteers but was hampered by the lack of a male chimp to provide the sperm.

In 1930, the scientist fell out of favor with the Russian government, was arrested, and spent the rest of his life in exile in Kazakhstan, where he died in 1932 without doing any additional ape-human hybrid studies.

After that early attempt failed, it was three-quarters of a century before the DNA code was cracked and the tools and methods of biogenetic engineering were invented.

Could a hybrid cross between a human and a chimp be created? We would assume so because male donkeys and female horses have differing chromosome counts, but they can mate and produce a mule, and a female donkey and a male horse can breed and produce a similar animal known as a hinny.

So it would seem, since they tell us that we are so similar, that there is nothing stopping a human-chimpanzee hybrid from being successfully engineered, though it, too, would be infertile, just like the mule.

It is an admittedly disturbing thought—though the cross between a horse and a donkey is not—just considering the scientific possibilities. (I am not promoting the idea.) However, as noted in earlier chapters, it turns out that humans and chimps are not as close as horses and donkeys or lions and tigers or other known hybrid combinations.

Though, as neo-Darwinians never fail to remind us, humans and chimps share 98 percent of the DNA code in common, several differences seem to prevent crossbreeding. There appear to be at least nine *pericentric inversions* in chimp chromosomes compared with our own. An inversion is when a section of the chromosome gets reversed end to end.

If the inversion doesn't involve the center of the chromosome where the arms are joined, it is called a *paracentric inversion* and seems to have little effect on the viability of the individual involved.

A pericentic inversion, however, does involve the section where the arms of the chromosome are joined and can cause medical problems.

This difference makes it less likely that an individual with such an inversion can produce a viable offspring when mating with an individual who does not have the inversion (chimp-human). The fact that nine pericentric inversions separate humans from chimps virtually eliminates the possibility of producing a hybrid.

Of course, the above involves sexual reproduction, but we know that there are ways to get around that natural process. Scientists could create a *human-chimp chimera* by inserting genes and cells from one species into the other.

Scientists think that the more humanlike an animal is, the better research model it becomes for testing drugs or growing "spare parts." Since chimps and gorillas are so close on the genetic tree, could they be used to produce donor livers that could be transplanted into humans?

We have already noted that pigs are being genetically altered in the hopes that they can produce organs to be transplanted into humans.

Human scientists are not squeamish about applying these gene-altering techniques on other species, but what about other people?

As we have seen, there is nothing all that special about the majority of the human genome. Could we not transgenically produce a race of superstrong individuals by inserting gorilla genes into our own genome?

After all, we have already engineered numerous chimeras out of combinations of other species, so human chimeras, from a geneticist's point of view, are nothing more than "living creatures that contain two or more genetically distinct lines of cells that originated from two or more different zygotes."[1]

In essence, chimeras are complexes of two genetically different animals. In fact, as previously noted, we have jumped across species classifications to give mammals an insect characteristic, creating *spoats that give silk milk.*

Geneticists have created supersized salmon and added fluorescence to dogs and cats, so why not add lion manes to the human genome? This all sounds so sci-fi and far out (as in *The Island of Dr. Moreau*), but is it? The following statement quickly eliminates that thought.

> A group of scientists from the Institute of Cancer/Stem Cell Biology have already successfully created mice with brains that have one percent human cells. Their next goal is to create mice with one hundred percent human brains. Their goal is to study Parkinson's and Alzheimer's diseases through analysis of the pattern of brain growth.[2]

Well, if human brain cells can be inserted into the mouse genome, they can surely be inserted into the chimp or gorilla genomes with far greater success and meaning for humans.

So was *Planet of the Apes* so farfetched? Perhaps when it was made, but not now.

We might not be able to create a hybrid race of self-reproducing primates today, but we can engineer transgenic variations of humans or other primate species. While the reader and I may agree that this whole scenario is extremely disturbing, most countries lack legal prohibitions against creating chimeras.

The Canadian government has issued the Assisted Human Reproduction Act, which specifically prohibits the production of a chimera, as stated in Section 5:

> No person shall knowingly . . . create a chimera, or transplant a chimera into either a human being or a non-human life form or . . . create a hybrid for the purpose of reproduction, or transplant a hybrid into either a human being or a non-human life form.[3]

However, the United States and the United Kingdom have yet to issue any strict regulations regarding chimera research. Even with restrictions, it would be difficult to monitor whether regulations are kept if research is being conducted illegally.

Heart transplants already use porcine valves; researchers have already produced pigs with human blood and sheep with partially human organs. Lacking regulations on chimera production, the possibilities are endless.

As we have seen, due to the nature of the *universal genetic code,* it is absolutely possible to splice a gene from another organism into the human genome. Theoretically, it is also possible to produce a hybrid between humans and one of the great apes or even an old-world monkey.

This brings us back to the topic of ancient civilizations and their allegedly imaginative chimeras, as we will see below. Were ancient Sumerian artisans using artistic license or were they depicting actual creatures that they used as models?

The mere suggestion would have been scoffed at and dismissed as absurd fifty years ago. Historians have always regarded these beings as mythological creatures, never real-life entities. But can they be so sure now, given the above developments in our as yet new science of bioengineering?

These kinds of genetic creations would be child's play to an advanced technological society even ten thousand years older than ours is. And we must wonder where artists got the idea to create these human-animal hybrids, if they did in fact emerge from their imaginations?

We find similar beings depicted in ancient Egyptian artwork as well.

What our geneticists have quickly discovered in this emerging new science is that manipulating the genetic code and reengineering it into bizarre new species is not nearly as difficult as was deciphering the genome. The universality of the code, which Crick and Orgel referred to, is the underlying reason for this surprising fact.

As they noted, and we must deeply consider now given where bioengineering is headed, this unexpected universality and the resultant closeness of all living things argues for an earlier origin and evolution of the DNA code on an extraterrestrial planet.

Microbiologists shrug this universality off as if it was to be expected, but they did not expect it, in fact. They harp on the closeness of chimps and humans, but not the 90 percent closeness of horses and humans and even the 80 percent closeness of mice and human DNA.

CONCLUSION

Science is still at the beginning stages of genetic engineering, and already the accomplishments are astonishing and the possibilities mind-boggling. To propose that an advanced race implanted the basic genome on Earth—and also genetically engineered the human race from it—is something that will not be at all outside the realm of even our biotechnology capabilities in the near future.

Clearly any advanced civilization would be capable of these feats and much more. One day we will be in the position to decide whether to create a new, transgenic species that is part ape and part human; that species may subsequently populate another planet that we terraform.

28

The Genetic Insertion Event

We were therefore interested in examining the gene content of the intra- and inter-chromosomal duplications involving 2qFus-related sequence. Because these duplications took place during hominid evolution, resulting variation in gene number and function might contribute to phenotypic differences among primates.

YUXIN FAN, TERA NEWMAN, ELENA LINARDOPOULOU, AND BARBARA J. TRASK, "GENE CONTENT AND FUNCTION OF THE ANCESTRAL CHROMOSOME FUSION SITE IN HUMAN CHROMOSOME 2Q13–2Q14.1 AND PARALOGOUS REGIONS"

As we saw in prior chapters, chromosomes compose the primary difference, in genetic terms, between humans and chimpanzees: humans have one fewer pair of chromosomes than do the great apes.

Evolutionary geneticists believe that in the human lineage, two ancestral ape chromosomes fused at their ends, which produced *human chromosome 2.*

According to the conclusions of the Chimpanzee Genome Project:

The results of the chimpanzee genome project suggest that when ancestral chromosomes 2A and 2B fused to produce human chromosome 2, no genes were lost from the fused ends of 2A and 2B. At the site of fusion, there are about 150,000 base pairs of sequence not found in chimpanzee chromosomes 2A and 2B.[1]

That is a very odd state of affairs. Logic would suggest that a *fusion event* would not add new base pairs that were lacking in the ancestor and the other great apes. In fact, we would expect to see a conservation or even a loss of pairs as complexity was shed in favor of simplification (i.e., two fewer chromosomes).

(Does not the theory of evolution argue for simplification and conservation?)

It is this chromosomal difference that prevents humans and the great apes from breeding and producing viable offspring. The entire "fusion" scenario is questionable. For the sake of argument, we will assume that the first protohuman mutant was born from the alleged common ancestral lineage, millions of years ago.

Question: Who would this mutant, with differing chromosomes, mate with to perpetuate this new genetic assembly?

It could not have been with the forty-eight-chromosome ancestral line, as the forty-six-chromosome mutation (fusion) represented a complete genetic departure. Additionally, are we to also assume that another member of the opposite sex—who had also mutated—was born at the same time? That seems quite improbable.

So how did we get from forty-eight down to forty-six chromosomes since there is a genetic wall preventing a reproductive union? Next, since mutations are rare and seldom successful, what gave a survival advantage to the mutant forty-six-chromosome individuals (our theoretical ancestors)?

This is where the external manipulation of the human genome appears to have occurred. While humans and chimpanzees have similar genomes to a point, they are not as similar as horse and donkey or lion and tiger genomes, as we have seen.

As we noted previously, those animals can mate and produce viable, if sterile, offspring. It is more accurate to say that these species are very similar genetically than it is to say that humans and chimps are.

The gene transfer that took place, via bioengineering by the

Genesis Race, added new information that did not exist in the ancestral lineage. The added (inserted) genes reveal another key difference that separates humans and the great apes.

An important feature of the human genome is a substance called cobalamin synthetase, a bacterial enzyme that makes cobalamin, also known as vitamin B_{12}. We humans are unusual in that we have several copies of cobalamin synthetase–like genes, including the one on chromosome 2. Chimpanzees only have one.

Why is cobalamin such a critical factor? It is vital for brain development in children and for energy and red blood cell production, as well as the all-critical effective DNA replication process.

The cobalamin synthetase gene in modern humans is inactive, which is an enigmatic fact.

Since plants do not contain cobalamin and the human B_{12} gene to synthesize it is inactive, *we have to obtain it* from various animal sources. (This is why strict vegans are warned to take a B_{12} supplement.)

Low cobalamin levels in the blood serum can lead to pernicious anemia and a host of other complications, including chronic fatigue.

In fact, vitamin B_{12} is important for brain development, and a deficiency during pregnancy or early childhood results in severe neurological defects in human children. Humans can survive on a vegetarian diet; however, we are not genetically programmed to function at an optimal level without cobalamin (B_{12}).

Note that in Genesis, the people after Adam and Eve are told they can eat meat; the reason for that was this genetic change, starting with Adam and Eve, that deactivated the cobalamin synthetase gene. *In reality, they had to eat meat.*

On the other hand, both chimpanzees and gorillas are largely vegetarians, the latter exclusively so. Chimpanzees primarily subsist on fruits, nuts, seeds, leaves, and insects and, on rare occasions, meat. The differences between human and great ape cobalamin metabolism are largely responsible for our greater postnatal brain growth, which is lacking in the great apes.

The only way we are able to import cobalamin into our human metabolism is by having the right bacteria in our guts; bacterial flora break down the cobalamin for us. While plants and fungi do not contain B_{12}, some bacteria and yeasts do.

I posit that the cobalamin difference, which stimulates brain growth in a way that does not occur in the great apes, was also the outcome of genetic engineering.

I make this claim because of the fact that it is in the fusion region where we find the *inactivated cobalamin synthetase* gene. The inactivation of this gene is curious because it does not appear to confer any kind of survival advantage; quite the opposite.

Obviously, it would be better if we could synthesize cobalamin without depending on external sources in the bacteria family. Nonetheless, we have to import the bacteria into the gut first, and the bacteria then extracts the B_{12}, which we can get only from animal sources.

When we add the fact that the major human ABO blood group is type O positive, which both chimpanzees and gorillas lack, it becomes clear that we humans are unique, outliers so to speak..

Taken as a whole, the chromosomal, cobalamin metabolism, and blood group data suggest that we modern humans were a fairly recent insertion into the mammal and primate genome mix. But that does not mean that we are not ancient in cosmic terms. Our genes tie back to the extraterrestrial planet that our progenitors came from.

How else could type O positive, which is recessive to both A and B blood types, still exist as the majority blood group if we have been evolving together with the great apes for millions of years?

Though scientists claim that the other primates also have ABO blood groups, the distribution is totally different; none but humans have the O positive predominance or the Rh negative blood type. (So where did *that* come from?)

Therefore, human beings represent an outlier species, a hybrid that was produced using the same genetic material that other animals display (up to a point) due to the relative uniformity of DNA.

The reason that evolutionists were confounded by our human short-age of genes, 23,000 compared with the *145,000 of the wheat genome,* is because we have not been in the mix that long on Earth. They expected the human genome to be five times that large and much more complex than that of a supposedly simple plant, but that did not turn out to be the case.

The constant focus on our supposed close genetic relationship with chimpanzees hides the fact that most animals and even plants have many similarities in their genomes. How else could we create cross-species hybrids?

If a corn plant was entirely different from a bacterium, then it would not be possible to insert the bacteria into the corn germ to produce Bt corn, a hybrid of the two. However, Bt corn exists, proving that most of the genomes are very compatible.

We should be very careful about how we interpret these emerging new genetic data. It was not that long ago those geneticists talked about large segments of the genome housing junk DNA. That has since been proven to have been a false interpretation of the data.

How many more misinterpretations have been made?

CONCLUSION

The alleged fusion event, the mutation that supposedly occurred in the ancestral ape population that gave rise to modern humans, presents anomalies. At the fusion site, we find an insertion of new genetic information that appears to be pivotal in distinguishing humans from the great apes.

It is curious to explain the two-chromosome human difference from apes by positing that a loss or subtraction of genes produced additional DNA, making the human genome more complex.

29
The Cobalamin Enigma

Cobalamin is usually found in one of two biologically active forms: methycobalamin and adocobalamin. Most prokaryotes, as well as animals, have cobalamin-dependent enzymes, whereas plants and fungi do not appear to use it.

In this chapter, we are going to further examine cobalamin's role in our investigation of the human genome, but please bear with me, as we need to get a bit more technical at this juncture.

Cobalamin, also known as vitamin B_{12}, is a micronutrient that is synthesized only by microorganisms yet is an essential nutrient in human metabolism. Genetic diseases of vitamin B_{12} use constitute an important fraction of inherited newborn disease.

Vitamin B_{12} is a large organometallic molecule, 1,300 to 1,500 daltons in size, and is the most chemically complex vitamin known. The focal point of vitamin B_{12} is the central cobalt atom.

The fact that only *prokaryotes* (bacteria) have the ability to synthesize cobalamin implies that all of the vitamin B_{12} found in algae, and indeed animals, must originally have been *produced by bacteria*.

Cobalamin is a structurally complex cofactor. It is usually found in one of two biologically active forms: methylcobalamin and adocobalamin, and it is the only vitamin that contains a metal atom.

Scientists consider it an ultratrace metal since it composes but 0.0029 percent of Earth's crust.

To function as a cofactor, B_{12} must be metabolized through a complex pathway that modifies its structure and takes it through subcellular compartments of the cell. As we shall see, this fact poses several striking problems for the theory that life began and evolved on Earth only.

As noted in the epigraph at the beginning of the chapter, "Most prokaryotes, as well as animals, have *cobalamin-dependent* enzymes, whereas *plants* and *fungi* do not appear to use it" (italics added). In bacteria and archaea (microorganisms similar to bacteria), these enzymes include methionine synthase, ribonucleotide reductase, glutamate, and methylmalonyl-CoA mutases.

In mammals, cobalamin is obtained through the diet and *is required* for methionine synthase and methylmalonyl-CoA mutase. This is because plants contain Me and Mh, whereas humans only have M.[1]

The fact that this trace element is necessary for proper enzymatic function in animals yet does not exist in plants presents several enigmas. If life began and evolved on Earth, then why did "evolution" select cobalt, a rare element, to play such a pivotal role in animal metabolism?

Would not iron, which is plentifully available on Earth, have better played this key metabolic role?

The chemical element cobalt, which plays a key role in cobalamin synthesis, does not exist in a free state and is found naturally only in a chemically combined form, usually in association with nickel deposits.

It appears that cobalamin (B_{12}) is the most critical ultratrace element in the human body. One could argue that its crucial role in human metabolism strongly suggests that its association with the chromosome 2 fusion site represents a deliberate insertion. (We shall examine this shortly.)

Cobalt is the active center of the cobalamin coenzymes, the most common example of which is vitamin B_{12}. As such it is an essential trace dietary mineral for *all* animals. Since animals, including humans, need cobalamin to survive—it is vital to red blood cell production and nerve and brain function—it represents a curious choice to become the base for such an important metabolic role.

Bacteria in the guts of ruminant animals convert cobalt salts into vitamin B_{12}. Nonruminant herbivores produce vitamin B_{12} from bacteria in their colons, which also synthesize the vitamin from simple cobalt salts.

However, the vitamin cannot be absorbed from their colons; therefore, nonruminants must ingest feces to obtain the nutrient. If you've ever wondered why your dog eats poop, there you have the real reason.

It seems a strange anomaly for natural selection to have taken this circuitous metabolic pathway. Since the majority of large animals are herbivores or ruminants, one would think that nature would have based the pathway on elements in the plant kingdom.

The rarity of cobalt in Earth's crust and oceans and the fact that plants do not depend on it or provide it to plant-eating animals poses a challenge to Darwinian evolution.

The vitamin B_{12} synthesized in the rumen and by bacteria in the colon is one of the most complex nonpolymeric natural products produced in nature. Then why did animals evolve such a complicated metabolism, based on an ultratrace element in short supply?

Once again, evolution is supposed to proceed by conserving energy and materials through the simplification of processes.

Animals that do not get vitamin B_{12} from their own gastrointestinal bacteria or that of other animals *must obtain the vitamin premade in other animal products in their diet, and they cannot benefit from ingesting simple cobalt salts.*

That includes predators as well as human beings.

As noted, in the wild, ingestion of feces is common among monogastric animals. Many of the B vitamins, including B_{12}, are synthesized as a result of bacterial fermentation in the large intestine, but B_{12} is excreted because it must be bound by an *intrinsic factor* produced in the stomach before it can be absorbed.

Studies have shown that when ruminants, such as cattle, are on a *cobalt-deficient diet,* there is a gradual loss of appetite, weight loss, muscle wasting, depraved appetite, anemia, and eventually death.[2] The animals appear as if they have been starved, the visible mucous membranes are blanched, and the skin is pale and fragile. Very similar symptoms occur in people with B_{12} deficiency.

Cobalt deprivation in ruminants leads to a vitamin B_{12} deficiency that can be corrected with cobalt supplementation because these animals have the right gut bacteria to break the salts down.

However, human beings and monogastric animals lack this ability. We have to eat animal products or take B_{12} supplements.

The underlying mystery: *Why did the cobalt pathway occur in the most primitive organisms and then skip the higher plants, to reappear again in complex animals?*

Equally as enigmatic: Why are there so many animal species that require cobalamin to trigger needed enzymes, yet their gastrointestinal systems are ill-equipped to obtain it?

Just as baffling is the fact that some sea algae have what is called *cobalamin acquisition protein* 1 (CBA1). This is a special protein that these species of sea algae use to grab cobalamin (B_{12}) from the ocean water and ingest it, similar to the way a sponge soaks up fluids.

The next question: Why do animals, including humans, lack this *lifesaving mechanism,* which confers an obvious survival advantage? If evolution originally took place on Earth, as is assumed by evolutionists, and this mechanism developed in the earliest microorganisms, why was it not passed on to animals? This supports the theory of panspermia and exoplanet origins for life on Earth.

Instead of a simple pathway based on a readily available element, we find a byzantine pathway based on a rare element. It seems clear that sea algae got it right by grabbing vitamin B_{12}, latching onto it, and escorting it through their digestive systems.

That way, they never had to risk suffering from B_{12} deficiency. We do have that risk.

Common side effects of B_{12} deficiency in humans include *peripheral sensory neuropathy causing symptoms such as numbness, tingling, burning, and complete lack of sensation; chronic fatigue; anemia; low red blood cell count; and digestive disorders, to name the most prevalent.*

It would seem that natural selection has monogastric animals skating on thin ice. Research has estimated that approximately 39 percent of the human population is vitamin B_{12} deficient. Many people over age fifty lose the ability to absorb B_{12} from foods.

This would indicate that B_{12} deficiency may have acted as a factor that limited life spans in human history. In fact, it will do so more in the future as our soils become more depleted. Although the average level of cobalt in soils is 8 parts per million, there are soils with as little as 0.1 parts per million and others with as much as 70 parts per million.

Because the cofactors such as B_{12} are complicated to synthesize and required in trace amounts only, it is possible that there is a selective advantage in dispensing with the need to produce them.

However, such mutations or gene inactivation can only have occurred if there was *a reliable external supply* of the cofactors in the environment. *But there is no evidence to suggest that Earth ever provided a reliable, sufficient source of cobalamin.*

As we saw above, cobalamin is an ultratrace element in short supply. In addition, only very minuscule amounts of this vitamin were ever present in natural waters.

David W. Menzel and Jane P. Spaeth reported that moderate diatom blooms occurred in the Sargasso Sea when cobalamin concentrations were at their highest, and several other studies have shown a link between algal productivity and vitamin B_{12} concentrations.

Taken together, the foregoing suggests that the cobalamin metabolic pathway is more likely to have evolved on a cobalt-rich planet. I have other reasons to suspect that this may, in fact, have been the case.

CONCLUSION

The crucial role that the trace mineral cobalamin plays in human metabolism is anomalous. Why natural selection would create a complex pathway that depends on a difficult to obtain substance that is often in short supply does not fit the Darwinian model.

It suggests that the origin of this B_{12} dependency was not Earth but a cobalamin-rich planet. As various researchers have suggested, the most primitive life-forms seemed to have arrived on Earth fully formed. These early organisms already had the ability to synthetize cobalamin and molybdenum.

30

Vimanas

The Flying Machines of Ancient India

Like the Old Testament, the Hebrew Torah, and the Sumerian Enumma Elish, the Vedas are a collection of ancient Sanskrit epics, scriptures, and written histories from India. However, the Vedas extend beyond those texts by containing references to flying airplanes and spacecraft known as *vimanas*.

Unlike the Hebrew and Sumerian traditions, which were unclear about the exact nature of the sophisticated mechanized technology the people were witness to, the Vedas are very specific about its nature and characteristics.

According to Venkataraman Raghavan, the former head of the Sanskrit Department of India's prestigious University of Madras, "Fifty years of researching this ancient work convinces me that there are livings beings on other planets and that they were visiting the earth as far back as 4000 B.C."[1]

This is consistent with the time line established for cosmic intervention prior to disseminating the tools of civilization, as in Sumer.

The Sanskrit scholar went on to note, "There is a just mass of fascinating information about flying machines, even fantastic science fiction weapons, that can be found in translations of the Vedas (scriptures), Indian epics, and other ancient Sanskrit text."[2]

The vimanas are variously described throughout the texts. Some accounts tell of their exact flight characteristics and also of the powerful weapons they harbored. Consider the following passage from the Yajur Veda:

> O royal skilled engineer, construct sea-boats, propelled on water by our experts, and airplanes, moving and flying upward, after the clouds that reside in the mid-region, that fly as the boats move on the sea, that fly high over and below the watery clouds. Be thou, thereby, prosperous in this world created by the Omnipresent God, and flier in both air and lightning.[3]

When we take into account the fact that the earliest Hindu religious traditions, entirely disconnected from the Hebrew or Sumerian traditions, also agree on the fact that extraterrestrial vehicles whirled through the skies over Earth, the evidence has gone from strong to compelling; as do the craft in eyewitness accounts given by the ancient Hebrews, the vimanas share many of their characteristics with the modern UFOs.

They are described as being able to navigate to great heights and speeds using quicksilver and a great propulsive wind. Another account, this one from the Sanskrit Hindu epic the Ramayana, says:

> The Puspaka car that resembles the Sun and belongs to my brother was brought by the powerful Ravan; that aerial and excellent car going everywhere at will . . . that car resembling a bright cloud in the sky. . . . And the King [Rama] got in, and the excellent car at the command of the Raghira, rose up into the higher atmosphere.[4]

Again, we find references to an extremely bright, shining light that is as brilliant as a white cloud reflecting direct sunlight. The Ramayana also describes a splendid chariot that "arrived shining, a wonderful divine car that sped through the air." In another passage, there is mention of a chariot being seen "sailing overhead like a moon."[5]

In the Mahabharata, a Sanskrit Hindu epic, we read that at Rama's command, "the magnificent chariot rose up to a mountain of cloud with a tremendous din." Another passage reads, "Bhima flew with his Vimana on an enormous ray which was as brilliant as the sun and made a noise like the thunder of a storm."

This sounds very much like Jehovah on Mount Sinai.

The *Vymanika-Shastra* (also known as *Vymaannidashaastra Aeronautics*) is a Sanskrit text on the science of aeronautics. It was written in the early twentieth century but was alleged to have been psychically delivered to the author by an ancient Hindu named Maharishi Bharadwaaja. In the work, there is a description of a Vimana: "An apparatus which can go by its own force, from one place to place or globe to globe."

The text also lists sixteen kinds of metal that are needed to construct the flying vehicle: "Metals suitable, light are of 6 kinds." However, only three of them are known to us today. The rest are lost to antiquity. Professor of aeronautics A. V. Krishna Murty at the Indian Institute of Science in Bangalore has studied these texts and has said:

It is true, that the ancient Indian Vedas and other text refer to aeronautics, spaceships, flying machines and ancient astronauts. A study of the Sanskrit texts has convinced me that ancient India did know the secret of building flying machines—and that those machines were patterned after spaceships coming from other planets.[6]

In the Mahabharata, the king, Asura Maya, has a vimana that measures twelve cubits (about 40 feet) and is equipped with missiles and has four wheels. The Samarangana Sutradhara goes beyond the Old Testament, which merely describes Jehovah hovering over Moses's tent and speaking with him, to give an actual description of the construction of the vimana, which follows:

Strong and durable must the body of the Vimana be made, like a great flying bird of light material. Inside one must put the mercury engine with its iron heating apparatus underneath. By means of the power latent in the mercury which sets the driving whirlwind in motion, a man sitting inside may travel a great distance in the sky. The movements of the Vimana are such that it can vertically ascend, vertically descend, moves slanting forwards and backwards. With the help of the machines human beings can fly in the air and heavenly beings can come down to Earth.[7]

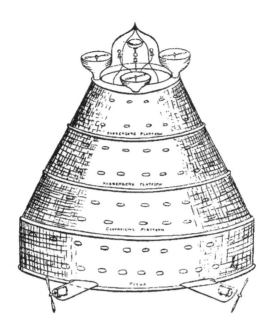

Fig. 30.1. The flying machines known as Vimanas.
Drawing by T. K. Ellappa, 1923

This passage evokes the *whirlwind* flight characteristic contained in the Torah and includes both human and extraterrestrial beings in flight together. The Rig Veda, along with the Enumma Elish, the oldest text document known, includes references to the following modes of transportation:

Jalayan: a vehicle designed to operate in the air and water (Rig Veda 6.58.3)

Kaara-Kaara-Kaara-Kaara-Kaara-Kaara: a vehicle that operates on the ground and water (Rig Veda 9.14.1)

Tritala-Tritala-Tritala: a vehicle consisting of three stories (Rig Veda 3.14.1)

Trichakra Ratha: a three-wheeled vehicle designed to operate in the air (Rig Veda 4.36.1)

Vaayu Ratha: a gas- or wind-powered chariot (Rig Veda 5.41.6)

Vidyut Ratha, Vidyut Ratha: a vehicle that operates on power (Rig Veda 3.14.1).

Flying vehicles were initially called *rathas* (vehicles or carriages) in the Rig Veda, as they were called *chariots* in the Old Testament. The ratha and later vimana could fly at a very high rate of speed. The ratha was triangular and very large, and it had three tiers and was piloted by at least three people (*tribandhura*). It had three wheels, and in one verse the chariot or carriage was said to have had three columns.

These craft were generally made of any one of the following three kinds of metals: gold, silver, or iron, but the metal that usually went into their makeup, according to the Vedic text, was gold; long nails or rivets held them together. The chariots had three different types of fuel.[8] References to flying vehicles occur in the Mahabharata forty-one times, of which one air attack deserves special attention. The account records the events surrounding the Asura king Salva, who had an aerial flying machine known as Saubha-pura, which he used to attack Krishna's capital, Dwaraka.

It tells how the king showered missiles from the sky. As Krishna chased him, the king flew near the sea and landed on the high seas. Then he came back with his flying machine and mounted a second attack against Krishna, hovering about one krosa (about four thousand feet) above the ground. Krishna retaliated with a powerful ground-to-air weapon, which hit the aircraft in the middle and shattered it into pieces. The damaged flying machine then crashed into the sea.

Another vivid description of this aerial battle also occurs in the Bhagavata Purana. There are similar references to missiles, armaments, sophisticated war machines, mechanical contrivances, and vimanas in the ever-popular Mahabharata.

It is interesting to note that among the types of vimanas mentioned in the Mahabharata are (1) the shakuna (bird-shaped), (2) the mandara (mountain-shaped), and (3) the mandala (circular-shaped), the latter being the type most typically observed in modern times. Vimanas are also mentioned in the Ramayana, and they have many qualities and descriptions that fit those described in the *Vymanika-Shastra*.

The Mayamanta draws on much older material from the Mayamata, which is ascribed to Maya Danava, the architect and artist of the demons, who is said to have created these flying machines for the gods and demons. The Padma Purana mentions that there are four hundred thousand types of "manusha-like," or *humanlike,* entities in the cosmos.

These references are of great interest since they allude to the existence of other humanlike races, which the Old Testament and the Enumma Elish do as well; that is, the gods who created man in their image, the Anunnaki, and the sons of the gods.

This harkens back to the biblical reference to the hybrid race created by the union between the sons of the gods and human women, as well as to the existence of the Nephelim at the same time.

Some of these races are superior (gods) and others inferior (demons). Then there are the nonhuman entities: the nagas, the monkey-type races, the cherubim, and so forth that also inhabit other worlds and occasionally interface with humans on Earth.

Like Egypt and Sumer, India has its very ancient and very mysterious artifacts, which have thus far defied scientific explanation. Though modern scholars pooh-pooh the tales of vimanas, ancient aerial wars, and the unleashing of weapons of mass destruction, there are reasons to pause and consider these historical accounts seriously.

The famous Iron Pillar is located near Delhi. At either 2,300 years old by the Puranic accounts of the Guptas or 1,500 years old by modern reckoning, it has been exposed to heat, rain, wind, and so forth for all this time and still has not rusted or decayed.

Such metal appears to have been scientifically engineered. Amulets made of similarly sophisticated metals have been found in association with five-thousand-year-old skeletons near Harappa. These skeletons have been found to have high levels of radioactivity, perhaps as the result of wars around the time of the Mahabharata.

Other physical evidence that supports the contention that there is far more to the ancient history of India than we know can be found in the Indus Valley civilization.

This civilization is much lesser known than its Egyptian or Mesopotamian counterparts, though it is every bit as mysterious; the Harappan cities in the Indus Valley are now in ruins that lie scattered across a thousand miles of desert terrain in northwestern India and eastern Pakistan.

These planned urban centers display a uniform pattern based on civil engineering principles that date back more than five thousand years. The cities, such as Mohenjo Daro, had two- and three-story houses, each with separate bathrooms, living rooms, and kitchens.

The houses had their own wells and indoor plumbing, outdoor drainage systems, even sit-down Western-style toilets that flushed into an underground sewage system via drains going to a septic tank.

Contrast these five-thousand-year-old cities to those of much of modern-day rural India and Pakistan, which still lack these civilized conveniences. In fact, urban planning is a recent development, even in the cities of Western Europe; how are we to understand cultural revolution in the context of this Indus Valley civilization that has lain in ruins for thousands of years?

We need to comprehend how the builders of this civilization created standardized bricks by the hundreds of millions, which were used to build the cities. Why were they so far advanced as to create uniform weights and measures? We also need to decipher their curious writing system, which remains one of the few completely unknown written languages in the world. We also ought to try to understand how the civilization came to an abrupt end.

The ruined ancient city of Dholavira has marble pillars, and the builders used stone architecture for its palace and an Athenian-like stadium, which included the world's oldest signboard (dating to 2500 BCE). The city also boasts a large water reservoir cut from rock.

Fourteen field seasons of excavation through an enormous deposit caused by the successive settlements at the site for over 1500 years during all through the 3rd millennium and unto the middle of the 2nd millennium BC have revealed seven significant cultural stages documenting the rise and fall of the Indus civilization in addition to bringing to light a major, a model city which is remarkable for its exquisite planning, monumental structures, aesthetic architecture, amazing water harvesting system and a variety in funerary architecture.

The other area in which the Harappans of Dholavira excelled spectacularly pertained to water harvesting with the aid of dams, drains, reservoirs and storm water management, which eloquently speak of tremendous engineering skill of the builders. Equally important is the fact that all those features were integrated parts of city planning and were surely the beauty aids, too. The Harappans created about sixteen or more reservoir of varying sizes and designs and arranged them in a series practically on all four sides.

A cursory estimate indicates that the water structures and relevant and related activities accounts for 10 hectares of area, in other words 10% of the total area that the city appropriated within its outer fortification. The 13 m of gradient between high and low areas from east to west within the walls was ideally suited for creating cascading reservoirs which were separated from each other by enormous and broad bunds and yet connected through feeding drains.[9]

The above level of sophistication has not been duplicated in terms of urban planning and civil engineering in Asia to this day or, in fact, in most of the world. It shows a level of engineering knowledge and skills that is virtually impossible to account for, given that this is one of Earth's first civilizations.

How was this level of advancement achieved and then so quickly forgotten by all of the other cultures of the Indian subcontinent?

Another Indus Valley city, Lothal, was recently excavated from February 13, 1955, to May 19, 1960, by the Archaeological Survey of India, the official Indian government agency for the preservation of ancient monuments. Lothal represents a very fresh site in archaeological terms.

The city's dock, the world's earliest known, connected the city to an ancient waterway, the Sabarmati River, which was on the trade route between Harappan cities in Sindh and the peninsula of Saurashtra when the surrounding Kutch district—now a desert—was a part of the Arabian Sea.

Lothal was a thriving trade center in ancient times. The city produced fine handmade beads, gems, and valuable ornaments, which reached the far corners of West Asia and Africa. The techniques and tools the city's people pioneered for precision bead making and metallurgy have stood the test of time. In fact, such beads still cannot be duplicated by modern craftsmen.

The city planners and engineers engaged themselves to protect the area from consistent floods in the following ways: The town was divided into blocks of 1–2-metre-high (3–6 feet) platforms of sun-dried bricks, each serving 20–30 houses of thick mud and brick walls. The city was divided into a citadel, or acropolis and a lower town.

The rulers of the town lived in the acropolis, which featured paved baths, underground and surface drains (built of kiln-fired bricks) and potable water well. The lower town was subdivided into two sectors. A north-south arterial street was the main commercial area. It was flanked by shops of rich and ordinary merchants and craftsman. The residential area was located to either side of the marketplace.[10]

In terms of managing the waterway, the dock was built on the eastern flank of the town, and it has become regarded by archaeologists as a great feat of civil engineering. It was located away from the main current of the river to avoid silting but provided access to ships in high tide as well. The warehouse was built close to the acropolis on a 3.5-meter-high (10.5 feet) podium of mud bricks.

The rulers could thus supervise the activity on the dock and warehouse simultaneously. Facilitating the movement of cargo was a mud-brick wharf, 220 meters (720 feet) long, built on the western arm of the dock, with a ramp leading to the warehouse.

Though the Harappan civilization does not overwhelm us with massive buildings, its overall urban organization and the sophisticated civil engineering required to facilitate indoor plumbing, public baths, river diversion, dams, canals, and so forth are on par with the Great Pyramid in terms of being anomalous artifacts.

The uniform organization of the townships, which spanned a thousand miles, and their standardized social and economic institutions attest to the Harappans being an advanced and highly disciplined society with a common purpose. Apparently, commerce and administrative duties were performed according to uniform standards, supposedly a fairly modern invention.

Municipal administration was strict; the width of most streets remained the same over a long time period. No structures were allowed to deviate from the building codes. These regulations were enforced throughout all the cities of the entire thousand-mile area.

Householders possessed a sump and a collection chamber in which to deposit solid waste to prevent the clogging of city drains. Drains, manholes, and cesspools kept the city clean and deposited the waste in the river, which was washed out during high tide.

Lothal imported en masse raw materials like copper, chert, and semiprecious stones from Mohenjo Daro and Harappa. These raw materials would be fashioned into sophisticated ornaments, selas, and other valuables. Then they were shipped out to inner villages and towns.

Does all of this sound strangely out of synch with our view of ancient history and how human culture was supposed to have gradually evolved from the Stone Age? In fact, the Harappan cities were every bit as sophisticated as our own today, perhaps even more minutely planned. There is nothing haphazard about them.

Archaeologists have found evidence that the Harappans had trade relations with the ancient Sumerians, and it is peculiar that these two enigmatic civilizations sprang up at the same time. Also worth noting is the fact that the Harappans were a bronze culture, though they lacked deposits of copper and tin ore—bronze's raw materials.

CONCLUSION

The ancient texts of India clearly describe flying machines and contact with extraterrestrial races having occurred when science tells us they should not have. Unlike the Old Testament and the Enumma Elish, the Indian texts directly portray the flight characteristics of these flying machines, the vimanas.

Last, the Indus Valley civilization, which built planned cities using modern-day civil engineering principles, stands as an anomaly that directly refutes the theories and time lines that cultural evolutionists currently propose.

Afterword

A few points need further clarification: Are the "gods" equivalent to God? No. Some people seem to think that if *gods,* a plurality of reasoning beings, created life on Earth, then they become the original creators of the universe and supplant the *One God.*

Not in my view.

The Genesis Race simply did what we are already aiming to do as our genetic and space technologies progress.

In a few short decades, we have gone from barely believing that space travel was possible to landing men on the moon and rovers on Mars. At the same time, bioengineers have brought transgenic plants and animals into existence that neither God nor nature produced.

Nevertheless, this does not put us in the position of having created life or the universe; we are just manipulating the genetic framework and natural resources that already exist.

Plans for terraforming other planets and satellites in the solar system have existed for decades, and they are not impossibly complicated.

In March 1979, NASA engineer and author James Oberg organized the First Terraforming Colloquium, a special session at the Lunar and Planetary Science Conference in Houston. He popularized the terraforming concepts discussed at the colloquium to the general public in his 1981 book *New Earths.*

Then planetologist Christopher McKay wrote "Terraforming Mars," a paper for the *Journal of the British Interplanetary Society.* The paper discussed the prospects of a self-regulating Martian biosphere; the word McKay used, *biosphere,* has since become the preferred term.

Michael Noah Mautner, research professor of chemistry at Virginia Commonwealth University, has written a paper, "Seeding the Universe with Life: Securing Our Cosmological Future," that proposes exactly how a terraforming operation could proceed.

> Life is unique in nature in complexity and in its drive for self-propagation. We are part of life, implying a human purpose to safeguard and propagate life. For this purpose we may settle the Solar System, and seed with life new solar systems, solar nebulae and start forming interstellar clouds. Directed panspermia to these targets can carry colonizing cyanobacteria, extremophile microorganisms, and eggs of multicellular rotifers to start higher evolution.[1]

In the first book in this series, I raised the notion that since we have DNA similar to that of the Genesis Race, we appear to be in the midst of recapitulating their evolutionary steps.

It is interesting to note how quickly modern civilization embraced the space exploration mission and cracked the genome as well. It could be that the transmission of the seeds of life throughout the universe is our ultimate calling.

However, moving along this path of terraforming, we humans are even now becoming "gods" by also creating new hybridized plants and animals. In this context (the entire context of this work) the term *gods* equals a technologically advanced race of beings, and that is all that it implies and means.

We conduct experiments on chimpanzees, gorillas, monkeys, and mice; they do not formulate their own research projects using humans as subjects.

Even in biblical terms, the foregoing makes us gods, as the Old Testament states and Christ reaffirms in the New Testament that *we are gods*. The reasons for that are obvious. We are the most intelligent and technologically advanced of all species.

Ironically, our bent toward applying our collective intelligence along technological lines could be our undoing, if we are not more careful.

We can already ponder the possibility of inserting human genes into the genome of rhesus monkeys or chimpanzees, not to create a complete hybrid but rather a simple transgenic variation of a monkey or an ape that would have some or even many human characteristics.

This is not something that the near future holds; it could be accomplished right now.

The technology already exists; it is only ethical considerations that are preventing its full use. Pandora's box is already wide open. This is a threshold moment for the entire human race.

We can either accept the fact that we are not alone in the universe— and the fact that our ancestors had contact with a more advanced civilization—or not.

The risks of rejecting the information that our ancient oral and written histories have tried to hand down is extreme. It is likely that if we were openly confronted by a highly advanced race of extraterrestrial beings, entirely unprepared, our civilization would quickly unravel.

Ironically, this unraveling would happen not because our religious institutions couldn't handle the interface, in fact, they could, but because scientists, politicians, and technocrats could not deal with it.

An unanticipated surprise like those that Moses experienced would quickly render all of our technologies obsolete. All the modern histories would collapse, as would archaeological chronologies. Evolution would fall apart.

We would be in the same position as the primitive cultures of Africa, South America, and Southeast Asia were in when the agents of Western civilization made contact with them.

If science continues to fail to objectively analyze the anomalous artifacts produced by ancient civilizations, such as the Great Pyramid, the Bible, the Enumma Elish, and so forth, then we have to face the risks and consequences.

If we are, in fact, the product of an extraterrestrial intervention and insertion of genetic material by an advanced civilization, then we may have strayed far off course already. Nuclear or genetic contamination of the biosphere could represent unacceptable breaches of the universal code of life.

We should not reject, out of hand, the notion that we are a

functioning part of the life that exists throughout the universe. This may and probably does come with conditions.

If we have violated those conditions, then this civilization is more than likely doomed to fail in the relatively near future.

That failure could come in the form of a massive solar storm that knocks out the electrical grid, an asteroid impact, squandering of resources, radioactive poisoning, pollution, et al.

That would put the modern surge in UFO sightings and contacts in perspective. The increased monitoring began right after the atomic bombs were dropped on Hiroshima and Nagasaki. The waves of sightings started in New Mexico, where the bombs were developed, which led to the Roswell crash.

That just happened to occur near the base of the only atomic air force group in the world. Then Washington, D.C., got buzzed, and the waves have kept increasing ever since.

In fact, we have no reason to doubt the existence of extraterrestrial civilizations, and most scientists do not. However, they do doubt that any have been able to span the vast distances that separate solar systems to get to Earth.

Nonetheless, the Genesis Race theory only requires that *one civilization*—out of all the myriad planets in the universe—conquered that obstacle. The galaxies do not have to contain solar systems crowded with life to prove this theory.

Astrophysicist Michio Kaku has even raised the possibility that we are living in a galaxy that could have been fabricated by another race. There is evidence, presented in the third chapter, that indicates some unknown engineering principles were at work in the forming of Earth's geology and geography.

There is nothing random about the arrangement of many of the world's major rivers emptying into gulfs on the 30° north latitude band around the globe.

The 120° separation between the Nile and Mississippi Rivers looks like a geometrical configuration (an inverted mirror image) since the former runs from south to north and the latter north to south. But the deltas of both sit on the 30° north parallel.

Another point should be made about the emergence of life in the universe and how it came into being. We, like our proposed benefactors, may seed other planets and bring life to them and may even insert various pieces of the earthly genome at appropriate times.

However, even if a new variant of the *Homo sapiens* lineage is created and it one day looks up to us as the "gods," we will know that all we had done was to transmit the process that we inherited.

In my view, pursuing a line of inquiry that is supposed to end with the discovery of the ultimate origin of life in the universe is a futile exercise. Our senses of perception and our brains are quite limited. Unfortunately, our minds can imagine questions that we have no chance of answering (i.e., the chicken and the egg).

Dig deeply enough, and life is infinite and eternal in all directions, what is . . . *is*.

It is in that sense and not a strictly biblical one that God must be understood. Too much time and too many trillions of discrete events have occurred to permit us to retrace the pathway that life took throughout the universe to get to Earth.

Our intellectual and perceptual limits (even with the aid of technology) constrain our limited conceptual framework; beyond that boundary is when and where the progression of life actually began. The astronomer Sir Fred Hoyle acquiesced to call that point "God," though not in the biblical meaning of the word.

He attributed the origin of life to "God" because the technical origin of life is logically unknowable. He arrived at this fact through various mathematical calculations that revealed that life's probability as a natural occurrence is impossible.

The microbiologist Sir Francis Crick reached the same conclusion but did not engage in the question of the ultimate origin of life. I take both positions: God is the ultimate creator of life in the universe, but there is no way to scientifically confirm that, nor is there any way to establish how and where life began using the scientific method.

However, we can engage our minds and quest for knowledge on the level of the transmission of life to the planet Earth and all that entails.

It is in that spirit that this series of books (this book and *The Genesis Race*) has been and is being written.

The astrobiologist Chandra Wickramasinghe summed up the situation when he wrote the following:

But the universe doesn't respect the boundaries between different disciplines. The differences between biology and astronomy and chemistry and so on, these are man-made artifacts of thinking. I think the whole system is doomed unless one decides that all these barriers are cleared.[2]

Notes

CHAPTER 1. COSMIC SEEDS OF LIFE

1. Crick and Orgel, "Directed Panspermia," 341–48.
2. Ibid.
3. Crick, *Life Itself.*
4. Hoyle, *Intelligent Universe.*

CHAPTER 2. WHERE IS EVERYBODY?

1. Sagan, *Cosmos.*
2. Drake and Sobel, *Is Anyone Out There?* 55–62.
3. Lemarchand, "Detectability of Extraterrestrial Technological Activities."
4. Ibid.
5. Ibid.
6. Kardashev, "Transmission of Information," 217.
7. Drake and Sobel, *Is Anyone Out There?* 55–62.

CHAPTER 4. ALIEN MESSAGE IN STONE

1. Smith, "Project Management B.C."

CHAPTER 5. THE ENIGMA OF PRECISION ENGINEERING

1. Dunn, *Giza Power Plant.*
2. Smith, "Project Management B.C.,"*Civil Engineering,* June 1999, 11.

CHAPTER 6.
BUILDING THE GREAT PYRAMID TODAY

1. www.africa-ata.org/aircargo.htm (accessed March 20, 2017).
2. Hitzik, *Turbulent, Thrilling Saga.*

CHAPTER 7. EGYPT:
CIVILIZATION WITHOUT CITIES?

1. Anderson, "Civilization without Cities?"
2. A report released by the Government of India's Archaeological Survey.

CHAPTER 8.
THE GIZA PYRAMIDS REPRESENT
THE THREE INNER PLANETS

1. Petrie, *Pyramids and Temples of Gizeh.*
2. Legon, "Plan of the Giza Pyramids."

CHAPTER 9. THE EARTH VORTEX

1. Leedskalnin, *Magic Current,* www.world-mysteries.com (accessed March 17, 2017).
2. Joseph, "Mystery of Coral Castle," 2.
3. Ibid.

PREFACE TO MODERN UFO CASES

1. Speigel, "Air Force UFO Rules Vanish."
2. Ibid.

CHAPTER 10. THE BATTLE OVER LOS ANGELES

1. *Los Angeles Times,* February 26, 1942.
2. Ibid.
3. *Glendale News-Press,* "Anti-aircraft Guns."
4. Craven and Cate. "West Coast Air Defenses," 277–88.

CHAPTER 11. ROSWELL: THE SMOKING GUN

1. https://en.wikipedia.org/wiki/Los_Alamos_National_Laboratory (accessed March 20, 2017).
2. *Roswell Daily Record,* "RAAF Captures Flying Saucer."
3. Marcel, The Roswell Files. www.roswellfiles.com (accessed March 17, 2017).
4. Brazel, Bessie, cited in ibid.
5. Brazel, Mac, cited in ibid.
6. Marcel, cited in ibid.
7. Marcel, *Roswell Daily Record,* July 8, 1947.
8. Rickett, Lewis, cited in Googelberg, *Ultimate Collection on UFOs: Edition 2012.*
9. Porter, Robert, cited in ibid.
10. Smith, Robert, cited in ibid.
11. Shirkey, Lt. Robert, cited in ibid.
12. Marcel, cited in ibid.
13. Dubose, cited in ibid.
14. Berlitz and Moore, *Roswell Incident.*
15. Randle and Schmitt, *UFO Crash at Roswell.*
16. Friedman and Berliner, *Crash at Corona.*
17. Roswell Report, "Transcript of Interview with W. Glenn Dennis," 211–26.

CHAPTER 12. UFOS BUZZ WASHINGTON, D.C., 1952

1. Clark, *UFO Book,* 653.
2. Ibid.
3. Ibid.
4. Ibid., 655.
5. Ibid.
6. Ibid.
7. Ruppelt, *Report on Unidentified Flying Objects,* 160.
8. Clark, *UFO Book,* 656.
9. Ibid.
10. Ibid., 658.
11. Ruppelt, *Report on Unidentified Flying Objects,* 164.
12. Peebles, *Watch the Skies!,* 76.
13. Clark, *UFO Book,* 659.

14. Peebles, *Watch the Skies!*, 76.
15. Ruppelt, *Report on Unidentified Flying Objects*, 166.
16. Clark, *UFO Book*, 660.
17. Michaels, *Sightings: UFOs*, 22.
18. Ruppelt, *Report on Unidentified Flying Objects*, 169.
19. Ibid.
20. Sampson, "'Saucer' Outran Jet, Pilot Reveals."
21. Ibid.
22. Ibid.
23. Ibid.
24. Ibid.

CHAPTER 13. THE SOCORRO INCIDENT

1. Zamora, Project Blue Book (case number 8766). www.ufocasebook.com /Zamorareport.html (accessed March 17, 2017).
2. Ibid.
3. Ibid.
4. Ibid.
5. Ibid.
6. Ibid.
7. Ibid.
8. Ibid.
9. Ibid.
10. Ibid.
11. Ibid.
12. Ibid.
13. Ibid.
14. Ibid.
15. Ibid.
16. Stanford, *Socorro "Saucer" in a Pentagon Pantry*, 85–87.
17. Ibid.
18. FBI field report on La Madera, April 29, 1964. www.verytopsecret.info/tag /lonnie-zamora (accessed March 20, 2017).
19. Ibid.
20. J. Allen Hynek, personal letter to Donald Menzel.
21. Druffel, *How to Defend Yourself*, 213.

22. Ibid.
23. Ibid.
24. Ibid.
25. Hynek, Project Blue Book. www.ufoevidence.org/documents/doc296.htm (accessed March 20, 2017).
26. Ibid.
27. Ibid.
28. Ibid.
29. Ibid.
30. Ibid.
31. Ibid.
32. Ibid., 219.
33. Quintanilla, www.abovetopsecret.com/forum/thread865564/pg1 (accessed March 20, 2017).

CHAPTER 14.
POLICEMAN ESCORTED ABOARD THE SHIP

1. Blum and Blum. *Beyond Earth,* 107.
2. Ibid.
3. Schirmer, www.ufoevidence.org/cases/case659.htm (accessed March 20, 2017).
4. Ibid.
5. Condon Report, "Scientific Study of Unidentified Flying Objects."
6. Vallée, *Confrontations,* 124. http://en.calameo.com/read/0005840376cfa 97053a4a (accessed March 20, 2017).

CHAPTER 17.
THE KELLY CAHILL ABDUCTION: AUSTRALIA

1. Cahill. *Encounter.*
2. Ibid.
3. Ibid.
4. Ibid.
5. Ibid.
6. Ibid.
7. Ibid.

8. Ibid.

9. NOUFORS, "Kelly Cahill Abduction."

10. Ibid.

11. Ibid.

CHAPTER 18. THE COMETA REPORT

1. UFO Evidence, "COMETA Report."

2. Ibid.

3. Ibid.

4. Ibid.

5. Ibid.

6. Ibid.

7. Ibid.

8. Ibid.

9. Ribes and Monnet, *The Extraterrestrial Life*.

CHAPTER 19.
THE RUSSIAN ROSWELL CASE

1. Popovich, "Ufology in the Commonwealth."

CHAPTER 20.
ENIGMAS OF THE SPACE PROGRAM

1. www.nasa.gov (accessed March 17, 2017).

2. NASA, Apollo 11 (Transcript).

3. Ibid.

4. Ibid.

5. Ibid.

6. Ibid.

7. Ibid.

CHAPTER 21.
ASTRONAUT GORDON COOPER

1. Cooper, "Message to the United Nations," 351.

2. Beckley, "Gordon Cooper and UFOs," 12–14.

CHAPTER 22.
ASTRONAUT MITCHELL TV INTERVIEW

1. UFO Evidence, "Edgar Mitchel Interview."

CHAPTER 24.
THE GENETICS OF THE ABO BLOOD GROUPS

1. Potts, "History and Blood Groups."

CHAPTER 25.
GENOME PROJECT REVELATIONS

1. Than, "Human Genome at Ten."

CHAPTER 26.
CLONES, CHIMERAS, AND HYBRIDS

1. Slonczewski, "Octavia Butler's *Xenogenesis* Trilogy."
2. Ibid.
3. Landsteiner and Wiener, "Agglutinable Factor in Human Blood," 223–24.
4. U.S. Food and Drug Administration, "Xenotransplantation."
5. Ekser and Cooper, "Genetically Engineered Pigs."
6. Komaroff, "Future of Medicine."

CHAPTER 27.
STALKING THE WILD HUMANZEE

1. Lam, "Truth about Chimeras."
2. Hecht, "Chimps Are Human."
3. Justice Laws Website: Canada, "Assisted Human Reproduction Act (S.C. 2004, c.2)."

CHAPTER 28.
THE GENETIC INSERTION EVENT

1. Chimpanzee Genome Project, "Chimpanzee Genome Project."

CHAPTER 29. THE COBALAMIN ENIGMA

1. Rodionov, Vitreschak, Mironov, and Gelfand, "Comparative Genomics of the Vitamin B12 Metabolism."

2. Underwood and Suttle, *Mineral Nutrition of Livestock.*

CHAPTER 30.
VIMANAS: THE FLYING MACHINES OF INDIA

1. Ivan, "Ancient Sanskrit Writing."

2. Ibid.

3. Yajur Veda 10:19.

4. Ramayana.

5. Ibid.

6. Veda, "Ancient Sanskrit from India."

7. Samarangana Sutradhara.

8. Chakravarti, *Indians and the Amerindians,* 141–46.

9. Archaeological Survey of India, "Excavations—Dholavira."

10. Ibid.

AFTERWORD

1. Mautner, "Seeding the Universe with Life."

2. Wickramasinghe, quoted in Varghese, "Science and the Divine Origin of Life: Professor Chandra Wickramasinghe."

Bibliography

Aaseng, Nathan. *Construction: Building the Impossible.* Minneapolis, Minn.: The Oliver Press, Inc., 1998.

Alamogordo Daily News, April 26, 1964.

Albuquerque Journal, April 27, 1964.

Albuquerque Tribune, April 29, 1964.

Anderson, Mike. "A Civilization without Cities? Mike Anderson's Ancient History Blog. www.mikeanderson.biz/2010/02/civilization-without-cities.html (accessed December 9, 2016).

Annis, James. "The 'Great Silence': The Controversy Concerning Extraterrestrial Intelligent Life." *Quarterly Journal of Royal Astronomical Society* 24 (1999): 283–309.

Archaeological Survey of India, "Excavations—Dholavira." Published by the Indian government.

Arrhenius, S. *Worlds in the Making: The Evolution of the Universe.* New York, Harper & Row, 1908.

Auchetti, John W. "Missing Pilot Valentich Final Sound Analysis Report." Phenomena Research Australia, 1982.

Badawy, Alexander. *A History of Egyptian Architecture.* Vol. III. Berkeley: University of California Press, 1968.

Banerjee, R. "B12 Trafficking in Mammals: A for Coenzyme Escort Service." *ACS Chemical Biology* 1, no. 3 (April 2006): 149–59.

Bard, Kathryn A. *Encyclopedia of the Archaeology of Ancient Egypt.* New York: Routledge, 1999.

Beckley, Timothy Green. "Gordon Cooper and UFOs: An Astronaut Speaks Out." In *MJ-12 and the Riddle of Hangar 18* by Timothy Green Beckley, 12–14.

New Brunswick, N.J.: Inner Light Publications, 1981. www.ufocasebook.com /gordoncooperufos.html, where it's cited as excerpted from Beckley's book.

Berger, Larry L. "COBALT: Cobalt in Ruminant Nutrition." GoatWorld. www.goatworld.com/articles/nutrition/cobaltsulfate2.shtml (accessed November 18, 2016).

Berlitz, Charles, and William L. Moore. *The Roswell Incident.* New York: Grosset & Dunlap, 1980.

Bharadwaaja, Maharishi. *Vymaannidashaastra Aeronautics.* Translated and published by G. R. Josyer Mysore, India: Press Trust, 1979.

Bloodbook.com: Information for Life. "Racial and Ethnic Distribution of ABO Blood Types." bloodbook.com/world-abo.html (accessed November 7, 2016)

Blum, Ralph, and Judy Blum. *Beyond Earth: Man's Contact with UFOs.* New York: Bantam Books, 1974.

Brazel, Mac. *Roswell Daily Record,* July 8, 1947.

Cahill, Kelly. *Encounter.* Sydney, Australia: HarperCollins, 1996.

California Military Department: California State Military Museums. "California in World War II: The Battle of Los Angeles." www.militarymuseum.org /BattleofLA.html (accessed November 7, 2016).

Camp, Frank R., Jr., Frank R. Ellis, and the Army Medical Research Laboratory (U.S.) Blood Transfusion Division, eds. *Selected Contributions to the Literature of Blood Groups and Immunology.* Fort Knox, Ky.: U.S. Army Medical Research Laboratory, 1971.

Cavalli-Sforza, L. L., and W. F. Bodmer. *The Genetics of Human Populations.* San Francisco: W. H. Freeman and Company, 1971.

Cedar Rapids Gazette. "Saucers Swarm over Capital," 1952.

Chakravarti, S. *The Indians and the Amerindians.* Harmondsworth, UK: Penguin Books, 1991.

Chalker, Bill. *The Oz Files: The Australian UFO Story.* Potts Point, Australia: Duffy and Snellgrove, 1996.

Cheng, Ze, Mario Ventura, Xinwei She, Philipp Khaitovich, Tina Graves, Kazutoyo Osoegawa, Deanna Church, et al. "A Genome-Wide Comparison of Recent Chimpanzee and Human Segmental Duplications." *Nature* 437 (September 2005): 88–93.

Chimpanzee Genome Project. "Chimpanzee Genome Project: Genes of the Chromosome 2 Fusion Site." www.liquisearch.com/chimpanzee_genome _project/genes_of_the_chromosome_2_fusion_site. (accessed November 4, 2016).

Chimpanzee Sequencing and Analysis Consortium. "Initial Sequence of the Chimpanzee Genome and Comparison with the Human Genome." *Nature* 437 (2005): 69–87. www.nature.com/nature/journal/v437/n7055/full /nature04072.html (accessed December 1, 2016).

Clark, Jerome. *The UFO Book: Encyclopedia of the Extraterrestrial.* Detroit, Mich.: Visible Ink, 1998.

Clarke, Somers, and Reginald Engelbach. *Ancient Egyptian Construction and Architecture.* New York: Dover Publications, 1990.

Condie, Kent C. *Plate Tectonics and Crustal Evolution.* Oxford, England: Butterworth-Heinemann, 1997.

Condon Report. "Scientific Study of Unidentified Flying Objects." Biblioteca Pleyades. www.bibliotecapleyades.net/sociopolitica/condonreport/full _report/contents.htm (accessed November 7, 2016).

Conneally, P. Michael. "Blood Type." Encyclopedia.com. www.encyclopedia.com /medicine/anatomy-and-physiology/anatomy-and-physiology/blood-groups (accessed November 7, 2016).

Cooper, Gordon. "Message to the United Nations Addressing a Panel Discussion on UFOs and ETs in 1985." *UFO Universe Magazine* 1, no. 3 (November 1988).

Cooper, Necia Grant. *The Human Genome Project: Deciphering the Blueprint of Heredity.* Mill Valley, Calif.: University Science Books, 1994.

Craven, Wesley Frank, and James Lea Cate, eds. "The Army Air Forces in World War II; Defense of the Western Hemisphere: 'The Battle of Los Angeles.'" Virtual Museum of the City of San Francisco. sfmuseum.net/hist9/aaf2 .html (accessed November 29, 2016).

———. "West Coast Air Defenses." In *The Army Air Forces in World War II: Defense of the Western Hemisphere.* Washington, D.C.: Office of Air Force History, 1983.

Crick, Francis H. *Life Itself: Its Origin and Nature.* New York: Simon and Schuster, 1981.

Crick, Francis H., and L. E. Orgel. "Directed Panspermia." *Icarus* 19 (1973): 341–48.

Davies, Kevin. *Cracking the Genome: Inside the Race to Unlock Human DNA.* Baltimore and London: Johns Hopkins University Press, 2001.

Dean, Laura. "Blood Groups and Red Cell Antigens." National Center for Biotechnology Information, United States Government, 2005.

De Grouchy, J. "Chromosome Phylogenies of Man, Great Apes, and Old World Monkeys." *Genetica* 73, no. 1–2 (August 1987): 37–52.

Department of Transport, Commonwealth of Australia (1982-04-27).

De Vera, J.-P., and Ulrich Kohler. "The Adaptation Potential of Extremophiles to Martian Surface Conditions and Its Implication for the Habitability of Mars." Abstract presented at European Geosciences Union General Assembly Conference, April 26, 2012.

Drake, Frank, and Dava Sobel. *Is Anyone Out There? The Scientific Search for Extraterrestrial Intelligence.* New York: Delacorte Press, 1992.

Druffel, Ann. *How to Defend Yourself against Alien Abduction.* New York: Three Rivers Press, 1998.

Dunn, Christopher. *The Giza Power Plant: Technologies of Ancient Egypt.* Rochester, Vt.: Bear & Company, 1998.

Dunn, Jimmy. "The Pyramids of Khufu at Giza, Egypt, the Three Queen's Pyramids." TourEgypt.com. www.touregypt.net/featurestories/great pyramid6.htm (accessed November 7, 2016).

Dutt, Romesh C., trans. *Ramayana.* Whitefish, Mont.: Kessinger Publishing, 2004.

Edgar, John, and Morton Edgar. *Great Pyramid Passages and Chambers.* Glasgow, Scotland: Bone and Hulley, 1910.

Ekser, Burcin, and David K. C. Cooper. "Genetically Engineered Pigs Have Brought Us to the Cusp of Xenotransplantation." EurekAlert! The Global Source for Science News. www.eurekalert.org/pub_releases/2011-10 /l-gep101811.php (accessed November 4, 2016).

El Defensor Chieftain. "Evidence of UFO Landing Here Observed," April 28, 1964.

Farr, A. "Blood Group Serology—The First Four Decades (1900–1939)." *Medical History* 23, no 2 (April 1, 1979): 215–26.

Fort MacArthur Museum. "The 9th Annual Great LA Air Raid Event." www .ftmac.org/AirRaid2010.htm (accessed November 7, 2016).

Friedman, Stanton T., and Don Berliner. *Crash at Corona.* St. Paul, Minn.: Paragon House Publishers, 1992.

Glendale News-Press, "Anti-aircraft Guns Blast at L.A. Mystery Invader," February 25, 1942.

Googelberg, Dr. *The Ultimate Collection on UFOs: Edition 2012.* Lulu.com.

Haines, Richard F. *Melbourne Episode; Case Study of a Missing Pilot.* Los Altos, Calif.: Lighting Design Association, 1987.

Harmon, Katherine. "Genome Sequencing for the Rest of Us." *Scientific American,* June 28, 2010.

Hecht, Jeff. "Chimps Are Human, Gene Study Implies." *New Scientist.* www

.newscientist.com/article/dn3744-chimps-are-human-gene-study-implies (accessed November 18, 2016).

Heppenheimer, T. A. *Countdown: A History of Space Flight.* New York: John Wiley & Sons, 1999.

Hitzik, Michael. *Colossus: The Turbulent, Thrilling Saga of the Building of Hoover Dam.* New York: Free Press, 2010.

Hoyle, Fred. *The Intelligent Universe.* London: Michael Joseph Limited, 1983.

Hoyle, Fred, Chandra Wickramasinghe, and John Watson. *Viruses from Space and Related Matters.* Cardiff, Wales: University College Cardiff Press, 1986.

Huang, Cheng-Han, Philip Z. Liu, and Jeffrey G. Cheng. "Molecular Biology and Genetics of the Rh Blood Group System." *Seminars in Hematology* 37, no. 2 (2000): 150–65.

Human Genome Management Information System. "About the Human Genome Project: What is the Human Genome Project?" July 18, 2011.

Hynek, Joseph Allan. *Project Blue Book.* www.ufoevidence.org/documents /doc296.htm (accessed November 7, 2016).

Ivan. "Ancient Sanskrit Writings: UFO's Visited Our Planet 6.000 Years Ago." Ancient Code. www.ancient-code.com/ancient-sanskrit-writings-ufos-vsited-our -planet-6-000-years-ago/ (accessed November 18, 2016).

Jones, Eric. "Where Is Everybody? An Account of Fermi's Question." Los Alamos Technical Report (LA-10311-MS), March 1985.

Joseph, Frank. "Mystery of Coral Castle." *Fate,* July 1998, 2.

Justice Laws Website: Canada. "Assisted Human Reproduction Act (S.C. 2004, c.2)." laws-lois.justice.gc.ca/eng/acts/a-13.4/ (accessed November 4, 2016).

Kanjilal, Dileep K. *Vimanas in Ancient India.* Calcutta, India: Sanskrit Pustak Bhandar, 1985.

Kardashev, Nikolai. "Transmission of Information by Extraterrestrial Civilizations." *Soviet Astronomy* 8 (1964): 217.

Komaroff, Anthony L. "Future of Medicine: Growing New Organs." *Newsweek,* December 7, 2010. www.newsweek.com/future-medicine-growing-new -organs-69037 (accessed November 4, 2016).

Korff, Kal K. *The Roswell UFO Crash: What They Don't Want You to Know.* Amherst, N.Y.: Prometheus Books, 1997.

Krulwich, Robert. *Cracking the Code of Life* (television show), April 17, 2001.

Lam, Vivienne. "The Truth about Chimeras." *The Science Creative Quarterly,*

November 20, 2007. www.scq.ubc.ca/the-truth-about-chimeras (accessed November 4, 2016).

Landsteiner, K., and A. S. Wiener. "An Agglutinable Factor in Human Blood Recognized by Immune Sera for Rhesus Blood." *Proceedings of the Society for Experimental Biology and Medicine* 43 (1940): 223–24.

Lawton, Ian, and Chris Ogilvie-Herald. *Giza Truth.* London: Virgin Publishing, 1999.

Leedskalnin, Edward. "Double Helical Magnetic Interaction." Leedskalnin.com: "Magnetic Current Research." www.leedskalnin.com (accessed November 7, 2016).

———. *Magic Current.* www.world-mysteries.com/ (accessed March 16, 2017).

Legon, John A. R. "The Giza Ground Plan and Sphinx." *DE* 14 (1989): 53–60.

———. "A Ground Plan at Giza." *DE* 10 (1988): 33–40.

———. "The Plan of the Giza Pyramids." *Archaeological Reports of the Archaeology Society of Staten Island* 10, no.1 (1979).

———. "The Plan of the Giza Pyramids." Egyptology and the Giza Pyramids: A Selection of Articles by John Legon. www.legon.demon.co.uk/gizaplan .htm (accessed November 7, 2016).

Lehner, Mark. *The Complete Pyramids (Solving the Ancient Mysteries).* London: Thames and Hudson, Ltd., 1997.

———. "The Sphinx." In *The Treasures of the Pyramids,* edited by Zahi Hawass. Vercelli, Italy: Barnes and Noble/White Star, 2003.

Lehner, Mark, and Brian Hunt. "Giza Plateau Mapping Project." The Oriental Institute: The University of Chicago. https://oi.uchicago.edu/sites /oi.uchicago.edu/files/uploads/shared/docs/03-04_Giza.pdf (accessed November 7, 2016).

Lemarchand, Guillermo A. "Detectability of Extraterrestrial Technological Activities." *SETIQuest* 1, no. 1 (1995): 3–13. www.coseti.org/lemarch1.htm (accessed January 1, 2017).

Lenntech. "Chemical Properties of Cobalt—Health Effects of Cobalt— Environmental Effects of Cobalt." www.lenntech.com/periodic/elements /co.htm (accessed November 29, 2016).

Los Angeles Times. February 26, 1942.

Matheson, Terry. *Alien Abduction: Creating A Modern Phenomenon.* Amherst, N.Y.: Prometheus Books, 1998.

Mautner, Michael Noah. "Seeding the Universe with Life: Securing Our Cosmological Future." *Journal of Cosmology* 5 (2010): 982–94.

Meyer, Robert. "First Attempt." NOVA Online Adventure. www.pbs.org/wgbh
    /nova/egypt/raising/first.html (accessed November 7, 2016).

Michaels, Susan. *Sightings: UFOs.* New York: Simon and Schuster, 1997.

Muir, Hazel. "Pyramid Precision." *New Scientist,* November 15, 2000.

National Aeronautics and Space Administration. "Apollo 15." www.nasa.gov
    /mission_pages/apollo/missions/apollo15.html (accessed November 7, 2016).

——. "Apollo 16." www.nasa.gov/mission_pages/apollo/missions/apollo16.html
    (accessed November 29, 2016).

——. "Apollo 17." www.nasa.gov/mission_pages/apollo/missions/apollo17.html
    (accessed November 29, 2016).

——. "NASA History." www.nasa.gov/topics/history/index.html (accessed
    November 7, 2016).

——. "Planetary Fact Sheet. http://nssdc.gsfc.nasa.gov/planetary/factsheet
    (accessed November 7, 2016).

National Aeronautics and Space Administration: Johnson Space Center. "Mission
    Transcripts: Apollo 11. www.jsc.nasa.gov/history/mission_trans/apollo11
    .htm (accessed November 7, 2016).

National Health Service (NHS) Blood and Transplant. "Frequency of Major
    Blood Groups in the UK." Blood.co.uk/why-give-blood/the-need-for
    -blood/blood-groups (accessed November 29, 2016).

Nelson, Gary. "A UFO Craft in Nebraska." *MUFON UFO Journal,* December 3,
    1967.

The New Encyclopaedia Britannica. Chicago: Encyclopedia Britannica, Inc., 2002.

Norman, Paul. "The Frederick Valentich Disappearance." Victorian U.F.O.
    Research Society. http://members.ozemail.com.au/~vufors/valensum.htm
    (accessed December 1, 2016).

Northern Ontario UFO Research & Study (NOUFORS). "Kelly Cahill
    Abduction." www.noufors.com/Kelly_Cahill_abduction.html (accessed
    December 31, 2016).

Ogasawara K., M. Bannai, N. Saitou, R. Yabe, K. Nakata, M. Takenaka,
    K. Fujisawa, et al. "Extensive Polymorphism of ABO Blood Group Gene:
    Three Major Lineages of the Alleles for the Common ABO Phenotypes."
    Human Genetics 97, no. 6 (1996): 777–83.

O'Leary, Margaret. *Anaxagoras and the Origin of Panspermia Theory.* Self-
    published by iUniverse Publishing Group, 2008.

Oreskes, Naomi, ed. *Plate Tectonics: An Insider's History of the Modern Theory of
    the Earth.* Boulder, Colo.: Westview Press, 2003.

Peebles, Curtis. *Watch the Skies!: A Chronicle of the Flying Saucer Myth.* New York: Berkley Books, 1994.

Petrie, W. M. Flinders. *The Pyramids and Temples of Gizeh.* London: Histories and Mysteries of Man Ltd., 1990.

———. *The Pyramids and Temples of Gizeh.* London: Field & Tuer, 1883.

Popovich, Pavel. "Ufology in the Commonwealth of Independent States: Organization Problems." *MUFON* International Symposium Proceedings, 1992.

Potts, W. T. W. "History and Blood Groups in the British Isles." In *Names, Words, and Graves: Early Medieval Settlement,* edited by P. H. Sawyer. New York: St. Martin's Press, 1979.

Puerto Rico UFO Network (PRUFON). "The Socorro, New Mexico UFO Landing." www.prufon.net/2010/07/socorro-new-mexico-ufo-landing_20 .html (accessed November 7, 2016).

Quintanilla, Major Hector. *Project Blue Book.* https://en.wikipedia.org/wiki /Project_Blue_Book.

Race, R. R., and Ruth Sanger. *Blood Groups in Man.* 6th ed. Oxford, U.K.: Blackwell Scientific Publications, 1975.

Rampelotto, P. H. "*Panspermia*: A Promising Field of Research." Abstract 5224, presented at the Astrobiology Science Conference, League City, Texas, April 26–29, 2010.

Randle, Kevin D. *Invasion Washington: UFOs over the Capitol.* New York: HarperTorch, 2001.

———. *Roswell UFO Crash Update: Exposing the Military Cover-Up of the Century.* New York: Global Communications, 1995.

Randle, Kevin D., and Donald R. Schmitt. *UFO Crash at Roswell.* New York: Avon Books, 1991.

Raux, E., H. L. Schubert, and M. J. Warren. "Biosynthesis of Cobalamin (Vitamin B12): A Bacterial Conundrum." *Cellular and Molecular Life Sciences* 57, no. 13–14 (December 2000): 1880–93.

Revolvy. "Lonnie Zamora." www.revolvy.com/main/index.php?s=Lonnie Zamora&item_type=topic (accessed November 7, 2016).

Ribes, Jean-Claude, and Guy Monnet. *The Extraterrestrial Life.* Paris: Larousse, 1990.

Rodionov, D. A., A. G. Vitreschak, A. A. Mironov, and M. S. Gelfand. "Comparative Genomics of the Vitamin B12 Metabolism and Regulation in Prokaryotes." *Journal of Biological Chemistry* 278, no. 42 (October 2003): 41148–59.

Roessner, C.A., P. J. Santander, and A. I. Scott. "Multiple Biosynthetic Pathways for Vitamin B12: Variations on a Central Theme." *Vitamins and Hormones* 61 (2001): 267–97.

Rood, Robert T., and James S. Trefil. *Are We Alone? The Possibility of Extraterrestrial Civilizations.* New York: Scribner, 1981.

Rossiianov, K. "Beyond Species: Il'ya Ivanov and His Experiments on Cross-Breeding Humans and Anthropoid Apes." *Science in Context* 15, no. 2 (2002): 277–316. www.ncbi.nlm.nih.gov/pubmed/12467272 (accessed January 1, 2017).

Roswell Daily Record, July 8, 1947.

Roswell Daily Record, "RAAF Captures Flying Saucer on Ranch in Roswell Region," July 8, 1947.

Roswell Files. www.roswellfiles.com (accessed November 7, 2016).

Roswell Report. "Case Closed: Transcript of Interview with W. Glenn Dennis." Interview by Karl T. Pflock and James McAndrews. Headquarters, United States Air Force, November 2, 1997.

Roy, Chandra, trans. *Mahabarata.* Calcutta, India: Bharata Press, 1889.

Ruppelt, Edward J. *The Report on Unidentified Flying Objects.* New York: Cosimo Classics, 2011.

Sacramento Bee. "Army Reveals It Has Fly Disk Found on Ranch in New Mexico," July 8, 1947. UFO Evidence. www.ufoevidence.org/documents /doc1256.htm (accessed November 7, 2016).

Sagan, Carl. *Cosmos.* New York: Random House, 2002.

Sampson, Paul. "'Saucer' Outran Jet, Pilot Reveals." *Washington Post*, July 28, 1952.

Schoch, Robert M. "Geological Evidence Pertaining to the Age of the Great Sphinx." The Official Website of Robert M. Schoch: Geological Data. www.robertschoch.com/geodatasphinx.html (accessed November 7, 2016).

Schoch, Robert M., with Robert Aquinas McNally. *Voyages of the Pyramid Builders.* New York: Tarcher/Putnam, 2003.

Science Clarified. "Genetics and the Definition of 'Human.'" www.scienceclarified .com/scitech/Genetics/Genetics-and-the-Definition-of-Human.html (accessed November 18, 2016).

Slonczewski, Joan. "Octavia Butler's *Xenogenesis* Trilogy: A Biologist's Response." Kenyon College: Department of Biology. http://biology.kenyon.edu/slonc /books/butler1.html (accessed November 18, 2016).

Smith, Craig. "Project Management B.C." *Civil Engineering Magazine,* June 1999.

Speigel, Lee. "Air Force UFO Rules Vanish after Huffington Post Inquiry." *Huffington Post.* www.huffingtonpost.com/2011/10/19/air-force-deletes -ufo-rep_n_982128.html (accessed December 13, 2016).

———. "Russian Roswell UFO Debris Is Part of Area 51 Exhibit at National Atomic Testing Museum." *Huffington Post,* March 27, 2012. www .huffingtonpost.com/2012/03/22/area-51-russian-roswell-ufo_n_1373352 .html (accessed December 1, 2016).

Stanford, Ray. *Socorro "Saucer" in a Pentagon Pantry.* Austin, Tex.: Blueapple Books, 1976.

Stanford Blood Center. "Blood Types." Bloodcenter.stanford.edu (accessed November 7, 2016).

Statham, Dominic. "Heads I Win, Tails You Lose: The Power of the Paradigm." Creation Ministries International. http://creation.mobi/human-ape-fused -chromosomes-paradigm (accessed November 18, 2016).

Steigerwald, John. "NASA Researchers: DNA Building Blocks Can Be Made in Space." NASA. www.nasa.gov/topics/solarsystem/features/dna-meteorites .html (accessed December 1, 2016).

Story, Ronald. *The Encyclopedia of Extraterrestrial Encounters.* New York: New American Library, 2001.

Than, Ker. "Human Genome at Ten: 5 Breakthroughs, 5 Predictions." *National Geographic News,* March 31, 2010. http://news.nationalgeographic.com /news/human-genome-project-tenth-anniversary/ (accessed December 30, 2016).

UFO Evidence. "COMETA Report." www.ufoevidence.org/topics/cometa.htm (accessed November 7, 2016).

———. "Edgar Mitchel Interview on Dateline NBC April 19, 1996." www .ufoevidence.org/documents/doc1923.htm (accessed December 24, 2016).

Underwood, E. J., and N. F. Suttle. *The Mineral Nutrition of Livestock.* Edinburgh, Scotland: Moredun Research Institute, 1999.

United States Army Medical Research Laboratory, Fort Knox, Kentucky.

United States Food and Drug Administration. "Xenotranspantation." www.fda .gov/BiologicsBloodVaccines/Xenotransplantation (accessed November 4, 2016).

Vallée, Jacque. *Confrontations: A Scientist's Search for Alien Contact.* San Antonio, Tex.: Anomalist Books, 2008.

Van der Leeden, Frits, Fred L. Troise, and David Keith Todd. *The Water Encyclopedia.* 2nd ed. Chelsea, Mich.: Lewis Publishers, 1990.

Varghese, Roy Abraham, gen. ed. "Science and the Divine Origin of Life: Professor Chandra Wickramasinghe." In *The Intellectuals Speak Out about God*. Chicago: Regnery Gateway, Inc., 1984.

Veda: Vedic Knowledge Online. "Ancient Sanskrit from India Tell of UFO Visit in 4,000 B.C." veda.wikidot.com/ancient-sanskrit-from-india-tell-of-ufo-visit (accessed November 4, 2016).

Walton, Travis. *Fire in the Sky*. New York: Marlowe & Co., 1996.

Waterloo Courier. "Pilot Missing after UFO Report," October 24, 1978.

Wesson, Paul. "Cosmology, Extraterrestrial Intelligence, and a Resolution of the Fermi-Hart Paradox." *Royal Astronomical Society Quarterly Journal* 31 (1990): 161–70.

Westhoff, C. M. "The Structure and Function of the Rh Antigen Complex." *Seminars in Hematology* 44, no. 1 (2007): 42–50.

Winston, Alan. "The Pyramid of Khufu at Giza in Egypt, the Pyramid Proper, Part II: Internal and Substructure." TourEgypt.com. www.touregypt.net/featurestories/greatpyramid3.htm (accessed December 1, 2016).

Yamamoto, F., H. Clausen, T. White, J. Marken, and S. Hakomori. "Molecular genetic basis of the histo-blood group ABO system." *Nature* 345 (1990): 229–33.

Zamora, Lonnie. *Project Blue Book* (case number 8766). https://en.wikipedia.org/wiki/Project_Blue_Book (accessed March 20, 2017).

Index